Jean Evan

NOT
BAD FOR A
FOREIGNER

To Grace
from one ex- Putney High School
girl to another.
  Jean (The author)
    September 22, 1996.

Safari Books (Export) Limited
Ibadan/London/Accra

First published 1996
by Safari Books (Export) Limited
Bel Royal House
Hilgrove Street
St. Helier
Jersey C.I. U.K.

in association with
Spectrum Books Limited
Sunshine House
1 Emmanuel Alayande Street
Oluyole Industrial Estate
PMB 5612
Ibadan
Nigeria

First published 1996

Design and production by Saxon Publishing Consultants
Edited by Ann Thompson
Typeset by Gilbert Composing Services
Printed by Lavenham Press, Suffolk

ISBN 0 946 480 99 0

Foreword

Whilst staying in Lagos at the home of Chief Ayo and Gbemi Rosiji, where I was always treated as one of the family, a visitor referred to me as a stranger. Quick off the mark, Ayo retorted: 'Madame is not a stranger. She is an honorary Nigerian'.

Acknowledgements

Many thanks are due to both European and Nigerian contributors to these memoirs. Top of the list must be dear, distinguished Uncle George, eighty-four years young, who told me what it was like living with my mother, Blanche, and the rest of the Ruf family in Huningue, Alsace Lorraine, and Basle, Switzerland. Ritou Dreyfus, his distant cousin, was eloquently moving about surviving in occupied France. My father's niece, Corrie Urquhart, gave me much information about the Jacoby side of the family.

Adding their knowledge to mine concerning my education were Jane Johnson, my old kindergarten buddy, and Helen Wiggins, ex-University College, London. Also I am especially grateful to Christine Sehgal at St Paul's Girls' School who gave me the run of the school library with its books, old magazines and records. My ex-flat mate, Phillis Tekkan, revived memories of Battersea Comprehensive School where we taught together, whilst my friends Oswin and Norah Howard of Putney proved to be walking encyclopedias concerning London, especially during the Blitz.

For information concerning Nigeria in general I am grateful to Dr Nnamdi Azikiwe, the First President of Nigeria, for his succinct appraisal of Nigerian political affairs.

Here is a list of the people, in alphabetic order, who supplied me with information in the form of notes, reports, articles, newspaper cuttings or diaries. Others imparted their views and information personally, interviews sometimes lasting for days. To all I am extremely grateful. Another book would be needed to absorb the plethora of material at my disposal. To anyone I have inadvertently forgotten to mention I apologise. As they would say in Nigeria 'Sorry O'.

M. S. Adigun CDN, BLA, Mr Jamal and Mrs Mary Akkare, Canon E. O. Alayande and his daughter Bukola, Chief Joop Berkhout, Professor Saburi Biobaku, Mrs Christine Bullock, Ms Dorothy Cooper, Chief Akin Delano and Mrs Kate Delano, Mr Alec Dickson, Chief S. L. Edu, Mr Salleh Haliru, Iyase (Samuel) Ighodaro (dec'd) and Dr Irene Ighodaro, Mrs Vera Kells, Mr Malcolm Maconochie, Chief Majekodumni, Dr Nina Mba, Mrs Kemi Morgan, Mr Thompson (Tommy) Ogbe and Mrs Hilda Ogbe, Dele Ayo Ogundipe, Head of Dept. of Sociology and Anthropology, University of Benin, Mr Oguntade, Judge Victor Omage and Mrs Christine Omage, Dr Tunde and Mrs Vera Osowole and Chief Ayo Rosiji and Mrs Gbemisola Rosiji and Dr Bimbi da Silva and Chief Akintola Williams.

The Rhodes House Library in Oxford proved a treasure house of information from people who had worked in West Africa and I would like to thank the staff for their readiness to give help when required.

A special word of appreciation must go to Mrs Grisell Davies for her on the spot reports of Adamawa and her photographs of the Provincial Girls' School Open Day.

Not only did Dr Nina Mba inspire me to start on the memoirs, she followed its progress step by step and edited them with academic precision. A final accolade must go to my friend/cum secretary, Adrienne Robson, who has worked tirelessly with me to produce the manuscript. To say that I could not have managed without her might sound trite — in her case it is absolutely true.

Contents

Illustrations

Part one – *Not bad for a foreigner*

Chapter one
Leo and Blanche

Although my parents gave my two sisters and myself a first-class British public school education we did not grow up typical products of the system. How could we when our roots were on the Continent?

My paternal grandfather Siegfried, was born in Altona in 1835. From early youth he was very gifted musically and soon won a reputation as a composer. Before he was twenty years of age he was engaged as a musical director in Hamburg. In 1865, he married my maternal grandmother, Bertha Iklè and they had eleven children: Mathilde (Tilly), Max, John, Adèle, Nelly (who died early), Henry, Clara, Charlotte, Ernest, Leopold (my father) and Adolph.

Siegfried had broken the mould when he took up music. Generally the Jacobys and the Iklès, his mother's family, were in the textile business. Traditionally the Levites were the assistants to the priests in the Jewish temple.

The firm, Iklè Frères, was famous for its manufacture of lace and had branches in New York, Paris, Berlin, Vienna and St Gallen. In 1867 Sir Charles Halle invited Siegfried to play as first violin in his orchestra which performed before Queen Victoria in Buckingham Palace.

After London, the orchestra moved to Manchester where the Halle concerts became a household word. Audiences still flock to hear them. Siegfried stayed on with the orchestra in Manchester. He bought a large house in Withington and took private students to help pay school fees for his large family. Leopold (whom everyone called Leo) and his five brothers went to Manchester Grammar School. His sisters went to humbler academies. The idea of women working for a living was unacceptable to English middle class parents in the nineteenth century.

After Leo completed his education at Manchester Grammar School, he returned to the family textile business, intending to work in the Paris branch with his brother, Max. He spent a year at a business college in Neuchâtel, Switzerland.

In the event, John, his older brother who had just set up on his own in London under the name of John Jacoby Iklè, persuaded him to work for him. Unwittingly, Leo had made the right choice. When the Germans occupied Paris in June 1940, Max's family and all the other French Jewish relatives were in great danger. Some managed to escape, some were imprisoned or shot.

Leo did well in London selling lace and embroidered trimmings, handkerchiefs and scarves to the big department stores in the West End, like Harrods, Selfridges and Fortnum and Mason. The lady buyers loved fussing over 'Mr Leo' who was always smart in appearance and gentlemanly in his manners. The bigger orders came, in fact, from the 'makers-up' in the rag trade who had their workshops in the back streets behind Oxford Circus or in the poverty stricken East End.

Impressed by Leo's high sales, John sent him to Australia and New Zealand to extend the business. When he became engaged to a Sydney belle, Cecily, it looked as if he would settle there for good. It was not to be. After three months Leo panicked. He wrote to Frank, his old flat mate in London, for advice on 'how to get myself out of this'. Frank wasted no time. He sent a telegram: SUGGEST TAKE LADY FOR DRIVE. BREAKING ENGAGEMENTS EASIER OPEN AIR. Leo wired back: WEATHER PERMITTING BREAKING IT OFF NEXT SUNDAY.

After five years in the Antipodes, Leo returned to England. He went first to Manchester to greet the family. He was thirty-one, tired of flirting around and ready for marriage. His sister, Addie Wheeler, was just as ready to help him. She introduced him to Blanche Ruf who came from Huningue in France and was staying two doors up the road with her uncle, Dr Charles Dreyfus and his wife, Hedwige.

Leo was completely smitten by this exquisitely dressed nineteen year old girl whose peachy cheeks were as bright and clear as her intellect. After courting her with invitations to parties, theatres, chaperoned walks, presents and respectfully worded letters addressed to MDSBBE (My dear, sweet, big, brown eyes), he proposed marriage. Blanche was delighted to accept. In her eyes, tall dandified charming Leo was the personification of an English gentleman. Compared to cosmopolitan Manchester, her life with her parents in the small provincial town of Huningue seemed drab and uninteresting.

In Huningue, Blanche had spoken German with her father, Leopold, and French with her mother, Alice. The reason for this is historical. In 1871, the Treaty of Frankfurt ceded Alsace Lorraine to Germany. From one day to another the German language had replaced French in education, administration and all official matters. Understandably the French resented having to change. Alphonse Daudet, a famous Alsatian writer describes their sense of loss in the story 'La Dernière Classe' (The Last Class). 'When a people is enslaved, hanging on to its language is like hanging on to the key of its prison.'

Alice's forbears had lived in Rixheim and Mulhouse and would have known what it meant to live under German occupation. Why then did she agree to marry Leopold Ruf, a representative in a textile firm in Sulzburg, Germany? The reason was purely financial. Her father had married again when his first wife died leaving eight children. His second wife was equally fertile; she had eight children as well. With eight boys and eight girls to feed, Herr Dreyfus had to leave his work in textiles and take a farm in the Argau in Switzerland. Even there he had a hard time since he was bound to provide each girl with a dowry, however small. Since it was necessary to find a neutral meeting place for the first encounter with Alice, the Schadchen (official matchmaker) who had already acquainted Leopold with details about Alice including her difficult financial situation, brought the two together in the home of a neighbour. Alice was both pretty and shrewd. Realising the chance of finding a better match was minimal, she stifled her anti-German feelings and set out to please. She succeeded. Leopold was bowled over. He, too, could switch on the charm, when necessary. They accepted each other and lived happily, if cantankerously together for over fifty years.

With Alice's minuscule dowry and some money of his own, Leopold bought a small store in Huningue, Lorraine, near the Swiss border. Together, they built it up into an efficient, moderate price enterprise like Woolworth's. Alice did the books in the store and supervised the staff of young boys who travelled in daily from the frontier town of Basle which was a couple of miles away. At lunch time the entire staff and family ate together in the big dining room of the family flat upstairs. She and Leopold had seven children in quick succession, beginning with two girls, Blanche and Yvonne and finishing with five sons called Henri, Max, Andrè, Gaston and Georges. The children were never told their mother was pregnant. When a certain Aunt Berthe came to stay and their mother disappeared with her into the spare room upstairs, they knew a baby would follow in a few days.

When Andrè was five, he told his sisters;
'I know what's in Tante Berthe's suitcase. It's a baby brother'.

Blanche was a kind, unselfish girl. Neither she nor Yvonne were allowed in the shop or the kitchen, so she did what she could to help the maid with the children when she came back from school. When they were sixteen, she and Yvonne spent a year in a finishing school for young ladies in Nancy. After this, they were expected to stay at home and wait for marriage. Although Mother Alice was an intelligent, musical woman herself, she had neither time nor money to spend on outside entertainment for her children. Social life was centred round the synagogue.

Everyone in the Jewish community in Huningue stopped all work on Friday night to prepare for the Sabbath by lighting the seven candles and preparing a special meal. The following morning they went to the synagogue. Leopold enjoyed taking his family to the service. Dressed in his best, black suit and wide brimmed hat he and the boys would don their praying shawls and sit downstairs whilst Alice, smart but soberly clad, would take her place with the other women in the gallery. The hard working Jewish citizens relied on these weekly get-togethers. How else could they discuss business or hear the local gossip and celebrate engagements and weddings?

Then as now the Jews celebrate five very important events in their history. Passover commemorates the exodus from Egypt under Moses, Shavuth and Sukkoth the beginning and the end of the harvest. Sukkoth also reminds the Jews of the wanderings of their ancestors in the wilderness before entering the promised land. Yom Kippur is a day of remembrance and the day of judgement, and, very important, Rosh Hashoneh heralds the New Year, a time to celebrate and a time to atone. Two other times of rejoicing are for the circumcision of a new born child, and for Bar Mitzvah, the day when a boy, having reached puberty, reads from the holy book, the Torah, in the synagogue for the first time.

Blanche's aunt and uncle in Manchester celebrated these as well, but the social life they led went beyond the barriers of the Jewish synagogue and into the main stream of Manchester society. Aunt Hedwige had no children and was able to afford to take Blanche to theatres, concerts and public lectures. She and Addie Wheeler were delighted by her engagement to Leo. It was, after all, what they had plotted and hoped for!

There was nothing to stop the young couple from being happy. Apart from being very much in love they were both Jewish, middle class and had not one but three languages in common. Leo had picked up French and German when studying in Neuchâtel. Although Blanche's English had improved during her time with the Dreyfus's and went from strength to strength once she settled in England permanently, she was never to lose her accent. Fortunately this was considered rather charming by the Jacoby sisters and brothers, including Henry who tended to put on airs.

'You're not a bad sort', he told her, 'even though you are a foreigner'.

Money too was no problem. Leo was already doing well in John Jacoby Ikles' before he went to Huningue to meet his bride's family. George Ruf, my mother's brother, who is eighty-two years old at the time of writing, remembers every detail of this visit.

'Le Vieux (Grandfather Ruf) handed Leo a dowry of twenty thousand French francs which was a princely sum in those days, and a far cry from the meagre marriage settlement he had received for his Alice. His early days of pushing a horse and cart with his goods around the villages were long since past. The store had made sufficient profit to enable him to set up a second business in Basle selling cloth wholesale which did even better, and he had bought a flat there to establish proof of residence for the Swiss bank.'

And money was not all Blanche and Leo received. Besides a host of presents for the house from relatives and friends, Le Vieux had ordered Alice (Grandmother Ruf) to buy the couple sufficient household linen to last a life time. The wedding took place on 7 July 1913.

George's eyes mist over as he conjures up that memorable day. 'They were married in the town hall in Huningue. The wedding party was held the next day in Basle in the Hôtel de l'Univers, the smartest venue in town. The marriage became a legend. Leo was so tall, so debonair, so different from everyone else, we all called him the 'Prince Charming from England'. His English accent in speaking French and German was very droll! He got on with everyone in the family and even endeared himself to the musicians in the orchestra. Well, he tipped them generously, didn't he? He gave all the children sweets, and even persuaded the hotel manager to organise fireworks at the end of the festivities. Blanche wore white, Yvonne had chosen pink chiffon. Like a true English gentleman, Leo wore a dress suit with tails made in Saville Row. Gaston and I were in sailor suits. Max, who was a student in Baden, had smartened himself up. Henri had persuaded his boss in the clothes firm where he worked to sell him some blue serge cheap. There must have been over a hundred guests. All in all 'le mariage' was talked about in Basle for months afterwards. George gives a soft, sentimental smile in happy reminiscence. 'Dear, dear Leo. I loved him then and always loved him'. So did the family, even crabby old 'Papa Ruf'. 'That husband of Blanche in England', he'd say. 'He's a real English gentleman'.

They left for their honeymoon in Brittany two days after the wedding and then went straight back to London. They wrote to the Ruf family regularly, of course, but it was difficult to meet. Blanche had her first daughter, Lilian, in March 1914. The Great War broke out the following September and Leo was called up six months later. Eventually he was posted to Salonika and stayed there for the duration of the war. Marion was born two years after the peace Treaty of Versailles in 1920 and Jean followed two years later'.

After Leo left for Salonika, Blanche joined his sister Addie and her husband Leslie in Manchester. She was happy enough with them personally, but her foreign accent attracted a lot of attention. A wave of anti-German feeling had swept over Great Britain once war was declared. Anyone German or speaking with a German accent was bitterly resented. Shops and businesses belonging to Germans who had been in Britain for years were vandalised and they were insulted in the streets.

Leo's family were glad that their father had a certificate proving Danish nationality since Schleswig-Holstein belonged to Denmark when he was living there. The two provinces were ceded to Germany in 1861, four years after his departure for Manchester. The Jacoby sisters flaunted their Danishness in company wherever possible to avoid a German label, nor did they really want a Jewish label as such. Their mother's early death and their father's Saturday commitments with the Halle Orchestra had meant there was no one to insist on them attending the synagogue. As an officer in the army Leo had been treated as an 'English gentleman' and he wanted this to continue. Blanche was not worried about going to a synagogue; she did what he wanted and if 'Anglicising' meant avoiding opprobrium from the British rank and file she was all for it. None of us children knew anything of the Jewish festivals mother had attended as a young girl.

Back in London after the war Leo bought a large flat in Overstrand Mansions, Prince of Wales Drive, Battersea, resumed work at the firm, John Jacoby Ikle, and settled down at last with Blanche and his three small daughters. He earned enough money to pay for Liza, the cook, and Violet Blow, our nanny. We children adored Nanny Blow; partly because she had a good way with children and partly because she was always there for us whilst mother, naturally, had shopping or sewing to do.

'You cannot expect me to look after the children and help as well.' Nanny Blow would say, quaffing tea in the kitchen and watching Blanche tear into the cooking. 'I brings up the little mites and talks to 'em, that's my job, Madam.'

And talk she did, over five years, virtually refusing to leave until Lilian and Marion were ensconced in their primary school, grandly named, Mrs Oakley's Academy for Young Ladies.

From our babyhood she included us in her conversations. 'Shall we eat our pudding, Marion duckie?' 'What shall we do about the tangled mass of black hair on that chubby head of yours, baby Jean?'

Once we were past the age of two we were privy to her world views and love life. 'Them aeroplanes should never have been allowed, if you ask me,' or 'Leslie, my gentleman friend in the marines tells me I'm putting on weight. Do you agree?'.

The afternoon pram parade in Battersea Park was the best time of all. Nanny and her cronies rocked and fed the babies, supervised the toddlers and gossiped in equal measure. Far from telling any child to go and play they encouraged our participation egging us on to repeat everything we had seen or heard.

Lilian announced that Isobel Luck, known by the servants as 'the sausage queen', because that was what she gave them every day for lunch, had sworn the butcher was putting bread in the sausages. Marion mentioned that Mummy had told Daddy the colonel upstairs should be ashamed of putting Mabel in the family way. As for the curate of St Saviour's, I nearly ruined him by telling the park assembly he had gone over to Rome. The news of his apostasy reached the bishop. He sent for the curate who explained he had gone to Rome on holiday.

We were heartbroken when Nanny left to marry her Leslie and live in Portsmouth. Listening, as usual, to Mummy's phone call to her bosom friend, Ethel Hill, I heard her say, 'I can't tell you how pleased I am that lazy woman has left. I only kept her on for the sake of the children.'

Thank God she did. We should have hated to miss those unforgettable conversations.

Chapter two
Growing up in the suburbs

In his bachelor days Leo had lived in the suburb of Putney. He had enjoyed the leafy, green commons in the vicinity and the boating scene along the river so much he bought a house there for his family. It had two storeys, all sorts of rooms and corners and a large garden to boot. Determined to become part of the Putney community, he and Blanche joined the local Conservative Association and played tennis at the Woodborough club near their house. Belonging to a club in London was also common with people working in the City or in the West End. It was somewhere to rest between business calls and a good place to talk and entertain clients and friends. Leo chose the Overseas League and later, when he could afford it, the French Club, both in the West End.

Like good Conservatives he and Blanche decided to send the three of us to the best school in the area, Putney High School. It was one of the twenty-six schools belonging to the Girls' Public Day School Trust set up in 1872, to provide a fine academic education at comparatively modest cost. Although many middle class parents, including Leo, sometimes found it a struggle to pay the fees, they saw no alternative. The idea of a 'council school' for their children was unthinkable.

We went first to Lytton House, the section for the five to eleven year olds. It was a few minutes up the road, and the grounds of the senior school were behind it, set in acres of pretty grounds with the main buildings fronting Putney Hill. Known locally as 'Millionaire Row' the Hill was lined with grand houses set back from the road with large gardens front and back. The poet, Algernon Swinburne and other worthies had lived in these houses which have plaques in front to prove it!

Putney High School had everything a school could need: airy classrooms, an impressive assembly hall, laboratories, a library, a studio and excellent sports facilities including a well equipped gymnasium, a rounders field and several tennis courts. A dedicated staff of highly qualified women worked hard to ensure we passed the School Certificate at the end of our fifth year. English, mathematics and a language were compulsory plus two other subjects. Some girls took as many as seven or eight. They could continue their education in the lower and upper sixth form where they took Higher School Certificate. This was often required by employers and essential for every other university except Oxford and Cambridge who held their own entrance examinations.

A board of honour with the names and dates of the girls who had acquired a University degree, stencilled in gold, ran the full length of the wall at the back of Putney High School Hall platform. The headmistress used to stand firmly in front of this board during the daily assembly which consisted of hymns, prayers, Bible readings and a short sermon. When the Old Testament texts dealt with A begetting B, and B begetting C, I would cut off and peruse the illustrious names on that board. Since that time, respect for intellect and awe of God have been linked together in my mind.

The school was non denominational and girls could be admitted irrespective of background and beliefs. In fact, only a small handful of Indians and Jews came to the school in our day and the teaching of Christianity according to the tenets of the Church of England was considered of paramount importance. Religious assemblies were held daily, conducted with great efficiency and reverence. Scripture was a subject in its own right and we learned Bible verses by the yard. One or two form teachers did, however, take scripture without much knowledge of how to set about it. One, I remember, insisted on our writing out our verses, so we used to learn them with punctuation. 'Our father, (comma) hallowed be thy name (full stop).

Miss Chester, the headmistress, came a year after the Jacobys and stayed for years and years. Here was a dedicated Christian indeed, whose scripture lessons were both inspiring and puzzling. Knowing that Jews did not accept Christ as the one and only true redeemer of mankind, I faced Dad with this question. 'What exactly are we, Dad, Jewish or Christian or what?' He parried by admitting that, 'yes, we were Jewish but er... the important thing is to lead a good life, believe in God, and well, fit in. And don't you think Mum needs some help in the kitchen?' I decided I would fit in as a Christian.

On a cultural plane different teachers organised visits to art galleries, places of interest like the United Dairies or Kew Gardens. We had concerts, lectures, school and staff plays and a reading aloud competition in which the whole school took part. If a student was discovered speaking or reading with a cockney accent, elocution lessons were recommended immediately. It was a social sin to speak 'badly'. Expressions like 'A pity about his speech. You can tell he's not from the top drawer. Murders the King's English, my dear', were common parlance and jokes told in a cockney accent, or what the speaker thought was a cockney accent, always raised a laugh.

I enjoyed drama immensely but failed to appreciate the value of music and dancing lessons. Hardly surprising since I had no sense of rhythm and could not sing a note. Although Miss Thornton, who sloped forward at forty-five degrees as she walked, was a wonderful teacher in class two in Lytton House; the Morris dancing she introduced had its comical side. Girls at the awkward age look even more awkward when they fail to 'set to' correctly, or changed to the wrong partner or sent flying all over the floor the sticks that represented swords of the brave warriors of old.

Alas! A further ordeal was in store — eurhythmics. Miss Phoebe Frensham, a scrawny female dressed in flying draperies, did her best to make us move through music. As her pianist, similarly bedraped, frenziedly tinkled all over the keyboard, she would utter commands like, 'Be leaves falling off the trees! You are the west wind blowing o'er the plain! You are waves lapping a stormy shore!' Fortunately all three Jacobys were too clumsy to be picked for a publicly performed eurhythmic mime telling the tale of Aneassin and Nicolette. This was quite ghastly and the source of many a family joke for years to come. Fortunately fluttering Phoebe left after this performance to get married. Teachers were not allowed to continue after marriage. It was the only time I appreciated this rule.

Following the public school dictate that a healthy mind can only exist in a healthy body, a lot of time was allotted to games and gymnastics, and an inordinate number of cups (often real silver), colours, sashes and badges were awarded to the individuals and teams who excelled in them. Whereas Doreen Slatter was acclaimed for astronomically high results (which eventually gained her a fellowship in Oxford), Molly Lincoln acquired a god-like status when she was picked for the ladies' team in the Davis Cup tennis tournament.

Whilst the glorification of sport remains unchanged to this day, the ideas and views of people vary from decade to decade. Many of the parents of the children at Putney High School in the thirties were terrible snobs and narrow in their outlook and, naturally, the children took on their views. Not many travelled abroad – it was too expensive – so they mistrusted foreigners', 'Jews' and 'Blacks'. 'Black' was a pejorative term then, the enlightened word was 'coloured'.

My parents went automatically to the Continent every year, Blanche to spend time with her parents in Basle and Leo to attend the fashion shows in Paris (Les Collections). He would return full of new ideas for using John Jacoby Ikle's lace and trimmings, extravagant presents for all of us, and invitations to visit which we did collectively or on our own. Australian friends and kinsmen who had emigrated to places like America and Canada never failed to call if they found themselves in London. I remember names like Ikle, Loevanthal, Keyras, Myer, Levy and, naturally, Dreyfus. When the Nazis started to persecute the Jews in Germany, Leo worked hard with the British Board of Guardians to get some families to England. Naturally they visited us when they arrived and many became firm friends.

At fourteen, I won a scholarship to the prestigious and even more expensive St Paul's Girls' School in Hammersmith which meant a twenty minutes bus journey each way every day. Once there it was another world! No one cared a fig how rich you were, what colour you were, where you lived or what you believed.

From its inception it had taken on board the traditions of St Paul's Boys' School which was founded in 1509 by John Colet, Dean of St Paul's. Three hundred years later, lack of space compelled them to move the school out to Hammersmith in the West of London. In 1895 a nearby site in Brook Green was selected for St Paul's School for Girls and this was officially opened on 15 April 1904 by HRH the Princess of Wales (later Queen Mary). Although many additions have been made since, the original red and grey stone buildings remain; impressive, dignified and functional. Since John Colet had always intended that a girls' school be established on his foundation, it is, perhaps, no surprise to see busts and portraits of him on the oak panelled walls of the entrance lobby and marbled tiled corridors running between the main hall and the classrooms. An old spacious library recently refurbished with identical wood, enhances this feeling of traditionalism.

Academically, socially and culturally the school was run on the same lines as Putney High School but everything was on a larger and more liberated scale. Competition for a place was intense. The pupils of the school as well as outsiders like myself could try for a scholarship. At Putney High School where the scholarship girls found it hard to win social recognition, the gold scholar's badge from St Paul's with the name of the wearer on the back, was a coveted status symbol.

Each year there were three mixed ability classes of twenty-five to thirty girls with separate divisions in Latin, French and Mathematics. A great help for anyone with a 'weak subject' and a chance to make friends from outside your own form. Most pupils stayed on for two years after taking school certificate or matriculation and the eighth form for the high flyers studying for the university entrance examinations was always full.

The form mistress moved up with her students for two to three years. We were lucky to have Miss Schofield who was like a personal friend to us all, organising outings together and a party in her flat at the end of term. Somehow she seemed to share rather than impart her deep knowledge of English language and literature.

A conscience clause was available to those who wished to opt out of morning prayers. A few Asian students, the kosher English Jews and some of the refugees from Europe stayed in a classroom and came into the hall for the notices. Except for a few music part-timers who arrived later in the day, the teachers, whom we called Ma'am, all attended assembly. The first sight of them in their robes filing in with great dignity filled me with awe but I soon found out that, by and large, they were as approachable and efficient as Miss Schofield.

Staff and school were present together for lunch in the dining room, which contained tables laid for ten pupils with a chair for a teacher at the head to serve and make conversation. The rest of the teachers sat apart at the 'high table' in front. We would stand behind our chairs watching them come in smiling and relaxed, with the exception of Miss Constance Geary, a Geography teacher of considerable merit. She had a purposeful, rolling gait and strode in like an admiral set to inspect the fleet. Ursula Bozman who took English would patter in behind her rather like a dinghy behind a battleship.

Miss Geary's family had worked in India for many generations and she had followed this tradition by teaching for three years in a mission school in Pune before coming to St Paul's. She stayed eight years then left in March 1937 on the invitation of the Punjabi government to take up the work of Principal of Lahore College where she suggested Ursula Bozman should join her as teacher. Partition between India and Pakistan was proclaimed on 15 August 1947 when Constance was on leave in Tibet. She returned to Lahore to find that all colleges had been closed and chaos reigned. She returned to the UK in January 1948, where she took her doctorate examinations. In June she went out to Nigeria as Chief Woman Education Officer (CWEO) in the Northern Region. Considering her experience of educating Muslim women it was a natural choice.

Fifteen years later, I too went out to Nigeria, to head the sixth government girls' school in the North which was situated in the small town of Yola in Adamawa Province. Dr Geary was stationed in the administrative capital of Kaduna. She kept in touch with Yola, naturally, by letter and by visitation, and I met up with Ursula in Maiduguri.

Coincidence or not, five other ex-Paulinas were working as WEOs in the North: Eileen Foster, Pauline Summer, Mary Kinton, Mary Hillersden and Grisell Roy. Grisell was actually stationed in Yola as Provincial Woman Education Officer, and she had done the spade work in setting it up in conjunction with Constance Geary (who had been her form teacher for three years).

Grisell and I overlapped at school without actually meeting since she had concentrated on music, playing the oboe and running the musical society. Her reports on its activities appear year after year in the 'Paulina' magazine. One concert where the players had played each others' instruments, inspired this comment, 'We are afraid that those of us who performed, enjoyed ourselves more than the listeners'.

Joking apart, many parents chose to send their girls to St Paul's because of the emphasis it put on music. Counting the part-time tutors in single instruments the music staff sometimes numbered fifteen with Dr Herbert Howells, the famous composer, as its overall director. He was expected to oversee the junior and senior orchestras, the junior and senior choirs, and the weekly singing lessons for every class. Concerts and recitals were given to the public and once 'Dido and Aeneas' by Purcell was performed. The grand finale came on the last day of every term when, under his direction, the orchestras played the music of works such as 'The Seasons' by Vivaldi or songs by Haydn. A few professional friends took the main solo roles, and every other girl in the school joined in the singing.

Besides music, a clutch of societies existed to capture every possible interest or hobby: debating, French, field studies, girl guides, history, photography and many others. Dr Howell's daughter, Ursula, always took a leading part in the plays staged by the drama and the John Colet Society which also organised lectures and excursions. Folk dancing, brain child of the geography teacher, Miss Stoddart, lost momentum when she failed to turn up. 'We hope she will visit us sometime for we have no hope of improvement without her aid'. (From the Paulina.) The parents supported all the concerts, plays, discussions, debates and meetings with great enthusiasm. Mr and Mrs Cole, authors of innumerable books on economics, were especially vocal. Their daughters persuaded them to offer a prize of ten shillings for the best essay on The Ideal School and I won!

Other parents frequently in the public eye were: Sir Allan Mawer, Provost of University College, Leon Underwood, the sculptor, John Howard QC (he helped daughter Rosemary and me with our Latin homework), and his excellency, Mr Rama Rau, the Commissioner for India in South Africa. His daughters, Premila and Santa had to be boarders in Bute House, up the road, which had playing fields at the back for hockey, lacrosse and cricket; the last two were unfamiliar to me and I hated both!

However, the netball and tennis courts and superb gymnasium were very enjoyable. The staff was big enough to allow daily team training in netball and tennis and the school won many tournaments. The swimming pool was an unusual feature for the thirties. I was thrilled to have swimming lessons weekly throughout the year. Everyone's enthusiasm waned, however, when the penetratingly cold fogs called 'pea soupers' reduced visibility to nearly nil. 'A fog holiday' was called if it was bad enough to hold up the traffic and we were sent home early. With the onset of adolescence, excuses were found or invented for not going into the water. The 'I've got period, ma'am,' was the safest. Unfortunately, Fuzzy, alias Joan Robinson, the bright and breezy PE teacher with a mane of frizzy hair, had an uncomfortably accurate memory and would get decidedly 'sarky' (sarcastic) if a girl used the excuse twice in a month!

A black shapeless costume was compulsory for swimming and an even more shapeless beige, square necked, flared skirted garment was worn for sport and gymnastics. Nicknamed the sack, it came in three sizes only: large, medium and small and was run up by two wispy seamstresses tucked away in a stuffy sewing room next to the stationery store. The new girls drowned in their 'sack' and the busty or quick growing young fourth and fifth formers were 'straining at the seams'. The school uniform was no improvement. A black square necked tunic hung over a white, square neck blouse and black or tan wool stockings thrusting through dark baggy knickers completed the uglification. A black or dark blue overcoat or gaberdine and a real bowler with a hard rim had to be worn. We were forbidden to dent it in any way. Of course we did and got detention if we were caught.

'I can always spot a Paulina on a bus', Mum used to say. 'She looks so awful'.

Socially, out of school hours, we dressed in our best to go to tea or to birthday parties at each others' houses. Sometimes we stayed the weekend or were invited for the school holidays. Dad's customers often let him have expensive dresses very cheap or gave him remnants of velvet or taffeta. Mother had a 'little woman who sews', Miss Andrews, come for a day a month to sew curtains, and make up lovely dresses from these materials, adding real lace collars and cuffs from John Jacoby Ikle. Far from being shabby I was often the 'belle of the ball'!

Nor was I ever, ever ashamed of my home even though many of my Paulina friends lived in larger residences and in smarter areas like Holland Park, Mayfair, Kensington or standing alone in the country. Mother had a gimlet eye for bargains, especially in the antique world. By dint of combing second hand shops, markets, especially one in the Caledonian Road, sales in auction rooms and old houses, she had built up a lovely home with Turkish carpets on the parquet in the lounge, period furniture for the other rooms, fine book cases here and there, real silver cutlery, needlework pictures dating from the 14th century, original paintings and a plethora of porcelain ornaments: Dresden, Meissen, Spode, Worcester and others.

When the economic slump of the thirties hit John Jacoby Iklé, they were forced to cut everyone's salary by half. Desperate to supplement the family income, mother decided to use our attractive, roomy house as a means of making money: she would take in paying guests.

Chapter three
Life begins to change

The majority of paying guests came from France. Others hailed from Germany, Austria, Scandinavia, Finland (including the daughter of the Poet Laureate, Zilliacus), Italy, Poland and Czechoslovakia. They stayed for three to six months as a rule, attending courses in English at the Regent Street Polytechnic during the day and returning for a superb three course meal at night cooked by my mother. Our storage facilities were poor — a very small fridge and a stuffy larder but food was always fresh since the baker, greengrocer, butcher and fishmonger called at the back door and errand boys delivered the orders mother made at the grocer's and elsewhere the same day. Mary, our young live-in maid helped the daily woman with the domestic work, did the washing and served at table. We were seldom less than six sitting at the beautifully laid dining room table at night, often more.

Mother would also show the guests round London when they arrived and liked me to accompany them — after all, they paid to be part of the family. As I grew older I was able to take them. London has always something new to offer, so I did not mind at all. I could practise my French with guests from France and Belgium as they were often lazy about speaking English.

Lilian and Marion played their part by including the guests in their parties and taking them to local dances. They were also encouraged to invite their own friends. Ellen Mosenthal, a Jewish girl from Wannsee, Berlin, was with us for a year, taking matric at a Tutorial College. In June 1936, she invited Hugh Russel-Davies, a fellow student, to make up the numbers for the Putney Conservative Ball. He fell in love with Marion the minute he saw her. She was too young to take him seriously. He remained her devoted suitor and after seven years and far more than seven suitors she finally said 'yes'.

When Ellen left, her sister Liz took her place and stayed two years. We shared a bedroom and went to St Paul's together. The school had accepted at least twenty refugees from the continent, including Liz, at a minimal fee. They all justified this concession by passing their exams with flying colours.

Paddy Jadeja, a little Indian boy, son of a senior civil servant in Delhi, was another delightful guest. He was a boarder in Haileybury College and regularly spent his holidays with us. His uncle and guardian, Singh, had great charm and soon became a friend of the family, coming over for meals and inviting us back to eat in one of the few Indian restaurants that then existed in London. He would pay the bill cheerfully but never, never left anything in the way of a tip. As a result the waiters made a point of putting us near a toilet the minute they saw us arrive. To this day, I associate onion bhajees with the smell of urine.

Older male guests tended to cause problems. Carl Schmidt accused mother of stealing his shirts and threatened police action. They turned up at the back of his cupboard just in time! Stephen Szabo and Robert Pinet both attempted to scale the drainpipe in order to climb through the window of the bedroom upstairs, inhabited respectively by Jantina, a hideously obese Dutch vegetarian and Nadia a French version of the film star, Deanna Durban. The first had hysterics, the second phoned her mother to protest and was removed forthwith to North London.

Ten years on, Nadia turned up in Putney. She had married Robert on her return from England. Now a huge, voluble matron, she did not allow him or her two cowering daughters to get a word in edgeways.

Even though we knew our livelihood depended on our paying guests we were often glad when they left and we could be alone in the house for a few days before the next arrival. A French proverb sums it up: 'Les visiteurs font toujours plaisir, si ce n'est pas en arrivant, c'est en partant' (Visitors always give pleasure. If it is not when they arrive, it is when they leave).

Domestic crises were soon overshadowed by world politics. Early in 1938 Ernest Bevin, a charismatic socialist politician, had warned the British people that Hitler 'intended at the right moment and when he was strong enough, to wage war in the world'. Sure enough, in 1938, the German army marched into Austria and stayed there. Ignoring protests from most parts of the world including a vain attempt at appeasement on the part of the British prime minister, Sir Neville Chamberlain, Hitler continued his aggression by sending his army into Czechoslovakia in March, 1939.

In May, the same year, a Polish girl of fifteen, Maria Eiger, came to stay for a month. She, Liz and I made a happy trio and her journalist father suggested we visit them after Christmas for a skiing holiday. Poignantly, I remember a remark he made about Hitler over dinner in Putney the day before he returned to Poland with Maria.

'It's a well known fact that man has a 'wanted list' in every country in Europe. I'm on the Polish list. We journalists are very outspoken you know. Ha! Ha!'

The skiing trip never materialised. Once the German army marched into Poland on 1 September 1939, we did not see or hear from the Eigers again.

The British cabinet took immediate action by sending an ultimatum to Hitler demanding the withdrawal of his troops. My parents and I were having elevenses in the lounge on 3 September 1939, listening to the radio and laughing over the antics of Tiggles, a newly acquired kitten, when Chamberlain came on the air at exactly eleven fifteen.

'This morning', he said, in that resonant, reassuring voice of his, 'the British ambassador in Berlin handed the German Government a final note saying that unless we heard from them by eleven o'clock that they were prepared at once to withdraw troops from Poland, a state of war would exist between us. I have to tell you now than no such undertaking has been received, and that consequently this country is at war with Germany'.

The outbreak of war was to change the lives of everyone in Britain including the

Jacobys. It was generally assumed that Germany would attack Britain from the air almost immediately and inflict thousands of casualties. Everyone was issued with a gas mask in case they used gas. In order to save the children from this imminent disaster most London schools decided to evacuate. Putney High School moved to St Anne's School, Caversham in Berkshire and St. Paul's Girls' School teamed up with Wykham Abbey in Buckinghamshire. The paying guest business had dried up except for Paddy and with no one wanting to pay for trimmings or lace in wartime, I had to leave school.

Inspired by Vera Brittain's book, 'The Testament of Youth', I decided to become a nurse as she had done in the 1914-18 War. Brighton Hospital agreed to take me when I was eighteen. Rather than wait around for six months, I took a job in a very odd school providing a home and tuition for children from babyhood to fourteen in Stow-on-the-Wold, Gloucestershire. The staff slept and worked in a bitterly cold, rambling house with a view of the churchyard on one side and the village stocks on the other. A nurse and a matron made sure the young ones were comfortable but the teaching side was abysmal. No one was trained, the books and equipment were inadequate, and Miss Chilcott the headmistress whose nickname was 'Weather' because of her varying moods, appeared to consider the welfare of her dog, Janie, more important than her charges.

I had been in Stow-on-the-Wold a month when Miss Chilcott received a written request from the mother of two of her students, Claire and Robert Lamb. She had divorced and was living in India. Instead of returning the children to school after the holidays, the father had left them with his old governess in Ruffec in the West of France and joined the army. Could someone from the school go and fetch them? With my knowledge of French I was the obvious choice. Dad organised the travel arrangements so I had to pick up my passport, special visa and tickets in London. It was bliss to be in the sane, warm atmosphere of a family after that crazy school. The train to Dover was crowded and blacked out but otherwise everything seemed normal and the Channel crossing to Calais was equally uneventful, even though the boat was surrounded by a convoy of warships looking out for mines. Apart from the presence of French service men on the trains and in Paris where I had to change and wait two days for the 'correspondence' to Ruffec, I saw little military activity. The French people I chatted to believed implicitly in the impregnability of the Maginot Line on their eastern frontier and were convinced that the enemy would never be able to break through it.

A middle-aged portly man called Commander Edward Fletcher engaged me in conversation over breakfast on my first morning in Paris. He told me he was an ex-naval officer staying at the Hotel Madeleine as a permanent guest. When he heard what had brought me to Paris, he summoned his secretary immediately and told him to take me to Cooks to change my money, to the Gare du Nord to book a seat on the train to Ruffec and to the Embassy to check on the childrens' visas. He finished by asking me to dinner that evening and it seemed churlish to refuse.

Thanks to his secretary, everything was done that needed to be done very quickly and I spent the rest of the day with my great uncle, Dr Yvan Dreyfus, his wife, Emma and their three sons, Paul, Charly and Bernard in their spacious flat in Boulevard Haussman. Mother's youngest brother, Georges and his wife, Jacquo, joined us for an exquisitely cooked lunch. Not long married, she was the epitome of chic in her haute couture black dress, pearls and 'Eiffel Tower' high heels. From time to time she took out her compact to powder her nose and pat her perfectly set curls.

My country garb: tweed coat, lisle stockings, thick sweater, shapeless skirt and flat sensible brogues were out of place in that elegant company. Even Paul who was on leave from the army looked like a character from an operetta in his immaculately cut officer's uniform emphasising the squareness of his shoulders and the slimness of his waist. Gallantly he put me on the bus back to the hotel and strode off gaily 'pour un rendezvous avec Marie', (for a date with Marie). Poor Paul! After the fall of France, he was imprisoned in a concentration camp and shot by the Germans as they were pulling out of France in 1944.

The dinner with the Commander was an intriguing experience. He took me to a select bistro, specialising in oysters which I had never tasted before. Lots of champagne gave me confidence and only three oysters slithered to the floor instead of down my gullet. Euphorically, I accepted an invitation to go to a night club the following evening. As we drove towards the Boîte de Joie, he started to fondle me. I drew back terrified, and started talking about home, Mum and Dad, Tiggles and Miss Chester's scripture lessons. He stopped, surprised by this torrent of wholesomeness, but rallied and tried again. The situation worsened once we arrived. Scantily dressed young ladies milled around us pawing my would-be seducer and promising him or me God knows what. At seventeen I did not know the English words, let alone the French! In spite of my efforts to shake it off, his hand kept crawling up my lisle stockinged right leg. He was plying me with drinks, ogling the girls and chuckling salaciously at the thought of the 'show' to come. 'That is really something, girlie fair. You'll see'. I did not wait to 'see'. Pretending I needed the toilet I left him, grabbed my coat from the cloakroom and a taxi outside in less time than it takes to write this sentence. Back in my hotel room with the door locked, I fell asleep only to be woken two hours later by the air raid siren and the hotel manager knocking at everyone's door and shouting: 'Descendez vite à la cave tout le monde. Descendez s'il vous plaît', (Will everyone please go down to the cellar).

Heart pounding I stayed put. Better death than embarrassment and further gropings in the cellar. Two long hours later, a second siren announced the all clear. I caught the Ruffec train early and had no trouble finding the children and taking them back to London by night fall. There was plenty of room for them. The paying guest business had died, except for Paddy in the holidays and both my sisters now lived away from home. Marion had joined the WAAF's and was training as a catering officer and Lilian had taken a 'top secret' job as secretary in the Ministry of Information in an equally secret location. (When this was no longer secret she told us she had been living in Woburn Abbey, the stately home of the Duke of Bedford, preparing propaganda leaflets to drop over Germany.)

Conditions in Stow-on-the-Wold school became worse, not better and the holidays could not come quickly enough. An unexpected phone call from Miss Chester just after Christmas in Putney asking us to see her, was to change the direction of my life. She urged me to return to Putney High School where I could resume studying for the Higher School Certificate and waived the fees as an inducement. I accepted with alacrity and the nursing profession lost a very unpromising student! The site on Putney Hill had been ceded to the Metropolitan Police 'for the duration', but part of Putney High school had returned to 378 Upper Richmond, just round the corner from 87

Howard's Lane. I had to work out my notice of three months and started there in May. With a number of students evacuated to Caversham near Reading, the Putney sixth form was down to two: a blonde prim girl called Jane Segar and myself. Fortunately we were taking the same subjects, French, Latin and English.

The scarcity of imported foods: meat, bananas and other exotic fruits irked us but we ate well enough on the ration system. Mum did marvels with meatless sausages, whale meat, dried eggs and powdered milk. When Dad balked at swallowing it she secretly poured it into a milk bottle and he drank it up without realising it was not the real thing!

Learning to live with minor privations is one thing, living with fear is something else. We were as anxious and scared as everyone else in Britain when the German forces invaded Norway and Denmark in April 1940 and followed up their attack in May by breaking through the Maginot line and occupying France. The British army found itself cut off from the French army and did its best to escape to England from Dunkirk. The efforts made by the navy and thousands of boats large and small from Britain to get them out is now a living legend. Invasion of our shores seemed imminent. The Luftwaffe started to bomb British towns, and were kept valiantly at bay by a small number of RAF fighter pilots. The Blitz on London in September landed the war on our doorstep.

At school the sirens announcing the onset of an air raid were the signal for everyone to go down to the cellar which ran the length of the basement. Each class had its appointed spot and continued the lesson there. Jane and myself were allocated the smallest space — a coal cellar furnished with three chairs and an electric fire. In spite of the discomfort and danger (which we seldom considered), we derived intense pleasure from studying together, especially with Esther Tomlin, an inspired teacher of English if ever there was one. She would continue discussing the lyricism and beauty of the verses of John Keats as calmly as if we were sitting in an Oxford tutorial. If the siren went before she was finished, the three of us were quite angry at being interrupted.

At night our family repaired to a communal air raid shelter in our neighbour's garden, equipped with blankets, 'Thermos flasks' and food for the night. Other Londoners had Anderson shelters in the garden, dived under reinforced kitchen tables or camped out on bunks or on blankets on the platforms of the London Underground tube stations. People chatted and sang together, determined to ignore the noise of the aeroplanes overhead, the thud of a bomb hitting its target and the constant sound of the anti-aircraft guns valiantly trying to defend their city.

Poor Mum was terrified and lost weight, feeling also the strain of not knowing what could be happening to her relatives in Switzerland and France. Dad was almost too busy to panic even though he saw a lot of death and destruction when acting as an air raid warden at night after working through the day. Old ladies in Putney used to love Mr Jacoby coming in to check their black-out precautions, finding him always so calm and reassuring. Some houses received direct hits. Frank Thoroughgood, the accountant at John Jacoby Iklé, returned home to find his wife dead in a pile of rubble. The bombing of the East End caused the most devastation. The strangely beautiful but terrible sight of the sky lit up all night by the red flames rising from its blazing buildings is a memory few Londoners will ever forget.

Jane and I passed our exams in spite of all the havoc around us and were both accepted by Oxford University. I also qualified for Exeter and London University but feeling that Oxford might prove too snobbish for me and too expensive for the parents, I opted for London which offered a three year degree course and a year's teacher training at its Institute of Education.

Like the schools, London University had evacuated to less dangerous places. Its Law school found itself in Cambridge and the Institute of Education had gone to Nottingham. University College had merged with the University Colleges of Wales, dividing according to departments: engineering in Swansea, medicine in Cardiff and french, history and science in Bangor. Students reading for an english or german degree plus students like myself, requiring the intermediate certificate, went to Aberystwyth.

I spent a very pleasant and peaceful year there, far away from the war. I lived with nineteen other female UCL students in an isolated luxury hotel with a huge garden called Cwmcynfelin three miles from the town itself. A special bus came to take us into college at half past eight each morning and collected us again at five o'clock. If we wanted to stay on we had to return on foot, round and round the mountain road behind Cwmcynfelin and down the long, dark, hotel drive hedged with rhododendrons, bristling with night jars, frogs and other nocturnal creatures. We judged the ardour of our escorts by their willingness to brave this long trek!

There were plenty of reasons to stay on in Aberystwyth. Our fellow students — mostly Welsh and English, with a sprinkling of Indian and West Indians — had the same broad-minded, open attitude as the Paulinas and we all got on very well together. The range of extra mural activities seemed boundless: drama and music groups, mountain climbing and field trips, religious and political societies and more besides.

Having been brought up as a Christian at school I concentrated on the inter denominational Student Christian Movement (SCM), attending their weekly meetings, bible study and prayer groups, weekend retreats and annual general conferences. I also accompanied my wealthy room mate, Pauline Blaxter, heiress to the Corona Drinks Consortium, to the meetings of the Labour Club which were dominated by the communists. I embraced socialism whole heartedly but refused to join the communist party like Pauline because its underlying philosophy of dialectical materialism was contrary to the tenets of Christianity. To be frank, this was the viewpoint of my SCM friends. In hindsight, I doubt if Pauline, or our friends or I knew too much about either!

'Anyone who is not a socialist at twenty has no heart. Anyone who is not a conservative at forty has no head', goes the saying.

However, we students discussed this and other ways of putting the world to right endlessly in the bus, in our meetings, in Cwmcynfelin, and in the crowded canteen at the top of the spiral staircase leading off the assembly hall. There was a lot of laughter and jokes and flippant conversation in that canteen as well. Many a time a Welsh boy or girl would suddenly stop in mid-slurp and break into song. Others would take up the tune and in a moment a whole group would be singing their hearts out in perfect harmony.

During the first long vacation in London I determined to put my socialistic principles to the test by working as a waitress in the canteen of the Civil Defence Headquarters which was based in the Geological Museum in Exhibition Road. I suppose I expected the working classes to be the goodies and the upper classes to be the baddies. I found out, of course, that some of the waitresses, kitchen staff, and workmen in the museum were nice and some were not. Similarly, the secretaries, army officers, civil defence and museum staff who came for their meals varied from pleasant and polite to difficult and rude whatever their class.

The menu was limited because of wartime restrictions and so were the cutlery and plates. We took different shifts and stayed the night in bunk beds in the basement if we were on late. We felt very safe there even when we had an air raid. After this somewhat troglodyte existence, it was a relief to leave the uncertain conditions of living in London and return to the peace and quiet of Wales.

Chapter four
Further education

The set-up in Bangor was different but just as enjoyable as Aberystwyth. Dr Leonard Tancock, (Tank), specialist in French Literature at University College was responsible for our accommodation. After a lot of running around, he had finally persuaded some families in a village called Llanfairfechan to take us in as lodgers. It was a perfect jewel of a place, backed by mountains full of waterfalls with a little stream bubbling through it to the sea.

Joan Todd, a history student from Todmorden in Lancashire, and I stayed in Mailor, Valley Road with Mr and Mrs Williams and their ten year old son Gwynn. They could not have been kinder or more hospitable. Like all Welsh parents they set tremendous store on education and their greatest ambition was to have a teacher or preacher or a professional man in the family. They asked us to coach Gwynn for his eleven plus exam and when he got into Grammar School, their happiness knew no bounds. After that Gywnn and I tackled French together.

Surnames seem to be in short supply in Wales. Most people in the village were called Evans, Jones, Hughes, Thomas, Roberts or Williams. Their trade or special feature was attached to the name to distinguish them from each other: Evans the Milk, Jones the Post or Hughes the Tall. Welsh was their first language and everyone was bi-lingual, switching from one to the other in a split second.

Bangor University was a solid, stone building on a hill rising out of the town itself with sheep grazing on its slopes. We had our lectures there from the staff of both colleges, studied in an excellent library and participated in all college activities if we felt like it.

Professor Jeffrey, Vice Principal of UCL, was a very caring man. He arranged for us to use the village institute as a social centre. Even though Bangor was not far away, we found it more convenient to form our own branch of the Student Christian Movement and hold meetings there combining with Bangor in services and conferences. Similarly UCL had its own French and history Society. With the history lecturers also resident in the village, they were seldom short of speakers: Dr Alfred Cobban could fill us in on European history, and the 'dishy' Dr Lepatourel lent charm to the Middle Ages. Once, just once, Professor John Neal vouchsafed to give a talk on the Age of Elizabeth. His recently published book on Queen Elizabeth had plunged him into the Tudor world and he found difficulty in emerging from it. Like King Charles' head haunts Mr Dick in David Copperfield, Queen Elizabeth completely absorbed John Neal. She popped up constantly in conversation, was referred to in every lecture and, if he did Vouchsafe to write an article for a college magazine, or any other publication, he chose to write about — you've guessed it — Queen Elizabeth.

Sunday evenings would find us all sprawling by the Institute's huge log fire engaged in lighter entertainment: family games, debates, discussions or amateur dramatics. We wrote a special show for Dr Pye, Managing Director of Pye Radio Products, when he came on a flying visit and he was so impressed by our wit and talent, he sponsored all the finalists for a month's intensive French Course held in Exeter during the Easter vacation. In peace time, all language students, then and now, spent a year abroad. This was impossible in war time so Dr Pye's offer was invaluable.

Since cinemas, theatres, pubs and restaurants were closed on Sundays and the bus service was curtailed, those get-togethers at the Institute were a godsend. The Welsh went to church or chapel regularly twice a day in towns and villages. I went to a service in the Methodist church with the Williams. The Welsh judge a speaker or a preacher by the length and eloquence of his sermon, happy if he holds an audience spellbound by the power of his emotion (called 'hwyl'). I experienced this several times and it made me understand the feelings of the German people listening to Hitler.

French films and plays in London in the vacation were few and far between. The village did have one cinema, the Regal, which must have shown the oldest B films in the world, one every two days. We went there for two reasons: to keep warm if the heating broke down in our digs or to hold hands with our boyfriends. Even they were thin on the ground at times as the military situation worsened and more and more men received their calling up papers. A popular song summed it up.

'They're either too young or too old,
They're either too grey or too grassy green'.

We used to meet members of the armed forces at the dances at Bangor which students were forbidden to attend! Twice Llanfairfechan was graced with a military presence. A small contingent of British boys did a month's course there and a few months later a host of Americans descended on us for half a year. Idealistic students are not the soldier's ideal fodder. We had some good times together, a few hearts were broken, then they left as if they had never been.

Radio and newspapers kept us informed of the progress of the allied forces. News films and occasional documentaries seen in London would bring it nearer but overall, the saying 'You wouldn't know there was a war on' certainly applied to rural Wales. Our efforts to help 'the war effort' by looking after evacuees and collecting sphagnum moss, used in medical dressings, by the Red Cross, were tame in comparison with the brave fire fighters, ambulance men and other volunteer workers in London.

During the vacations my parents encouraged me to escape the danger of doodle bombs by picking fruit or potatoes in special agriculture camps organised by the government and by the students. When it was essential to cram for exams I went to Todmorden in Yorkshire to stay with Joan Todd and her family. Although coal was rationed her mother insisted on lighting a fire for us 'in the parlour'. A touching act of generosity since mill workers in Todmorden and other Lancashire cotton towns reserved this room for very special occasions such as a wedding or a funeral.

Our studies paid off and we each got a 2.2 grade in our degree. Mum and Dad came up to Llanfairfechan for a fortnight's holiday to celebrate. They arrived haggard and exhausted after weeks of fear from the 'doodle bugs', pilotless aircraft programmed to drop their bombs over London. Several had exploded on the platform as the train pulled out of Paddington Station.

Our final year was spent at the Institute of Education which had moved back to London from Nottingham and was functioning in a handsome Regency house in Portman Square as The Ministry of Information was in its original premises in the London University House, Malet Street. Joan Todd lodged with us in Putney and we were determined to enjoy ourselves in spite of a new German threat: the rocket bombs which suddenly exploded with an ear splitting bang. It was all right if you heard them, if you did not 'you'd had it'. If the siren sounded at night, all four of us squashed into the shelter which had been installed under the kitchen table downstairs.

We attended lectures on education, psychology, teaching method, and, a new venture, sociology. This was given by Karl Mannheim in King's College and attracted a vast audience. With less academic work to do we spent a fair amount of time mooching around London — I remember an extraordinary visit to a captured German U Boat moored on the Thames. It was difficult to imagine how so many people could live under water in such cramped conditions. Joan dragged me to political and student union meetings, and I persuaded her to go to an occasional cinema or theatre. Black-out and transport difficulties at night did not deter us from dancing at King's College or the elegant Lyceum theatre which had been converted into a ballroom for the troops.

Karl Mannheim had proclaimed: 'Every activity is an educational experience'. We found that a splendid reason for doing what we liked!

The majority of students at the Institute of Education, including Joan and myself, studied for the Diploma of Education. Mature students with previous teaching experience took a different exam. Two Roman Catholic priests and Sam Amissah from Ghana were in that category. In spite of my international background I had never met a priest socially or anyone from West Africa. Sam had been teaching in Wesley College, Kumasi and was appointed vice principal on his return. He and his wife, Margaret, often came over to Putney with their daughter, Araba.

We sobered down when it came to teaching practice which took up two days a week and two months during the final term. Joan taught history in Richmond Hill School and I went to the Green School in Isleworth working under the French teacher, Mrs Nemet, a bright, proficient teacher who sat in for all my lessons and offered excellent advice and tips on teaching. After seeing 'Le Malade Imaginaire' (The Hypochondriac) at Portman Place, which a few of us had produced and staged ourselves, she invited us to repeat it at the Green School. We followed that up by giving performances at St Paul's Girls' School, Putney High School and other London schools. As the pompous, foolish young Thomas, I got the most laughs and my friends told me I was a natural for the part! This production which was done for our own amusement, paid off in the end. Out of the hundred plus students, only four passed with distinction and I was one of them! As a result, I had offers to teach from several schools and chose to go out of London, to High Storrs Grammar School for Girls, Sheffield, Yorkshire.

Pleased to have a daughter with BA (Hons), Dip Ed, after her name, Dad offered me a holiday before starting in Sheffield at the beginning of September. I went to an international centre in Stratford-upon-Avon with Singh Jadeja. It was run by a Quaker couple, Arthur and Elsie Walters, under the aegis of the United Nations Association. He was Professor of Agriculture in Cambridge and they generally had a student from abroad lodging with them, more out of kindness than for profit. They held international get-togethers monthly in their Cambridge house during term-time and ran informal, inexpensive holiday courses in interesting places like Stratford-upon-Avon and Cambridge in the vacation.

There were about forty of us in Stratford. Elsie and Arthur made everyone feel at home from the moment they arrived by enlisting their help in organising the programme. During the day we went sightseeing or boating on the Avon, or wandered about in twos and threes. In the evening we would have a brains trust or a discussion or a dance or an informal concert where we could learn each other's songs and dance each other's dances.

British nationals were in the minority. The other guests that summer included refugees from Europe who had settled in Britain, or students and professional people from India, Ceylon, Burma and West Africa. Elsie had brought along her lodger, Christopher Chukwuemeka Mojekwu, a law student at the London School of Economics which had moved to Cambridge for the duration (a topical phrase meaning for the duration of the war). Christopher, in his turn, had mustered his friends: Godfrey Nkemena, Clifford Ogadazi, Emmanuel Uku, Raymond Njoku, and Joseph Ojukwu.

On 14 August 1945, three months after the surrender of Germany to the allied forces, we heard a momentous announcement on the radio. The atom bomb on Hiroshima had finally brought the Japanese to their knees and they too had surrendered. Our group joined the citizens of Stratford in the street to celebrate. We danced, we clapped and we shouted in wild relief that the carnage of war had come to an end. Christopher Mojekwu and I danced and chatted together all evening.

Unlike Raymond Njoku, who had all the girls swooning at his charm and classic good looks, Christopher had fully African features with pronounced thick lips and a very dark complexion. Seeing his dark eyes light up when he smiled and hearing his gentle voice dispelled my initial discomfort at such an unfamiliar appearance. He was only a little taller than myself but his very broad shoulders, tapering to a surprisingly small waist made him look taller. He dressed simply, student style, in a rough, brown tweed sports jacket, mostly, and grey Oxford bags (flannel trousers). The overall impression was of a very virile and attractive man. Like most of his friends he preferred his Nigerian name, Emeka, to Christopher.

We kept up the acquaintance by correspondence after we got home. He had returned with the LSE to London and I had begun teaching French in Sheffield. When he had time and money enough, he came up North to see me. My kindly, somewhat simple landlady, Mrs Downing, whom I called 'Ma' did not honestly approve of him. When I mentioned him or whenever she saw his frequent letters slide through the letter box in the kitchen, she'd say in her broad Yorkshire accent, 'Ee luv, I don't know why tha can't have a proper fellow'.

At first she was reluctant to put him up in the spare bedroom but relented eventually as she loved me like a daughter. 'Ah suppose 'e can cum', she said. 'The neighbours won't like it but it'll just 'ave to be a nine days wonder.'

Her decision was courageous for there was no way of keeping his visit a secret. Ma's house was one of ten in a row without any fencing back or front. The neighbours were bound to see Emeka 'going up yard'. This was a euphemism for going to the outside toilets which were at least fifteen sloping metres away from the houses. My first winter we had to dig a path through the snow and take a bucket of water with us as the cistern had frozen up! It was still cold when Emeka came up in February for a few days. We went for long walks in the wild Yorkshire dales, then huddled round the fire in the kitchen which was used for cooking and heating. We never liked to ask Ma to bring in more coal from the shed outside since it was rationed and expensive.

Later the British Council invited Emeka and other foreign students to attend a summer course at Sheffield University. They were taken to see a glass factory, stainless steel works and some ancient caves. Emeka got tickets for me and my gym teacher friend, Jane Cherry, for their Saturday evening dance and Sunday social. We enjoyed meeting everyone including a rather smooth law student from his class in Cambridge called Ayo Rosiji and his slim, serenely pretty, quietly spoken fiancée, Clara Mann, who was taking a general degree in Exeter. She was one of three Nigerians studying there, the other two were men: Andrew Sagay and Saburi Biobaku.

Emeka and I also met during the holidays in London. After our first kiss, he wrote: 'What have you done to me? Are you using magic? I am more used to the company of men. This friendship is so different and yet, darling it makes me so happy.'

True he was the very opposite of a flirt. His two main interests were in the Anglican Church and most importantly the Scout Movement. He had been a local preacher at home and the Church Mission society in London sent him to preach in places as far away as Liverpool and Manchester. One Sunday in Easter we were hitch hiking to Cambridge and far away from a church. Emeka recited the anglican service in a wood instead. His ardent faith persuaded me to be confirmed — a step I had not taken at Putney High School.

He was equally devoted to scouting. He attended scout councils in Croydon, led weekend and summer camps in Gilwell Park Centre in Epping Forest and finished up by representing Nigeria at the world jamboree in Paris in 1946. The final accolade was an invitation to a garden party at Buckingham Palace given by King George V and Queen Elizabeth. The King had loved to attend scout camps when he was Duke of York and was a great patron of the organisation. A shy man with a stammer to overcome when speaking in public he was completely at ease singing and laughing with the boys round the camp fire.

Emeka rang me the minute he returned from the garden party.

'How was the King?' I asked.

'Almost speechless', he replied.

'And Queen Elizabeth?'

'Absolutely charming.'

During the school and university holidays we went with Elsie, Arthur and the group to Stratford and Cambridge. I have two particular memories: shuddering with cold as we said good night one icy winter outside my digs in Cambridge, then, the following spring, singing and laughing with joy in a boat for two, gliding softly under the willows beside the River Cam.

After two years in Sheffield I returned to London where I taught general subjects, including french, in the newly founded comprehensive school in Battersea. This move enabled Emeka and myself to meet on a more regular basis.

Chapter five
Mainly Mojekwu

I travelled by train to the school in Battersea every day, changing at Clapham Junction which had a regular service to East Croydon. The International Club, where Emeka was staying, was two minutes from the station. This club was the brain child of a go-ahead Irish entrepreneur called Terry Driscoll who had bought up a number of houses near to each other and converted them into boarding houses.

Many Nigerians stayed at the Club and were often calling in. I remember in particular, Sam and Irene Ighadaro, because they were older than the others. He was pursuing his studies in law and Irene had been the first woman from Sierra Leone to qualify as a doctor. The Club possessed a large sitting room suitable for dances and meetings and a dining room serving regular meals on demand. Butter, meat, eggs and other foodstuffs were still in short supply immediately after the war, so many students ate at the Club regularly. For what they paid, the food was good enough. The special fare for Christmas or similar festive occasions was tasty and plentiful. Terry Driscoll made up for this generosity by cutting down on rations for the next two weeks.

In fact, Terry worked hard for his lodgers, organising sight seeing trips and persuading London theatres to reduce the cost of tickets for a group of ten. He also had a special arrangement with Fairfield Hall which was near the Club and put on concerts, plays and all manner of entertainment. It was there we had an evening of song by the African American singer, Paul Robeson. The Hall was full to capacity and never in my life had I seen so many black people together. Remember, few black people lived in the suburbs. Once, Emeka and I crossed the road deliberately in Putney just to speak to a black stranger walking on the other side. It was such an event.

As a former teacher in Nigeria, Emeka was interested, if somewhat bemused, by the school in Battersea which was one of the first five comprehensive schools in London. The idea was for students to be together in one large secondary school instead of dividing into separate establishments according to the standard of the pupils. No more 'grammar', 'central', 'technical', 'secondary modern', just SECONDARY. The classes in Battersea were graded for practical purposes from A-B with a PB division for the students with learning difficulties. The PB came from the initials of their two teachers. Unfortunately and accurately, they were known as the 'practically barmy'.

It was rated old-fashioned to use the 'talk and chalk' teaching method. Whatever their ability, the pupils were encouraged to work everything out for themselves. The teacher was there to guide and elucidate knowledge, not to impart it directly. The London County Council — later, the Inner London Education Authority or ILEA — provided plenty of literature and equipment to enable them to do so. A good thing considering the parents of some of my cockney students were too poor to buy a pair of shoes, let alone a book. We teachers set projects in motion, showed films and did plenty of practical work. We were also free to take our students out to libraries, or museums or factories in school time if we thought the visit would help the learning process. Mr Cayley, the very approachable Head Teacher, happily provided free bus or train passes. Socially and culturally, the system was completely democratic especially where sport and drama were concerned. However, with so many new ideas flying about, the three Rs suffered and many left school unable to read and backward in writing and arithmetic.

The LCC also encouraged the teachers to use the extensive library in County Hall and to follow one of their many study courses, which ranged from 'Tennis for the Over Twenties' to 'A Study of Race Relations in Britain' given by Graham Little. The persecution of the Jews had made me all too conscious of racial discrimination but I had never had to consider the question of colour before meeting Emeka. I was merely aware that the ports of Liverpool, London and Cardiff had communities of black seamen married to white women (often rumoured to be prostitutes) and that Limehouse in the London docks was full of Chinese. I had met the Amissahs, a few West Africans at the vast SCM conferences during my university days and two Jamaicans: Capildeo, the President of the Students' Union in Bangor who had married a Welsh girl, and Michael, the storeman at John Jacoby Iklé.

My parents encouraged all three daughters to bring their friends home. When Marion came on leave she introduced them to 'Air Force types' and goodness knows how many members of the American forces. An engagement to a GI ended when she found out he had a wife already! Lilian, too, had a married man in her life, Dr Roman Sas, a brilliant expert on radar and electronics when the subject was still in its infancy. He was honest enough to tell her he had a wife in Poland who had left him a good time ago and was believed to have died. Once the European War ended he confirmed this and the two were married during my first term in Sheffield after a courtship of seven years.

Mum and Dad welcomed Emeka and his friends as warmly as everyone else: his cousin Emmanuel; his old teacher, Christopher; his Croydon neighbour, Michael (who died in London of high blood pressure); his classmate, Chukwu, who suffered from persecution mania; Clifford Ogadazi, Raymond Njokwu, Denis Osadebey, and many others came over for tea or dinner or table tennis parties in the garden. What was one nationality more or less, after all our paying guests, not to mention Indian, Burmese, Ceylonese and other international folk from the Stratford Centre.

Emeka had stayed earlier at Nutford House in Marble Arch and took me to dances and meetings there. We also frequented the African Students Union which was ably run by Mr and Mrs Solanke. They gave occasional receptions for important guests like Dr Nnamdi Azikiwe. He impressed me tremendously and I invited him to dinner in Putney. The parents found him an easy man to entertain, speaking urbanely about all manner of subjects. Whereas Emeka and his friends had barely started their professional careers, 'Zik' was already a wealthy and distinguished politician, fighting fiercely for the cause of his country's independence in his book, 'Renascent African' and in other publications, including his own newspaper, the 'West African Pilot'. Published in Lagos, it had a countrywide circulation and was, thereby, able to persuade its readers to join the NCNC formed in 1944 which was headed by Zik himself. When Nigeria did gain her independence in 1960 Zik became the Governor General. Later, when Nigeria became a republic, he was appointed the first President.

Emeka admired him as a fellow Igbo, and shared his desire for freedom without committing himself to any political party. Realising they might be dealing with the future leaders of Africa and India, the British political parties deliberately set out to woo the students from overseas. By this time, it was obvious that with the Labour Party's commitment to de-colonisation, independence was no longer a matter of 'if' but 'when'. Influenced by their propaganda many Nigerians joined their ranks. The spell binding lectures on economics and political economy delivered by Professor Laski at the London School of Economics did much to fan the flame of socialism. The Communist Party had an even greater appeal, presenting as it did the image of Russia as a modern Utopia created by the people and governed by the people. It vowed to support the Nigerian freedom fighters in their bid for liberty. Many joined the party for this reason.

The Colonial Office kept a vigilant eye, a dossier in fact, on those who did join the Communist and Labour Parties and it was rumoured they tried to stop them working in important posts on their return to Nigeria. True or not, law students were considered 'potential trouble makers' and were seldom given government scholarships. These were awarded to students of dentistry, engineering and medicine, such as David Ofamata, Emeka's cousin, who joined him in the UK as a medical student at Guy's Hospital in September, 1948.

Naturally the Government had no objection to the conservative party. Their propaganda organisation, The Primrose League, was equally busy rooting out possible party members like pigs sniffing for truffles. Emeka and his friends were invited to their meetings and to parties at the homes of the Duke of this and the Duchess of that. Emeka went along because he was interested in meeting people whoever they were. By the same token, he could not resist an invitation from the Moral Rearmament Group to spend a week at their expense in Caux, a spectacular conference centre in the Swiss Alps.

The last holiday he and I spent together was at Christmas in Cambridge with the Waltons and the 'Group'. David Ofamata came along as well and the three of us had interminable conversations together back in our digs after the evening's festivities. By March, 1949, it was time for Emeka to prepare to return to Nigeria. He had passed his degree in June and eaten the requisite number of dinners in the Temple to qualify for the bar. He had told me at the beginning of our friendship that his family would object to him marrying an English girl. If he disregarded their feeling he might lose their support in fulfilling his ambition to found schools in and around Onitsha.

I would have loved to marry Emeka even though I felt it might be difficult but if that was the situation I could not argue and enjoyed the close friendship which lasted until he finally left England. My parents were relieved. As early as 1946, my father had sent me this letter.

Dearest Jean

Mum and I like Emeka's intelligence and nice manners but I must confess that when it comes to a possible marriage with a coloured man, I am a little prejudiced but it is a strong innate characteristic and many people, otherwise kindly and tolerant, cannot help feeling the same. Remember, dear, prejudice will not only occur frequently to you but to your children. It is a heavy responsibility. Such a marriage would be a bitter disappointment to Mum and myself and grieve us very much.

Four months after Emeka had left, he wrote from Onitsha to say he was engaged to Lily Oruche a sixteen year old girl from Nnewi, his family home and was sending her to Akure Training Centre. This had been founded by the seasoned missionary, Miss Mars of the CMS, to provide further, suitable education for girls engaged to men of higher education than themselves. Although I knew I should have been glad for the sake of our respective families, I was, in fact grief stricken and shattered by the news. I concealed my feelings, congratulated him bravely and we continued to write intermittently. Unsettled and depressed I started to think about taking a new job abroad. I applied for a job in Guyana but did not get it. Then Stella Abbot, an old college friend returned from working as an 'Assistante' in Lille, France.

Apart from the terrible pay, she told me, 'it was the best possible way of perfecting my French. You should follow suit.' I took her advice and started to save up with a view to applying when I had a bit of money in the bank.

'Man proposes, God disposes'. In this case David Ofomata did the disposing in a totally unexpected manner. He had continued visiting me after Emeka's departure, at home at first and then in one of my father's flats which I shared with Phyllis Baker and Diana Rimmington, teachers of Geography and Music respectively. Phillip Tekkam, Phyl's constant companion, was a Chinese medical student from Mauritius and a superb cook. The smallness of the flat did not stop us from keeping open house. We shared our friends and welcomed strangers. One evening David brought Dr Oke Ikejiani, his Canadian wife Marjorie, and Dr Kenneth Dike.

The short holiday in London had been a welcome hiatus in the busy life of the Ikejianis. Oke had studied and worked in Canada for some years. Now he was heading for an even tougher assignment – a lectureship in Nigeria's first university which was just starting up in Ibadan. Chandos Hoskins-Abrahall, the Chief Commissioner of the Province had opened it officially on 2 February 1948. Dike was already a History lecturer there.

Dr Kenneth Mellanby, the Principal, who had been responsible for Oke's appointment, invited him and Marjorie to a cocktail party in order to introduce them to Ibadan society. There they met a true son of the soil, the Reverend Emmanuel Oladipo Alayande, the Principal of Ibadan Grammar School for boys. Struck by Oke's dynamic personality, he invited him to the school to give a talk on 'Medicine as a Career'. Afterwards, over coffee, the two men discussed education in general and Alayande's staffing problems in particular.

'Now Ibadan has a university, my boys stand a better chance of higher education' Alayande said. 'At the moment I am the only member of the staff with a degree. Until Ibadan produces graduates of its own, I must recruit qualified staff from outside

Nigeria. Tell me, Oke, would you know anyone I could ask?'

Oke mentioned a couple of Canadian students, then added as an afterthought. 'If you do not mind taking a lady teacher, we met a girl called Jean Jacoby in London who might be interested', Alayande's face lit up. 'I know her', he exclaimed. 'Mojekwu used to bring her to the parties at Croydon International Club where I was staying. Could you write to her on my behalf?'

Oke sent a letter at once. Why not? I thought. After meeting so many Nigerians this would be a unique opportunity to see them at home. I vaguely remembered Alayande as a friendly, sensible man. By the end of November I had signed a contract with Ibadan Diocesan requiring me to start in January, 1950. As a sort of preparation the Church Mission Society in London put me in touch with two of their members: Una Price and Joyce Herklots.

Una Price, recently retired from their Head Office in Salisbury Square, invited me to coffee one evening in her small flat off the King's Road, Chelsea. Her pale, drained, bespectacled face, bobbed grey hair kirby-gripped back above each ear, lisle stockings and simple beige dress were quaintly at odds with the Bohemian types crowding the Chelsea streets outside. She gave me the standard list of clothing issued to missionaries going out to West Africa for the first time. It included: dresses (cotton), mosquito boots (white canvas), twelve brassieres, a long evening dress, nightwear and a terai. This, Miss Price explained (no question of first names) was a double felt hat. It had replaced the pith helmet, obligatory for all Colonial workers since the dawn of the British Empire.

Clothes, she said, should be packed in a tin box. Ordinary suitcases let in flies, moths and other insects. Bakers, Griffiths McAlisters, or Army and Navy Stores were the best places to look for tropical wear. I asked her to clarify 'nightwear'. Should it be cotton or rayon? How many would be needed.

'Two or three long or short sleeved cotton nightdresses would be advisable', she answered, adding with a twinkle 'Take a couple of pretty silky ones as well. It's good for the morale'.

Determined to get the wardrobe right, I went to all three stores. Griffiths McAllister was the most entertaining. Old Colonel Blimpish characters with very white hair and military moustaches were casting an expert eye on the displays of camp beds, guns, water filters, mosquito nets, khaki shirts, shorts, safari clothing, fishing rods, and other 'bush-whacking' paraphernalia. Pale young cadets for the Colonial Service were nervously ordering everything the natty Assistant recommended. It did not stock pith helmets or terais. Nor could I find them in the London markets, not even in the Caledonian road where you could buy everything under the sun from antique commodes to old bicycles.

Una's drab appearance had concealed a warm, loving heart. Joyce Herklots, whom I met over tea and scones in the dining room of the Strand Palace Hotel, was a pigeon-chested maiden lady of forty who looked every inch a missionary and spoke like the chairman of an important business meeting: briskly and without emotion. She thawed slightly when she heard I had taught her niece, Sylvia in Sheffield who was the daughter of Canon Herklots at the Cathedral. It was an informative but cheerless meeting and my heart sank when she told me to see yet another missionary called Christine Groves. Dutifully I asked the lady to tea. I dressed as simply as possible without my usual lipstick and nail polish. Far from dashing to the door when the bell rang, I walked decorously looking as sober, steadfast and demure as I could manage. Standing on the threshold was a pretty, plumpish woman in her early thirties. She was beautifully made-up and smartly dressed.

Christine Groves was a most inspiring person. Her dedication to the Christian faith had manifested itself already at the University in the Student Christian Auxiliary Movement. The fact that many of its overseas members were in Britain because they had been educated in a Mission school was one of the reasons she decided to join the Church Mission Society.

After a year's training in Foxbury College, she worked in a general hospital for a month and spent time in a maternity hospital as well. She told me missionaries were expected to commit themselves for life and to be ready to go anywhere. Because of this they might end up knowing very little about the place to which they were sent. In her case, as a graduate in biological science she had expected to be posted to Nigeria since its secondary school education was far ahead of East Africa at that time. Sure enough, she had gone to the CMS secondary school, Lagos, and would be moving to Ibadan with the school at the end of her leave.

Many people in Europe had the impression that the job of a missionary was to present the uncivilised natives with the gift of Christianity. If this 'changed their lives', if they 'became Westernised', all the better. Christine approached her vocation quite differently. 'I did not go to take the gospel from Britain to Nigeria. I went as a member of the world church to assist the Nigerian church in uncovering the work of God's holy spirit there!' We met again before we left. I felt she would be a good friend, and a great support. She turned out to be that and even more.

Two weeks before my departure, Dad brought home Hilda Gerson, a dress designer whom he had met when visiting a dress factory in the East End. She told him she had many friends in Nigeria and would like to meet me. I found out later that the reason for her great interest was a law student, Thompson Ogbe, whom she eventually married. Hilda was as glamorous as she was charming and that meeting was the beginning of a very, very long friendship.

Eventually the time came for me to leave England as well. The first time I ever saw my father cry was at the airport. His 'baby' Jean (I was twenty four!) would be in Nigeria for eighteen whole months. Her many nice African friends had assured him that Nigeria was no longer 'the white man's grave'. His mind understood that but his secret self still harboured the image of Africa as a strange and primitive continent that was unhealthy and unkind to white men, let alone young women as innocent and unworldly as his darling Jeannie.

Maybe it was not 'a first step for mankind', but I felt like the astronaut Armstrong was to feel as I boarded the Avro-York plane at London Airport. Noisy and far from glossy, it had done long service in the Second World war and looked it. The moment the world of fluffy clouds blotted out the doll's patchwork of tiny fields and houses below, excitement banished all my fears. I was actually on the way to Nigeria. In fact I was on my way to see Emeka. Yes indeed. Amazed and delighted to hear that I was due to work in Ibadan, he had written back immediately, asking me to take a mere three hundred miles detour in order to visit him in Onitsha beforehand.

2. Parents.
Leo and Blanche Jacoby.

1. The Jacoby sisters 1938. L-R. Lilian,
Jean, Marion.

3. Paying guests in garden 1938.

4. 1946 Paris. Surrounded by his family, Dr. Ivan Dreyfus receives the légion d'honneur for work in the
Resistance.

6. Party with friends in Putney (guests from Nigeria, Ghana, Austria, France and U.K.)

5. Author as graduate. July 1938.

7. David Ofomata, Emeka's cousin.

8. Sam Amissah from Institute of Education, London.

9. Later promoted as Principal of Wesley College, Kumasi.

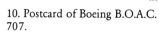

10. Postcard of Boeing B.O.A.C. 707.

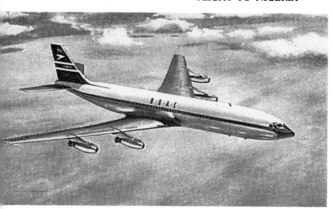

B·O·A·C
Britannia

FIRST FLIGHT CERTIFICATE

LAGOS - LONDON

This is to certify that

Mrs Jean Lorna Evans

was a passenger on the first B.O.A.C commercial flight

by the Britannia jet-prop airliner

from Kano to London

Captain

Elapsed flying time 11 hrs 5mins Date 14 April 59

BRITISH OVERSEAS AIRWAYS CORPORATION

11. First Flight Certificate on B.O.A.C. Britannia to Kano.

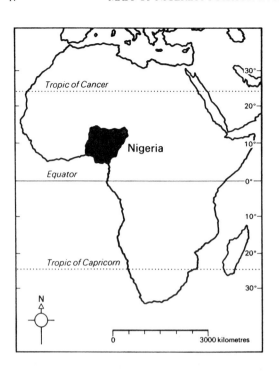

11. Map of Nigeria's position in Africa.

12. Map showing Nigeria with principal road connections and distances between towns.

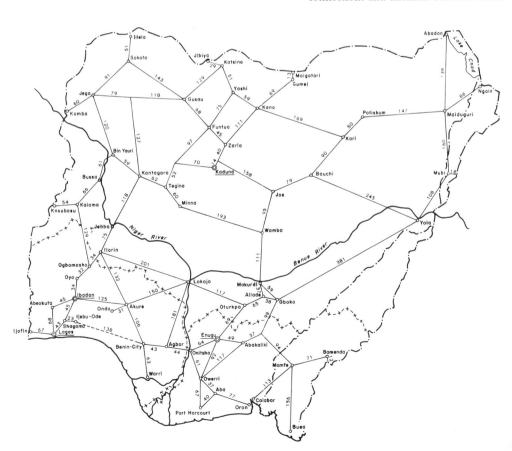

Part two — *Madame is not a stranger*

Chapter six
The clamour of Kano

My neighbour on the plane was a chocolate-box pretty, newly married girl called Brenda Invald. She was flying out to join her Czech husband, Jan, a forestry officer working near Ondo. She chatted ten to the dozen. The plane was too noisy to hear or talk, so I nodded assent and dozed off till we stopped at Castel Benito, Tripoli.

The shabby desert airport seemed empty except for a few muffled figures hanging about near the York plane and the terminal. They were probably workmen with something to do, covered up against the cold. To greenhorns like Brenda and myself, the whole scene was mysterious, sombre and frightening. We were glad we were together.

We were the only people in the scruffy restaurant. The superb waiter made up for the food which was insipid and tasteless. For dessert there were oranges. Without once touching them, he peeled off their skins with a knife, separated and skinned the quarters, then arranged them on separate plates in the shape of a rose. A seven hour dark flight over the Sahara desert finally terminated at Kano airport. 'We'll call on you when we come to Ibadan. We can practise cutting roses together', Brenda said before hurrying off to get her connection to Lagos where Jan would meet her.

My plane to Enugu—the airport nearest to Onitsha—was due in three days time. Emeka had instructed me to phone his uncle, Mr Okonkwo as soon as I arrived at the Airport Hotel. He had spoken a lot about this uncle who worked for the country-wide Ojukwu transport company and other commercial companies. It was he who had been mainly responsible for Emeka's training in England and his decision in family matters appeared to be absolute.

Mr Okonkwo and Joel, Emeka's younger brother, arrived on the dot in a kitcar marked OJUKWU transport. 'We are punctual, you see.' Uncle's voice was brisk and decisive.

I did not realise that first day how exceptional such punctuality was. I was to learn in the years ahead that 'African time' could be anything from an hour to a day late. We set out immediately to tour the city.

Joel, a slimmer, quieter edition of his brother, was shy at first, but gained confidence as he pointed out the Emir's palace, the ancient red city walls, the hospitals, the simple primary schools and the Koranic classes held outside with the children writing their

Arabic symbols on the sand or simple slates. What struck me at first as a Londoner was the total lack of obvious things like pavements, street lamps, traffic lights or policemen controlling the cars, lorries, camels, donkeys and people jostling each other in the dry dusty, uneven streets. Okonkwo stopped a moment to point out the ancient vats where the dyers were busy dipping white cloth into the dark blue indigo dye. 'These have been here, unchanged, for thousands and thousands of years', he said. 'I suppose they'll be here for many thousands more. Now, I'll take you to the main market'.

What a place! The clamour and colour of it all assaulted ears, eyes and senses. By contrast, London's Petticoat Lane was as tame as a stall in a village fete. Everyone in Nigeria seemed to be there: Hausas clothed in light coloured robes and turbans; slim, light coloured Fulanis with straight brown hair oiled with sour butter, plaited and twisted in a dozen different styles; scantily clothed pagans from the bush villages outside the city; Igbos like Mr Okonkwo who had come from the Eastern region to settle in Sabongari (New Town); Yoruba, Nupe and people from many other ethnic groups.

Fresh food was laid out on the sandy ground: mouthwatering displays of pawpaws, coconuts, limes, oranges, lemons, grapefruits, bananas and pineapples: vegetables like okra, spinach, chillies, red and white peppers, onions, garlic, tomatoes and loose salt: all this juxtaposing fly-covered chunks of raw meat, scrawny clucking chickens and queer inexplicable, disgusting looking 'juju' objects.

'Do a lot of Nigerians use "juju"? What is each one for?' I asked.

'Some do, of course, especially the less educated', Joel admitted sheepishly. 'The men you would call "witch doctors" sell all sorts of spells to help people get what they want, and, to punish their enemies as well.'

'Don't forget our native doctors have used drugs and herbs like quinine and rosemary for years before the West discovered them'. Okonkwo was quick to remind me. 'Come on. Let me show you the rest of the market'.

After pushing our way past piles of saddles, horse brasses, stirrups, spurs and fancy fly whisks — destined for the camels and horses seen everywhere in the North, we lingered by stalls laden with jewellery, beaded slippers, embroidered caps, fezzes, brocade, light cottons and baft. The tailors who sewed these materials up into pyjama-like suits or long white robes with wide sleeves called 'rigas' were treadling away on very old Singer sewing machines. Their needles whirred like dervishes as they traced the most intricate designs imaginable on the garment and around the neck and sleeves without a pattern or pin to guide them.

Young boys carrying tin trays on their heads piled with sweets, kola nuts, biscuits, separate cigarettes, sugar cane and little cakes weaved their way through the shouting, gesticulating traders, adding their cries to the general pandemonium. Their sisters, eyes rimmed with kohl and nails dipped in red dye, sold the same goods or acted as nannies with their baby sisters or brothers strapped to their backs.

Groundnuts were very much in evidence: in piles on the ground, unshelled or in their kernels and in sacks as well. Kano was the main depot, Mr Okonkwo explained (he had left the light chatter to his nephew but he owned a groundnut plantation and knew all about it). The farmers in the outlying districts would bring them to the local traders by trucks if they could afford it, on horseback or by camel if they could not. More often than not they had been given money before they produced the nuts. The sacks were stacked in pyramid form besides the railway tracks and freight trains took them down to Lagos daily. The large firms each had their plot and there was a big wahalla (trouble) if anyone else dared to use them. Joel pointed to calabashes full of cowrie shells. 'Credit transactions have a long tradition in Nigeria', he said. 'These are for decoration now. In the 19th century, they were currency in some villages. It was not unknown for traders to leave so many cowrie shells in an appointed place, unguarded, knowing for sure that the farmer would leave the right amount of produce in exchange.'

Dusk was beginning to fall when we arrived at the main mosque, the heart of this enormous Muslim centre. The caretaker agreed to let us climb to the top of the minaret. The steps were caked with bird droppings but the view of the pink roofs of the Kano houses was worth the sticky climb.

Returning to the kitcar, we passed several small groups of women with veils drawn over their faces, who were strolling along and chatting happily with each other. 'These are Muslim wives', Joel whispered. 'The evening outing is the only time they leave the compound. They come out as the muezzin is about to call the evening prayers.'

We did see him as we were driving back to the hotel: a thin chanting figure silhouetted against the splendour of a blazing scarlet sunset. Mr Okonkwo dropped me at the hotel after inviting me to meet his family and have dinner afterwards the following evening.

A Mr Lawson who had been attending a conference at the Sudan Interior Mission hospital for the blind joined me for dinner. He was a kindly, serious man, devoted to his wife who worked with him in a small remote mission station. Unlike many British people working abroad who sent their children to public boarding schools from the age of seven, he and his fellow missionaries kept their children with them and educated them by following a correspondence course.

As soon as he left to prepare a lecture, Mitch, the hotel manager, came over to sit beside me.

'So what is your job, young lady, and where are you heading?' He asked.

'I'm a teacher'.

'Hm. That's strange. I didn't think you were in government. Women education officers tend to be chaperoned by their superior officers. On the other hand you are far too glamorous to be a missionary. They generally wear shapeless dresses and ankle socks with sandals like boats.'

I was soon to find out that Europeans always wanted to pigeon-hole you as soon as they met you in Nigeria. Before Mitch could grill me further we were joined by five other men. White women were in the minority in the fifties. It was the situation, and not my Californian poppy perfume which brought them buzzing around!

After a surprising number of drinks, someone suggested we repair to the club. Mitch was slightly drunk already. He felt I needed protection and insisted on me sitting beside him in his station wagon. The others crowded in at the back, singing and laughing at nothing whilst the vehicle whizzed, buzzed and skidded along a dark, lampless road towards the club.

The bright lights of the lounge inside contrasted strongly with the pitch black trees outside in the compound. People were drinking at the bar in one corner, playing snooker in another or sitting around tables chatting. More people joined our group including a government hides & skins officer called Dusty Miller. As the whiskies and the pink gins flowed, conversation became more and more trivial.

'It's been an exhausting day. Could someone take me home?' I got up to show I was serious.

'My driver's outside. He'll take you', Dusty offered. He called a steward to fetch him. 'How about me showing you the town, tomorrow afternoon?'

'That would be lovely,' I said. 'I have to contact some people and give them a letter from their son in London in the morning. I'll be free after that.'

'I finish at the tanning shed about two and I'll pick you up at three', he said. 'What's the name of the people you want to see?. After fifteen years in this town, I probably know them'.

'Nwosu', I answered frankly. 'Mr and Mrs Nwosu. They live somewhere in Sabongari. I have to phone them first.'

'Did you say NWOSU?' Dusty spoke loudly and with complete disbelief. Every single person at our table, drunk or sober, stopped talking and stared at me, horrified. 'Do you realise that's a Nigerian name?'.

'Of course I do.' I answered stoutly. 'Dominic Nwosu, their son, is a cousin of a friend of mine in London and has just recovered from tuberculosis. He knows his family must be anxious about him.'

'Jean, you've got to be very careful with these fellows?' Dusty spoke slowly and with infinite concern.

'Very, very careful', echoed Mitch standing up quickly as if my sitting next to him might be contaminating.

I had been so fiery in Putney to the less liberal-minded amongst my parents' friends who had dared to utter one derogatory word against the Africans. Yet here in this colonial stronghold, I was too green and too embarrassed to vouchsafe anything except a feeble 'I don't see why'. The appearance of Dusty's driver stopped short the conversation. He was told to take me to the hotel and that was that.

Dominic Nwosu's cousin called the next morning and took me to his parents who lived in Sabongari, the Igbo part of the town. They were so delighted to have news of him I stopped caring about the approval of Dusty, Mitch and their boozy friends.

Yet, to be honest, later that afternoon sitting in Mr Okonwo's rather shabby house in Sabongida, surrounded by his wife, children and other relatives I felt a little constrained myself. However I smiled and drank fizzy lemonade and tried to crunch kola nuts, knowing they were a must at every gathering and finding them bitter and hard to swallow. Later, Emeka told me Mrs Okonkwo was embarrassed too as she had never before entertained a European lady in her home.

The evening dinner at the Central Hotel with just Joel, his uncle and Dominic Nwosu's brother was far more relaxed. The European food was tasty and we got on well together. Underneath his rough diamond exterior, Mr Okonkwo was an impressive character: intelligent, shrewd, reliable and generous. We did get funny looks from some British old coasters at the next table but none of us allowed that to spoil our enjoyment.

The Ojukwu transport kitcar took me to the airport the following morning. Emeka was there in Enugu as promised, accompanied by several friends I had never seen before. I had hoped he would be alone for our first meeting after so many months but also knew how Nigerians seldom think of doing anything social on their own. His wonderful new Hudson car was waiting outside to take us to his simple one storey house, 10 Market Road, Onitsha. Tenants occupied the ground floor and a bare wooden staircase led to the rooms upstairs. Emeka was still struggling to make his way as a new barrister in town against fierce competition so the furniture was quite simple and the only modern appliance was a fridge. Food was never wanting. It was cheap to buy and his clients often brought him eggs, fruits, chickens and just before I arrived, a goat, which was kept in a store room next to the kitchen.

I'd wake in the early morning to the baa baa of the goat, the hooting of cars, the roar of lorries and the sound of passers-by shouting to each other in the street outside. The primary school children were going to school carrying their books and even their inkpots on their heads. The small shops, the market stalls, the colourful clothes everyone wore seemed bright and beautiful in the sunshine, and no one looked miserable or depressed, least of all Godfrey Nkemena, newly married to a capable young nurse, and Theo Ojiaku and other friends of Emeka who entertained us royally. We visited Nnewi one day to meet Emeka's mother and father. They knew no English so we smiled and nodded, whilst his affable uncle 'Homer' Nguibe, a government accountant on leave from Minna and nicknamed Homer because of the way he told a good story, did the honours and insisted on us returning to Nnewi the next day to have bowl of Jolof rice in his house.

Another time we drove for miles into the bush where Emeka had already laid the foundations of Akuma primary school. The headmaster designate knew we were coming and the whole village danced out to greet him. Both Emeka and I were expected to make speeches. All right for him. He was in his country, with his people, in his school. What does a young suburban English woman teacher say who has not yet spent a week in Nigeria? Vague words of encouragement and thanks for the welcome were all I could muster. The applause was tumultuous!

On Christmas day, Emeka preached in the Anglican church in Igbo and introduced me to the mission families afterwards. I spent the rest of the day with them as he was expected to attend a large family meeting in the afternoon. The archdeacon's daughters had come for Christmas and their presence made it feel like home. We even had a typically English meal of turkey and mince pies!

Last, but not least, I met Lily, Emeka's fiancée at her parents' home. She was shy but friendly. Her father less so. He thought I might stop negotiations over the bride price! He had no need to worry. Lily married Emeka the following year and they had two boys and four girls.

That short stay in the bustling friendly town of Onitsha was a splendid prelude to the new life I was to lead in the larger metropolis of Ibadan.

Chapter Seven
Red Heat
(Written by Gbemi Rosiji)

When Reverend Alayande asked me to go with him to Ikeja airport to meet Jean Evans who was to join the staff at Ibadan Grammar School, I accepted with enthusiasm. It was a chance to show my gratitude to him for his support when I was teaching there just before my marriage. I had also met Jean once in Sheffield, England, with her friend, Emeka Mojekwu, and she seemed a friendly, out-going sort of person.

We stood waiting in front of the small, low terminal building and I recognised her tall, slim figure a soon as she got off the plane and began walking slowly towards us. Ikeja Airport was ten miles out of Lagos in an isolated area beyond the residential government centre on the outskirts of the city, and there was nothing to stop the blazing rays of the sun from blistering the tarmac. Nowadays, it is the terminal centre for internal flights only: at that time only BOAC was in operation and its flights were once a week.

Jean was obviously bowled over by the searing, stifling heat and grateful for a quick cup of tea in the terminal's indifferent canteen. Without wasting more time, we got into the principal's Ford Consul and made for Lagos centre. Its crowded, dusty, narrow streets full of bumps and ditches aggravated her discomfort. When we finally reached the wide, red laterite road leading to Ibadan with only the tropical forest of iroko, kola nut and other trees to look at, Jean brightened up. 'This is Tarzan country!' she joked.

She was less enthusiastic about the constant stream of enormous timber lorries charging towards us overladen with iroko and mahogany trunks from the forests around Ondo and Ibadan. How they stayed put at the back was a miracle. The drivers disregarded all speed limits and hogged the middle of the road with their headlights full on.

Overwhelmed by the volume of traffic thundering towards him and blinded by the glare, Reverend Alayande was forced to swerve quickly to the side and wait for them to pass. Jean's eyes closed every time he stopped, afraid to look at the steep perpendicular culverts lining the route which seemed to slope away under our very wheels.

The drivers of the passenger lorries, known as 'mammy wagons' were equally heedless. Jean was much amused by the slogans they sported above the front windows, on the sides and at the back: 'God proposes, no disposal', 'Sea never dry', 'God is my friend', 'Do not rush', or 'God's time is best'. The terrible wrecks of vehicles which had skidded off the road and crashed into smithereens told the tale of dangerous driving, little or no maintenance and insufficient regard for human life. After travelling about sixty miles through the forest, we passed scattered villages heralding the approach to the very old town of Abeokuta. Like so many travellers before her, Jean was fascinated by the huge, grey, threatening rocks and hills surrounding the town (hence its name 'under the rocks').

Dusk was falling as we passed through a large market dotted with wicker oil lamps. Not all of the traders had gone home, many were still shouting loudly to the passers-by to come and buy cooked foods, or fresh produce.

The various pots and pans for sale gleamed in the flickering shadows as we drove past. Abeokuta (Egba women) are famous for their tie-dyed fabrics, specialising in the colour blue. Every other lady seemed to have chosen indigo, saxe, turquoise or marine for their wrap-around skirt and over blouse, crowning the ensemble with a blue patterned head-tie. Jean loved every minute of it and said she was sorry to leave this splendid symphony of blue behind.

She nodded off as more villages surfaced through more forest. After driving for an hour and a half, I woke her up to point out the large notice by the roadside, saying Moor Plantation, sometimes called the gateway to Ibadan. This agriculture centre of research and development straddled both sides of the road and its colourful hedges and wide canna-bordered drives were visible to the passer-by. When the first university in Nigeria was founded in Ibadan, January 1948, it automatically became the choice for its department of agriculture.

The university itself had its beginnings in the buildings and compound of a general hospital which had been vacated by the army. It had been converted into a temporary site for the university pending the completion of the main buildings. All educated Nigerians were thrilled that the idea of a university was finally come to fruition and welcomed the staff, Nigerian and foreign, with open arms.

As we neared Ibadan, Jean was peering out eagerly to catch sight of the town where she was to live for the next eighteen months. She had expected houses, but that area was a forest of mud dwellings with roofs of corrugated iron. Then came hilly streets full of little houses with bedrooms above and shops below and crowds of wayside stalls selling foodstuffs and virtually everything under the sun, by the flicker of tiny wicker lamps. Everywhere in Ibadan is hilly and Mapo Hall, the town hall with its Grecian pillars, towers above the narrow streets, the smarter areas and Ojaba market. 'Whatever time do people shut up shop?' Jean asked. 'Very seldom in Ojaba market', I said. 'It is the social centre for everyone around'.

Up one more hill, Oke Are, and we were at the school compound. It was too dark to see the principal's house to the left, or the school buildings on the right. The principal's wife, Ebun, and her teenage daughters, Keye and Bukola, had seen the car lights and were waiting at the front door, smiling. Their ten year old brother, Funsho, who had been sent to bed, was hovering on the stairs, curious to see the new arrival.

The school had electricity which did not always work. That evening it did and the bright yellow bulbs hanging on tenuous wires glared like search lights in contrast to the guttering wicker gleams in the market and the little houses at the bottom of the hill. Mrs Alayande, genial and welcoming ushered an exhausted Jean to bed immediately.

Rev Alayande drove me home, he looked tired and a little worried. 'It's been difficult persuading the mission, the director of education, and the diocesan council to agree to this appointment', he confessed. 'They were surprised Jean is not a member of any mission and criticised me when I found accommodation for her outside the school compound. Personally, I think they were looking for objections because it is something new. She and I between us must prove them wrong.'

'Don't you worry', I said. 'Her appointment will be a great success. You'll see.'

Chapter eight
The drummer's boy

From January 1950 to May 1953, Ibadan Grammar School played a major part in my life. For eighteen months the Alayandes were next door neighbours and good friends. The principal was not only my boss, he was councillor, advisor, guardian and confidante rolled into one.

Before describing my time as teacher there, I must first explain how and why the school was founded in the first place. Like all great chiefs the Balogun of Iwo had his band of drummers. Their 'iya-ilu', 'gangan', 'opan' and 'kokolo' would be heard at each and every important occasion from weddings to funerals, from naming ceremonies to betrothals, from meetings, councils and negotiations to the greatest occasion of all — war. When the Balogun attacked Ibadan, the Alayandes (traditional drummers as their name implies) went with them. They settled there when victory was declared. That is how Oladipo Alayande came to be born in Agodi in 1910.

His mother who was a Sango priestess, earned a good living dealing in kola nuts with the people of Oyo, Ogun and Ilorin. She became a Muslim on her marriage. How was it then that this Muslim boy grew up to be a Christian priest in the Anglican church? In his early days he had to attend Koranic classes before and after a full day's session at the normal school. David Okesina, his grandfather, who was a farmer, had taught himself on Western lines and became a Christian in the process. The early church tended to disapprove of drumming, associating it with the old 'primitive' beliefs. Wanting Oladipo to reach a greater height in life, 'Pa' David insisted on him attending St Peter's School. Oladipo was quite happy to change. Even as a child he had been curious about Pa Campbell's Christian school which he had to pass daily on the way to his own Koranic class. He lived four years with Mr Olatinrin, the catechist of St Peter's Church, Aremo. Hardly surprising, he became a Christian, took the name 'Emmanuel' and was told to forget all about drumming.

His life was quite hard. Sometimes the evening meal would be the remnants of three days food and, like many of his contemporaries, he had to work on the farm before and after school. He did not mind so long as he could study. An intelligent diligent student he passed every exam. In 1929 he was awarded a place in St Andrew's College, Oyo, where he trained as a teacher for three years. His first post was at St Stephen's School, Ondo. Ebun Akinyele joined the staff in 1936 and they were married in 1938. Their three children, Ogunkeye, Bukola and Funso remember him as a fine, intelligent man as well as being a good husband and a loving, caring father.

In 1943 they moved to Ondo Boys High School where Oladipo taught geography as well as latin, maths and religious knowledge. He was a first class teacher with a genuine interest in his students. He got on well with his colleagues and worked hard for the church.

He had married into the right family. Ebun's father, Alexander Babatunde Akinyele and all his brothers were highly respected for their character as well as for their achievements. After working as a pupil teacher at the CMS College, Lagos, Alexander had been sent to a school in Abeokuta. A few years later, he went to Fourah Bay College, Sierra Leone which prepared its students for a degree and for a diploma in holy orders at the same time. He returned to Ibadan, his native town in 1912 to teach and to work as curate under the Reverend Olubi in St David's Church, Kudeti. As the only graduate in Ibadan he was the obvious choice for the post of secretary to the Ibadan district council.

Realising the need for a school on the lines of Abeokuta Grammar School — founded by the famous pioneer of education, Reverend I. O. Ransome-Kuti in 1908 — Akinyele kept urging the Diocesan Council to let him do the same. Some money was raised but it was difficult to find a site they could afford. Eventually Okewu, a prominent trader friend of his, offered a house in Alekuso. On 31 March 1913 the foundation stone of Ibadan Grammar School was laid with the Reverend Akinyele as its first principal. He began with one class and trailed up there daily from Kudeti.

Chief Ayotunde Rosiji compares him with the Reverend Ransome-Kuti: 'As my family were Egba (natives of Abekuta) my early life was spent there and I expected to go to Abeokuta Grammar School. I dreaded the thought as Ransome-Kuti's harsh discipline was a byword throughout the region. What I did not appreciate as a young boy was that this man had rescued the school from collapse and built it up into a very fine institution. Moreover, he was a conscientious pastor, an advocate of womens' rights and the founding father of the National Union of Teachers. Anyway, we moved to Ibadan during my last year in primary school and I was able to go to the Grammar School there under the gentler tutelage of Reverend Akinyele. He controlled the boys by sheer force of character. On the rare occasions, when the crime was really bad, he would give the boy a gentle tap or two holding the cane in his left hand, the arm of which was withered. The effect was terrific. The boy would shrink away, cowed and ashamed to have offended this great Christian.'

The school house in Alekuso was a start but Akinyele was determined to find a better site. He persuaded and cajoled eminent Ibadan citizens to give money to the cause and in four years they had enough to move to Oke Are, the highest of the many hills in Ibadan. What a contrast! There was space, palm trees and green slopes.

The principal and his family occupied the top floor of a one storey house on top of the hill and lessons took place in the two rooms below, with an average of thirty boys to a class. A large building opposite housed the assembly hall, the office, the stores, another classroom, euphemistically labelled the science room, with hardly any scientific equipment in it, and two more classrooms. A staff was recruited and the school went from strength to strength.

A large playing field for football and athletics and the school farm were a little below the school in the shadow of the rediffusion centre, popularly known as 'Bawa

Tawa' (Bower Tower). This one hundred and twenty foot high edifice is on top of Oke Are and was built as a memorial to the first administration officer in Ibadan, Captain R. L. Bower. He eventually finished up as resident and travelling commissioner of what was known as Interior Yoruba and was respected by Nigerians and Europeans alike.

As for Alayande, he won an Agbebi Scholarship to Fourah Bay in 1943 where, following in the footsteps of his father-in-law, he took a general degree and a diploma in divinity. From there he went straight to England for a year to take the post-graduate diploma of education at the University of London. This was made possible by a generous grant from the colonial government. With the idea of independence firmly established — if not the date — the British had realised Nigeria would be needing a supply of leaders for the political, commercial and social development of the nation.

The year in London was a unique opportunity for Alayande to get to know the British better. During his school practice, he found the London Cockney children had all sorts of strange ideas about Nigerians. They thought he lived in a jungle like Tarzan and wanted to know how many lions and tigers he had killed. One little boy asked him if he only washed the palms of his hands since the rest of his body was dirty. Alayande was too good a teacher to let this worry him and soon established a good relationship with them all.

The adults he met were pleasant too, especially when they met socially. However, he was disappointed in the emptiness of the English churches and the chilly atmosphere compared to the friendly warmth of the crowded churches he had known back home. Very few Londoners seemed to know where Nigeria was. To them, it was a small black spot, possibly East, possibly West, already known for its gold and other minerals, and many presumed Nigeria was in the Gold Coast or even in Accra.

Accommodation was a big problem for African students in the fifties. Alayande was lucky to have stayed the whole time in the International Club in Croydon, but many of his friends told a different tale. His cousin, Dele, used to go to the office of the local paper so as to be the first to see the advertisements. Even so, as soon as the landlady opened the door and saw his black face, she would tell him the room had gone. Others would receive a blunt refusal as soon as they heard he was black. Thompson Ogbe was turned away because he told his prospective hostess his girlfriend, Hilde Gerson, was white. Another friend, Solanke, had an experience he would never forget. It was summer, so, dressed in his native robes, he went along to see the lady as arranged on the phone. She opened the door, took one look and fell down in a dead faint!

Not only did his countrymen tell Alayande about their housing problems, they consulted him about their money problems and their girlfriends as well. They did not understand why the girls said 'no' to sex when they let them kiss and cuddle them. Realising the girls might object if they said they were married, a few claimed to be single when they were not. Like all young men anxious to impress, many gave themselves or their parents gratuitous titles such as 'prince' or 'chief'. Language can be a funny thing. Without meaning to tell lies, a fellow could say his father was the 'director of a firm', 'head of a school', lived in the 'manse' or a 'vicarage' without meaning to deceive, but the firm, school, manse or vicarage could be very humble and the girl might think they were the same as in the UK. Had Alayande known certain Europeans better in Ibadan he would have found out they were often shooting a line too — relying on the fact they were far from home and there was no way their boasts could be verified.

The year flew by. In July 1944, Rev E. O. Alayande, with a Dip. Ed. to add to the BA after his name, sailed for home on the MV *Apapa*. The thirteen days voyage, full of sunshine, rich, unrationed food and entertainment were very welcome after his year of slogging and teaching in alien surroundings and he enjoyed every minute. Always a good mixer, he made friends with black and white alike. His neighbour in the dining room had a high position in the Education Department. He was very impressed with this enthusiastic graduate and offered him a job as principal in a school out East at five times the salary he was expecting to receive. Thrilled by such a prospect Alayande was all set to take up his offer.

At Accra, his father-in-law came on board by rowing boat, that being the only way to reach a ship then, and Akinyele was too excited to wait for his beloved son-in-law in Lagos. When he heard about the new job, this sweet, mild man exploded with rage. 'There's no question of you taking that post. I haven't worked for years to set up the Grammar School to have my own son-in-law go anywhere else. You start at five times less than that princely sum the minute we get back home.'

In his heart Alayande had known that the other offer was a pipe dream. He was a son of the soil, a dedicated Christian and money, up to that brief voyage, had never been a priority with him or his wife. Realising where his duty lay, he began work as principal of Ibadan Grammar School, ready and eager to try out all that he had learned at the Institute of Education in London. Sooner or later Nigeria would get its independence. His task was to prepare his students to be ready for that great day.

Chapter nine
First days in Ibadan

What was I doing lying here with bright sunshine on my face? The noises coming from downstairs did not sound like Mum and Dad. Why on earth were they playing such loud noises on the radio? A knock on the door and the cheerful face of Rev. Alayande announcing breakfast restored me to consciousness. I was not in London. I was in Nigeria, ready to start a new life as teacher in Ibadan Grammmar School. My bedroom window looked over the principal's pretty garden, which was full of shrubs planted in a lawn dividing it from the school buildings. Fields and palm trees stretched away in the distance and the pink houses and corrugated iron roofs in the village below shimmered hazily in the morning sun.

The first day was chock-full of surprises, a combination of the normal and the abnormal. No exotic foods and no drums or tomtoms in the Alayandes' compound. We ate a simple breakfast of bread, butter and tea and joked about the pint size of Rev. Alayande's tea cup whilst the rediffusion box on the wall blared forth the popular tunes of the day: 'Irene, good night Irene', 'Have I told you lately that I love you?', 'A man without a woman', 'No, there aint nobody here but us chickens', and the music called 'Quicksilver'. I was to hear these tunes time and time again.

It had been decided to introduce me to the members of the Board of IGS before I set foot in the school itself. As we drove down the hill we met the day students walking up with large piles of books in their hands — the more prosperous had satchels. They looked clean and smart in the school uniform of khaki shorts, brown sandals or white canvas plimsolls and white shirts. The school motto, Deo et Patriae (for God and the Fatherland), embroidered in black and white, was pinned on to the top right pocket of their shirts.

'Some of them seem quite old', I observed. 'They look more like university students than schoolboys.' 'We do have quite a number of students over the compulsory age', the principal replied. 'We try to take them in at the age of twelve but more often than not they have no birth certificate. If they are over age, look young, and are on the small side they will knock off a few years as they are all so desperate for education.'

We called first on Bishop Akinyele and his pleasant smiling wife. Physically he was a small, old man with a withered arm. Once he began to speak he was strength, intellect and spirituality rolled into one. At the same time, he was disarmingly simple with a gentle sense of humour. Kemi, Ebun's sister who had read history at Cambridge, was there with her lawyer husband, Yinka Morgan, on leave from Lagos. He was later chief justice of the western region. I took to the whole family there and then. They proved loyal, true and unfailingly helpful throughout my time in Ibadan. Archdeacon Latunde, chairman of the diocesan council was a more difficult person for a newcomer to understand. A towering figure of a man, he had an important presence which made it hard to relate to. He welcomed me politely, that was as far as I ever got with him, even though we met afterwards at various functions. Our next port of call was the department of education where we found Mr C. R. Butler, the director, ensconced in an airy office. He reminded me of certain school inspectors I had encountered in Britain, distant, appraising and very conscious of their 'superior' position. He addressed Alayande with condescension. Fortunately my shrewd principal had acquired a thick skin over the years. Humble, yes, but confident, he noted but ignored like the true Christian that he was — all attempts to snub him. Using tenacity and tact he had a knack of making the very people who thought they had got the better of him to do exactly what he wanted!

Off we went again, with the driver honking and hooting his way through the crowded streets, until we reached the large post office building at Dugbe, where Alayande collected the school mail. 'Remember the school is Box 21 Ibadan, Jean. There's no postman knocking at your door in Nigeria.' After a few minutes the driver turned into a much wider road called the Oke Ado road. This joined Oke Bola Road and the two together were known as the Ijebu by-pass. Apart from a series of lorries thundering towards the Ijebu road two miles further on, there was not much traffic and no shops to speak of. The houses were spaced-out and generally set in their own compound. Here and there a half constructed building would stand crumbling and lonely in a bare site awaiting money that never seemed to come.

'I'll take you first to the place I've found for you Jean, and then we'll have lunch with Linda Gardner. She is helping out with the English at the Grammar School for the time being.' Alayande announced 'Our new university has appointed Robert, her husband, as the first director of extra-mural studies throughout Nigeria. He's away on tour at the moment. Ah, here we are'.

The driver had stopped outside a distinctive, two storey house with a flat on each floor. I was to be downstairs. Hank Williams, a Baptist missionary and his family were already in the flat above, which was reached by an outside staircase. This continued up to a flat roof with a pillared balustrade all round it. The straight, smooth whiteness of the walls and the elaborate balustrade had the air of a giant wedding cake.

'You won't see much of the Yoruba lady who owns the house as the school pays your rent. The principal explained 'I hope you like the way I've furnished it.' Bless him, the principal had bent over backwards to bring colour and comfort to a large flat containing one very large room to serve as lounge and dining room combined and two smaller rooms of the same size. He had bought local mats for the concrete floors and organised a carpenter for the furniture: two armchairs, a two-seater sofa, a bookcase and a long, rectangular table with four upright chairs for the main room; a cupboard, a small chair for one room and another cupboard for the third room to be used as a store.

Since the house lacked electricity he had purchased three Alladin lamps, a Tilly lamp and a high stool for it to stand on. A market tailor had run up bright orange and gold curtains for all three rooms and cushion covers of the same material for the sofa and armchairs. The kitchen contained a few pots and pans and a cast iron stove fuelled by wood. Cutlery, tinned goods and provisions were kept in the store and so was a water filter.

Alayande had even organised a 'boy', called Peter, to come in daily. Thank goodness he had. I had never cooked on anything except a gas cooker and the thought of cleaning the concrete floors of the shower room and the latrine filled me with dread. This 'thunder box', I found out, was emptied from the back of the house. The fellow came about the same time every day and took it away whether I was on it or not!

Chief Adigun, an ex Ibadan Grammar School pupil remembers: 'every activity had its own time. For example, you dared not go to the toilet during lessons. To this very day, I can still go through a whole day without visiting a toilet because of the early training.'

Before leaving for the Gardner's house Rev. Alayande suggested I send Peter to the market at once to buy food as I was moving in that day. He finished with the instruction: 'Give madam yam or rice or gari with her stews and don't spend too much of her money.'

Linda Gardner's house was a few minutes up the By-pass on the same side. She was waiting for us in the living room upstairs with the table laid. An office and stores were downstairs and an outside staircase led to the first floor. Her three children were sitting primly at the table: Charlotte, aged nine, Georgie six, and the three year old, Roberta. Linda's husband, Robert, from Ghana, had worked for the United Nations Organisation in New York before coming to Nigeria and the children had attended the United Nations school. As a result they were delightfully friendly and outgoing. Linda was a very cultured, clever lady with a degree in fine arts from Reading University, in the UK. Making clothes for herself and the children, running the house, dealing with queries in the office and looking after clients calling for Rob, who spent more time away than at home, kept her very busy indeed.

Although Alayande himself never rested a moment he insisted on me taking a siesta at Linda's before we visited the United Mission College which was almost opposite the house. We could see its bold sign and the long entrance drive lined with flame trees from her verandah. The compound was beautifully laid out. Neatly trimmed flower beds encircled the classrooms, the dormitories, the chapel, the staff quarters and the mission house. Trees and shrubs with exotic names like frangipani, hibiscus, plumbago, bougainvillea and amaryllis were everywhere. The crickets sang, weaver birds were building their upside down nests in the cassuarina trees, and lizards, thin, fat, long and short darted across the pathways.

The Methodists and the Anglicans had struck a blow for ecumenism by uniting to form this college which trained girls to be primary or secondary teachers according to their previous education. Enid Holmes, a young Methodist teacher from Manchester and Mary Hodgson, the principal, were staying put in the mission whilst the rest of the staff were on holiday. Mary, a thin, bespectacled, rather tense lady in her forties, never really relaxed. Her 'principles' were constantly stopping her from doing this and that, including having a good laugh. Enid and I were to become close friends. She was engaged to a Methodist missionary who was doing a course in

England and counting the days till they met again. She had a cosy, sympathetic manner and listened without criticising to my descriptions of the suitable and unsuitable men I was meeting. She was excellent as a teacher, but very conscious of being a Methodist and sensitive to any college activity which seemed too Anglican.

The next person on the visiting list was Joyce Herklots in the diocesan office which was a few minutes away. She was courteous and correct and it was obvious her office was run with great efficiency. Mr Osibo, her assistant, was gentle, tactful, intelligent, hard working and uxorious. He had six children! His wife was in England for further training — she was already a qualified teacher. As I got to know him I was able to see the little twinkle in his eyes behind the glasses. He understood people and saw their funny side, but his face did not betray him! He was a perfect darling of a man and popular with everyone. 'You'll be living in an educational area, Jean', the principal explained. 'You're ten minutes walk from St Teresa's Catholic School for Girls, which has a convent, a secondary and a primary school in its compound. Oke Are and St James' Primary school are within walking distance. The Ibadan Boys' High School is down the road and the government training college for men, under Reverend Banjo, is five minutes away by car. Then, of course, there's St Anne's.' 'A lot of education' I ventured faintly.

He was such an energetic, enthusiastic man, I was terrified he was going to show me the lot that very day! What with the strong sunshine, the bumpy driving and meeting new people, my head was swimming. Fortunately, he restricted himself to St Anne's. Its gardens were as lush and as lovely as UMC, with less formality. Nancy Wedmore, the headmistress, and maths specialist, a daunting looking woman in her mid thirties and every inch a school marm, was at the mission house when we called. Evelyn Shepherd, who taught English, joined us for tea, Scottish oatcakes and shortbread. I munched happily, (headache forgotten) and listened to Nancy explaining how the school had developed.

It had been inaugurated on the spot of a much older school called Kudeti Girls' School. When the CMS School, Lagos, closed — which had attracted students from as far afield as the Cameroons in the East — its students came to Ibadan and the newly formed school was renamed St Anne after the mother of the Virgin Mary and, also, to honour Anna Hinderer who had pioneered so many schemes in education in the early days of the mission in the nineteenth century.

The idea of the merger was to form a secondary school offering a full range of arts and science subjects as well as religious knowledge and domestic science. It was hoped the students would eventually progress from the Cambridge School Certificate to higher studies. There were facilities for debates, music and physical education. Chris Groves, who was still on leave, was, they told me, the life and soul of the drama group when she was not teaching science.

All the staff, Nigerian and expatriates, lived on the premises. They had breakfast and lunch with the girls and ate together in the dining room of the mission house at night. 'I lived in a room at the end of a dormitory for the girls' Chris recalls. 'It was a very tiny sitting room' with a divider made from bookshelves and a louvre to separate it from the bed. It was small but it was my own room, my own territory. The girls could see me resting. They had to get my permission to go out of the compound for a debate or something. I'd hear them whisper 'She's asleep'. I had to set up, of course. It was only fair to them.' Nancy Wedmore had a kind heart under her brusqueness. Knowing the principle was taking a service later, she offered to take me home after showing me round. The airy classrooms each had a little library. The compound was large enough to have a playing field, a tennis court and a beautiful chapel. 'The tennis court is open to visitors', Nancy said as she was driving me back to the wedding cake flat. 'So is the church. You'll be welcome at either.'

Before flopping out on the small bed in the flat, I wrote a letter home describing everything, concluding with these words: 'However much the mission society doubted the wisdom of my appointment, the folk I met today gave me a polite, friendly welcome and I've a feeling we shall get on all right if I remember my own manners'. I was asleep in a minute. It had been a long, full, unforgettable day.

Chapter ten
The old site

Linda and Robert Gardener called at 8 o'clock the next morning as we needed to go to the University to drop Rob at his office first and then continue on to the university staff school under the headship of Miss Plumtree. The Gardner children loved this bright, well-equipped school which was also available to the townspeople who could afford the fees. Chubby little Roberta would practically fall out of the car in her haste to go to 'cool', with Georgie hard on her heels whilst Charlotte, ever the young lady, would do her best to hide her own eagerness to be gone.

Another ten minutes drive took us up Oke Are to the grammar school. We found Reverend Alayande in the small office which was opposite his house on the other side of the road. He was giving the orders of the day to Kayode, the cashier, who was a brisk, cheerful rotund family man and Ebenezer, the young clerk who was neither one nor the other. A slim, pleasant, mild-looking man in his thirties, called Samuel Charles was also in the office. He came from Freetown, Sierra Leone where English was the main language and he spoke it quietly, accurately and with easy eloquence.

We discussed what subjects I could teach. French was not yet on the grammar school time-table, so it had to be english and history. I was to be class teacher for 5A and before taking me there, the principal handed me the time-table which was given to the day school boys and the boarders alike on the first day of the term. It ran as follows:

6.00 am	Boarders wake up. Do morning work.
6.30-7.00	Private devotion
7.00-7.30	Bathroom
7.30-8.30	Breakfast
8.30-8.45	**Assembly**
9.00-9.45	First lesson
9.45-10.30	Second lesson
10.30-11.15	Third lesson
11.15-11.30	**Break** (water for students)
11.30-12.15	Fourth lesson

12.15-1.00	**BREAK FOR LUNCH**
1.00-1.45	Fifth Lesson
1.45-2.30	Sixth Lesson
2.30	**Fridays – assembly's summing up**

As there was no noise coming from the classroom, I presumed a teacher was sitting with the boys. Not at all. They were sitting, unsupervised, in rows of hard desks bunched close together, hard at work reading or writing. In front of the desks stood the teacher's table, shabby and stained with ink and behind that was a faded blackboard running the length of the wall. A university library could not have contained quieter and keener students. They stood up as we came in and chorused: 'Good morning, sah. Good morning, madame'.

The principal introduced me and left. I sat down at the teacher's table staring nervously at the sea of black faces in front of me. They stared back, devoured by curiosity and interest. Some of them looked as old as I was. 'Er, er' I said, anxious to get something going. 'What must I do now? Do you have a class prefect to help me?' A tall brawny six-footer with the face of a seasoned boxer, stood up. 'The principal has chosen me as class monitor, madame. I see the board is clean, fetch the chalk and bring the register which must be called every morning.' He pointed to a small, slim serious boy sitting in front of me. 'Akerele is the class captain. It is he who is responsible for the discipline of the class.' Akerele acknowledged the accolade seriously. He had all the makings then of a typical university professor and this is what he became. 'Open the register, Akande' he said. 'Let the Mistress call our names'. I obeyed. They laughed a little as I mispronounced Ademola, Akande Dele, Ige, Ojo, Olatunde, Onadeko, Uju and others. London boys would have guffawed and played about.

'Would you tell me your tribe and town of origin as we go through it again?' I asked. We repeated the names together and this time I got them nearly right. The majority were Yoruba from Oyo, Ilesha, Ijebu and Ibadan district. Two came from Delta and one from Benin in this class. Alayande made no invidious tribal distinction.

In those days there was no discrimination in the South, Akin Delano, an old student explained that Alayande was ready to take children from all over the country, regardless of their religion. We had students as far east as the Cameroons and a few came from the north as well. It was lucky that English was the accepted language. Another old boy, Chief Adigun, remembers a lad who had never left Ijebuland. 'When he spoke in his Yoruba dialect I was at a loss as to what he was saying.'

By now it was time for morning assembly in the school hall. Knowing the boys could be relied on to stand quietly without fidgeting, the teachers stayed at the back. In Battersea they would have been on guard at the end of every row to keep order. Rev. Alayande was a good public speaker and said the prayers with true reverence. Incidentally, the boys and the staff always addressed him as 'Principal' so I soon followed suit.

After assembly, I tried to get my class to talk about themselves, their hobbies and their ambitions. That day they were telling me only what they thought I wanted to know. They were happier when I said: 'Now you ask me questions'.

Does the mistress live in a town? What does the mistress do about the snow? Did the mistress teach in a school in England? Where are the mistress's children?

My descriptions of British schools providing free tuition, free milk and free text books met with clicks of the throat and incredulous exclamations of 'Aha!' If the Ibadan boys did not pay their fees within the first fortnight they were sent away and not allowed back until they had. More questions followed till the bell rang for the next class. I stood up ready to go. Akande stood up too. 'Would the mistress please write her name and qualifications on the board?' Diffidently I wrote: Jean Evans BA. Hons. The class applauded loudly. Enjoying this accolade, I added: Diploma of Education. This time they practically hit the roof with their clapping.

At lunch break Linda and I went to the principal's house where Ebun had laid out bread, butter and a flask of tea. She did this daily all the time we were at the old site and refused payment. Two more lessons followed with different classes and we broke up at 2.30. This was the established daily routine, except for Friday when the principal conducted prayers and gave a moral talk, bringing in the events of the week. The sun was at its height and sometimes he got carried away with his own eloquence. Occasionally, a day boy who had worked hard in his compound before walking two or three miles to the school, would be overcome by fatigue. Feeling his eyes begin to close he would stand up and go to the back, out of courtesy. Other boys might follow suit and no one said anything.

As day succeeded day, the boys and I adapted to each other. Teaching them was both rewarding and frustrating. They worked hard, listened well and always did their homework. They did not let a single new expression or point of grammar go unchallenged. If I could not explain, Akinyele, another academic in the making, would help out. The boys disapproved of my attitude to vocabulary. I wanted them to use simple language whilst they judged the value of a word by its length. The trouble was — like public school boys in Britain — they and the teachers had been reared on the classics and thought they should speak and write like Thackeray, Trollope, Macaulay, Samuel Johnson or Shakespeare. These are all superb writers but can they help a foreign student speak good, everyday English?' 'I-faith! All hail. No!'

It took hours and hours to correct the weekly essay. First, it was necessary to find out what the long string of pompous sentences meant. Then, care had to be taken to preserve as much of their vocabulary as possible in the corrections. Finally, notes had to be appended to explain every change. At the other end of the scale their English could be too explicit. When I suggested euphemisms for phrases like: I ate till my belly was full', 'I went behind a bush to ease myself', 'I urinated in the compound', they would reply: 'Aha! But the mistress told us to write naturally'. I wrote three conversations incorporating the common errors in English and used them in my classes. The principal showed it to the broadcasting officer who relayed it on re-diffusion from 'Bawa Tawa'.

Here is a short extract:

J. J: Do we still have time for a few more points?
Kola: We still have time.
J.J: Just reply: Yes, we do. Do not make it a sentence. Now let us take the word 'knicker', which you use for shorts. It means any undergarment worn by ladies.

Small wonder that the boys compounded their mistakes since reading books were not readily available. The school library was in a classroom containing a few dull-looking books and a collection of Palgrave's Golden Treasury of Verse. Hanging unevenly on the walls were unrecognisable, large photographs of past alumni faded with time. A 1930 portrait of King George and Queen Mary in bright red, yellow and blue was the one spot of colour in this paper symphony of grey and brown. It was difficult and expensive to buy reading matter in Ibadan town itself. The few paperbacks and magazines on a shelf in Kingsway were more for the colonial taste. The CMS bookshop was bright and attractive in appearance but it catered for students with examinations in mind, only selling dictionaries or atlases, a handful of the English classics, and the set books for the current year. Books promising instant knowledge like Pass Your Exams in Six Months, The Key to Success, or Instant English were very popular indeed and so was the Teach Yourself series. Its yellow shiny jackets covered dozens of topics from science to languages to dressmaking. I, personally, found the small black print as intolerable as the ponderous English used by the authors to explain their subjects and admired my students for ploughing through them with such persistence.

Borrowing books from libraries was equally daunting. The Native Authority reading rooms offered out-of-date newspapers untidily scattered about on tables in an otherwise empty room. The only reasonable public library was in the British Council complex and was popular with both Nigerians and Europeans. Finally, the University library with a vast stock of reading matter was miles away and available only to its own staff and students. Joan Parkes, the government librarian for the region travelled round the Western Region to promote interest in reading. Institutions like Government College with money to spend welcomed her advice and their students profited immensely from having a good stock of books to consult.

Relying on the one set book, some of my students — and many of their contemporaries — would learn several pages, even chapters, by heart and regurgitate them in toto in their essays without selecting the relevant passages. I tried to introduce the project method to encourage them to compare texts, discuss and work in groups. They preferred the time honoured talk and chalk method. I did not persist. It was difficult to organise anyway with the desks so close together. Funnily enough, the news of this avant-garde method spread to the town and I was asked to lecture on it to The United Mission College and other training institutions.

With their sights set on passing the school certificate examination, the boys could not be blamed for rejecting anything which appeared to waste valuable study time. The need to pass this qualification hung like a shadow over every boy from the day he arrived until the day he left. Without it he could not apply for a white collar job. With it, he still had to face competition from hundreds of other applicants.

The teachers were there to feed them the syllabus like mothers giving their babies gruel. Realising the need for paper qualifications, they too were studying in their spare time: for the higher elementary, London matriculation or British external degrees. Most of the staff were untrained, they had picked up their trade by dint of teaching in primary and secondary schools, and were poorly paid. They practised private trading or taught privately to make ends meet!

Alayande's biographers, writing in 1993, commented that: 'Due to inadequacy of staff Alayande started with a total of seven teachers, two of whom were university graduates and ended with a staff of 45, 32 of whom had university degrees'. (Alayande and I constituted the two graduate teachers!).

Those of them who had acquired training diplomas from St Andrew's, Oyo, or Sierra Leone or elsewhere earned far, far less than their former classmates who had become lawyers, engineers, or doctors, and it was galling to see them, living in fine houses, wearing smart clothes and travelling around in cars, whilst they, the teachers, counted themselves lucky to have a bicycle.

The best teacher in the school was Mr Ayeni. He had attended St Andrew's College and taught history, geography and mathematics. He knew how to present his subjects and achieve good examination results at the same time. With or without a training diploma the staff worked hard and conscientiously. Illiteracy was high and the oral tradition strong as a result. It was wonderful to watch the way some teachers used their hands, their face, their whole body to tell a story.

Chief Sunday Adigun pokes gentle fun at the weaving teacher, Odutola. Since he was a mere technician, he could not boast of good spoken English. Always contemptuous of English grammar his verbal utterances were a veritable source of amusement to us. Supervising examinations in the hall he would call out: 'Don't talk! Don't talk! Your paper will be teared'. Be that as it may I remember his work was superb. He received orders to weave wedding garments. Unfortunately, he was such a perfectionist the garment often failed to arrive. 'Odutola, my friend', Adesina complained once during break when he was given a beautiful agbada, 'This was ordered for my wedding which took place a year ago. Next Saturday sees the christening of my baby'.

Mr Ojo, his friend, the woodwork teacher, whom the boys nicknamed Okukuku was more prompt. As I write I am looking at an exquisite wooden figure of a Yoruba mother carrying her baby on her back. It was given as a farewell present to me when I left Ibadan in 1953.

The worst teacher was Mr Femi Akinrele. 'He began his teaching by letting us know the exceptions rather than the rule.' (I quote Chief Adigun.) I, also, was unimpressed. One of my students had asked him if Julius Caesar, the play, had anything to do with the historical Roman Emperor, and his reply was: 'Drama is not my subject. You must ask your English tutor'.

Occasionally of course some students got into trouble. They failed to hand in the homework or forgot to do an essay for one of the teachers. Never for Mr Charles! He demanded and got work in on time and unstinting attention to his history and geography classes. The boys listened to every word partly because he was good at teaching, partly because they were too frightened to do otherwise. His low key, mild exterior was deceptive. He beat the boys for the smallest misdemeanour. The culprit would be ordered to 'mount' another boy who would hold his arms whilst he, Mr. Charles, administered the thrashing. The other teachers beat the students too, but not so fiercely. I have seen a young teacher order a miscreant break off a branch from a tree nearby and bring it to him. He stripped the leaves off, made a cane out of the rest and beat the poor lad with it.

Alayande himself used to lash out at times but he caned his own son, Funso, more than the boys. Akin Delano recalls: 'You must understand that the Yoruba way was not to bring up the children too softly. Some spoilt children were even sent away to a recognised disciplinarian, such as the Reverend Israel Oludotun Ransome Kuti in Abeokuta Grammar School.'

No teacher could have worked as hard as the Principal. With true Christian spirit he went from task to task without a thought of financial reward. Kayode was a loyal and honest cashier. Ebenezer was too young and inexperienced to do more than the typing in the office. Everything else concerning school administration fell on Alayande's shoulders: purchasing text books; planning the school meals with Ebun and finding the cheapest suppliers; overseeing labour; the list went on an on.

The government had provided money from the development fund to build a new site for the school in Molete. It was up to the Principal to run around for building materials, drive down to Lagos to buy concrete, check the contractors were not cheating them, and negotiate with the director of education concerning the funds needed for the building of a science laboratory.

It was he who found teachers and recommended them to the diocesan education committee. He was on the committee of the National Union of Teachers, not forgetting the principals' committee and various other committees connected with the church. As deacon he had to take services in the town and was much in demand as a preacher.

Over the years he has been made an archdeacon and a chief. '. . . take him for all in all, I shall not look upon his like again.'

Chapter eleven
The Ijebu By-pass

A daily pattern of life established itself. For the first month I had lunch with Linda, then returned home for a shower which was never cold as the pipes were laid too near the outside wall. After a long sweaty siesta, I would have tea and a banana then take a stroll when I would often meet the Rosijis doing the same thing!

If Linda was busy, she would sometimes ask me to have the children for tea. When they got too hot playing in the gravel outside, they would come in for one of my stories. The two girls enjoyed them immensely. Georgie who always played the toughie, was a softie at heart. If he heard anything too sad or too dramatic his lips began to tremble and I would change tack. Thomas the terrible, a tale about a naughty elephant, was their favourite. (It was broadcast four years later from Lagos.)

They would return home before dark and I would shower again and change into mosquito boots and a gorgeous floral housecoat from Liberty's. Tropical sunsets are short, sharp and seldom later than seven o'clock so Peter had to make certain the lamps were ready before then. Aladdin lamps were cheap and easy to light. One each went into the bedroom, the passage and the kitchen.

The Tilly lamp was trickier. The delicate mantles needed gentle handling and caught fire easily. Replacements could not always be found. We had to make do with the dim light of an Aladdin until Peter managed to find one in the market. Once alight the Tilly was every bit as bright as electricity. Unfortunately it attracted swarms of insects and flying ants which buzzed about it all evening. If they went too near they singed their wings and fell into an enamel bowl of water, which Peter had placed on the floor below the stand. How I loathed those Tillies and that noxious, black insect stew! Once I inadvertently kicked the bowl over and a mass of squelching bodies and wings streamed over the concrete floor like a picture from Dante's Inferno. Ugh! In time Peter got the lighting ceremony to a fine art. I never did!

Nothing, however, could discourage the mosquitoes. They penetrated everything I wore, ate me alive and recommended this fresh, juicy blood to their friends. I remember itching and praying at night with equal intensity. 'Oh God. Do you realise I'll have to go back to London if this continues? Is this what you want?'

He obviously did not. Eventually, the mosquitoes attacked with less intensity and I got used to the other living creatures who shared my abode: lizards and gheckos on the walls, ants in the food unless it was covered, and cockroaches in the kitchen. Passing the open door of the kitchen one night en route to the latrine, my torch lit up a rat that was sitting on the stove chewing the remains of my supper.

Peter's efforts at cooking were far from impressive. The food he served was unappetising and poor in quality, owing to the fact that too much money went into his own pocket. Also, he had not boiled the water before filtering it. After a week I went down with diarrhoea. The principal was most concerned and warned Peter he would be dismissed if he did not mend his ways. It was a help when a friend of the Principal gave me his old fridge — it never made ice, but it stopped the butter from running and the Peak milk from going off. The Rosijis called with medicine and comfort and continued to be unfailingly kind and helpful all my time in Ibadan.

Alayande felt vaguely worried about me being alone so much and suggested asking someone to nominate me as a member of the European Club. I refused. Apart from the offputting experience of club life in Kano, I did not want the critics of my appointment to say 'I told you so'. One of their objections to my coming had been the difficulty of finding me suitable accommodation. I was reluctant to visit the missions, uninvited, for the same reason.

The Rosijis introduced me to their neighbours and relatives and generally did their best to ease me into a new way of life. They lived five minutes away on the side of the By-pass which had electricity, sharing a recently built duplex storey house with the historian, Saburi Biobaku. Not only were he and Ayo old school and university friends, they had got married within a month of each other. With twelve rooms at their disposal, they used the ground floor for dining room and living room and the first storey for bedrooms, studies and offices. Ayo had a clerk to see to the office routine as he was often on tour. He was becoming well known for his eloquence and efficiency and had cases, especially divorce, in Ijebu, Ondo, Abeokuta, Lagos and many other towns in the Western region.

Gbemi was a most versatile wife. She could cook both Nigerian and European dishes and often went to the market herself instead of the boy. The flowers in the little garden in front sprang to life at her touch. So did the canna lillies growing outside the kitchen which was connected to the house by a narrow bridge. Her mother, Amelia Omotayo Mann, who had died when Gbemi was fifteen, had been famous for her expertise in dressmaking and fashion design and had trained her daughters to follow in her footsteps. Gbemi spent hours in her workroom next door to Ayo's room, running up curtains and cushion covers, not to mention dresses and tailored jackets from her own patterns.

Her resourcefulness had no limits. 'Once I was badly in need of a stiff hat for a wedding', she recalls. 'Since I could not find one anywhere, I bought a length of cotton, starched it stiffly and made a hat out of that.' She and I went to Dugbe market together and bought a length of deep red cotton with blue and white flowers for my first 'Nigerian dress'. Gbemi decided on the 'up and down' style — a wrap around skirt, a loose over-blouse of the same material with a frill round the neck, cup sleeves and an extra length to drape around the top at will. A matching head tie of red rayon completed the ensemble. The origin of the design was, of course, the long skirt and blouse worn by the early missionaries.

Three children — Esimaje Sagay, Roland Durante and Bola Sodeinde, lived with the Rosijis. Their parents had been posted far away from Ibadan and they wanted them to continue at the university staff school which provided an exceptionally good pre-school and primary education. Gbemi turned out to be a wonderful surrogate mother. The hand-smocked dresses she made for Esimaje and Bola were the envy of all the other little girls.

Gbemi had also lived away from her parents when she was young. Her father, Jacob Tejumola Mann, had begun life as a teacher in Faj and had transferred to the railway to get more money. It was a problem when he was posted to Jos as Gbemi knew no Hausa which is spoken throughout the Northern Region. She had to stay on in Lagos in the house of Archdeacon Phillips of the Cathedral Church of Christ, Marina, Lagos. His daughter, Bimbe, soon made friends with this shy, new edition to the household. They went to CMS grammar school together and their friendship has survived over fifty years!

Since the Durantes and the Sagays were friends of very long standing Gbemi did not like charging them too much. Ayo was just making his way as a lawyer and he still had to repay the people who had enabled him to study abroad. Gbemi had to husband her money carefully. She knew exactly where to find the best bargains and took me round the small shops in the town. Had I bought the extra kitchen utensils we needed in the main European stores, I would have spent twice as much money.

These stores were situated in the centre of town: a collection of large un-pretentious buildings with warehouse style interiors lined with shelves of tinned food, drinks, cloth, coloured bowls, tools, kerosene and God knows what else, juxtaposed haphazardly with no thought of hygiene or order. Paterson Zochonis was owned by Greeks: SCOA and CFAO were French, UTC was Swiss — in Ibadan it specialised in motors and spare parts and ran large general stores in Lagos and other towns. The British firms in order of importance were: The United Africa Company (UAC), GB Ollivant, and London & Kano Trading Co. Gottschalck, which was German, ran a regular back page spread in the monthly 'Nigerian Scouter', it began with:

GOTTSCHALCK
for
SERVICE AND SUPPLIES
*

Whatever is needed for **WORK**,
HOBBIES, and **HANDICRAFTS**.
Special **TYPEWRITER** Dept.
Repairs and Service.

and finished by saying that it also stocks: Carpenters Tools, Metal Workers Kit, Paint, Oil, Varnish & Distemper, Textiles, Shirting Drills etc.

The most popular centre for shopping and, certainly the most attractive, was Kingsway which was a subsidiary of UAC. This, in its turn, was founded by George Taubman Goldie in the mid nineteenth century under the name of the Royal Niger Company. He did not hesitate to use strong methods to protect his trading posts. When these failed to stop the French, the Portuguese and the indigenes from demanding — and literally fighting for — a piece of the commercial expansion cake, he persuaded the British Government to send troops in to flush them out.

Historians claim that the main reason Britain took over the Government of Nigeria was to give the British trade monopoly legal backing. J. F. Ade Ajayi comments: 'In this piecemeal fashion the British brought the country under control before considering how to administer it, before knowing in fact the extent and the nature of the country and its products'.

All the big stores, including the United Africa Company bought local produce and sold wholesale as well as retail. The other firms were also household names. There was no real specialisation or laws about what they could or could not trade in; nor any limit to the size of the transaction. The same companies would be in overall control of large wholesale operations, development schemes and retail businesses. Their salesmen ranged from expatriate agents in charge of huge sums of money, private traders with or without much money down to an army of small lads selling sweets, cigarettes and a variety of small items by the handful in the markets.

Kingsway Store was the place to go to on a Saturday. The Nigerian élite arrived in smart cars to buy the European goodies they had enjoyed abroad. Chiefs came with their wives and families. The Hausas from the North were after cigarettes in bulk. The expatriates and British colonials crowded round the cold store fridges like bees round a honey pot. (The men wearing embarrassingly short shorts were usually French!) Cars, kitcars and lorries were loaded up with coldstore and tinned goods by the boys whilst the cooks were despatched to the market to purchase the fresh meat, vegetables and fruits required for the weekend. If curry was on the menu they reckoned on one chicken per two guests. Wives who were bored with no job and no housework to occupy them used the Saturday Kingsway morning to spot the new men in town, offer them advice over the frozen vegetables and take it from there!

Although most missionaries in Ibadan and in the field lived off the land, they still needed basics like tea, sugar, coffee, and maybe bacon and flour from Kingsway. Once the new senior service rates were introduced in April, I was able to treat myself to a few luxuries like tins of fruit, soup and meats and English biscuits. Ayo chided me for extravagance and urged me to manage on thirty shillings a week like Gbemi.

The Moor Plantation staff and the university folks, both a little out on a limb, would pool cars and share jeeps to come in for one good shop and take the chance to gossip with people they could not see very often. District officers about to go on tour would stock up with kerosene, tinned goods, cold stores, extra lamps and spare bullets for their guns which they used to 'bag something for the pot' more than for their own protection. Bush fowl, when in season, wild duck or dyeka, were a welcome change from tough market meat.

Conversely, their colleagues would leave the bush to come up to Ibadan for supplies. They could claim mileage for this and it gave the 'missus' a good break. That is how I met up with Brenda Invald. She turned up one Saturday morning about six weeks after we'd met on the plane out, together with Jan, her husband. He was a friendly exuberant, handsome fellow with plenty to say. Unfortunately, his thick Czech accent prevented him from being understood! He invited me to a dinner party that same evening, given by a Lebanese couple called Louis and Teresa Abizakhem whose brother, John, ran a saw-mill near Ondo and did business with Jan.

Louis Abizakhem ran various successful business enterprises including a small textile shop in Lebanon Street. There was nothing else but textile shops the length and breadth of this street and its continuation. The shop owners were Lebanese or Syrian and one display was very much like the next. Rolls of baft, cotton, muslin, African prints sold in six yard lengths, velvets, plush brocades and taffetas were stacked on shelf upon shelf lining the walls, with more on trestle tables in the middle. They were helpful, persuasive salesmen offering credit if you did not have enough money with you. The Abizakhems had a smart upstairs flat in town but most families lived above the shop and many wives came downstairs to help out whilst their children played around them or upstairs or peeped around the door at the back.

I would linger in these shops for hours, drooling over the African cottons especially, marvelling at the variety of colour and designs — animals, flowers, people, slogans, vegetables, kitchen utensils, buildings, every aspect of life would end up wrapped around the cuddly capacious bodies of the ladies in Ibadan! Because the middle Eastern men tended to go home to fetch a wife once they had the money or desire or both to settle down and, because the community was very close knit, their women had little chance to learn good English and often spoke pidgin which was not too easy to understand.

It was easier to speak to the ladies who had attended French speaking schools in Lebanon or Syria. When Teresa Abizakhem heard I spoke French she asked me to call again for French conversation. Then her sister-in-law asked if she could bring her three children to my flat for English conversation. They were most generous and hospitable to me and I appreciated going out and eating delicious Lebanese food in a family atmosphere. Always hungry and adventurous where food was concerned, I relished the superb fare of kebabs, brains in white sauce, and roasted goat. Eating alone, especially when the weather got hotter and hotter, was often an effort. I was glad to repay their hospitality. Like most Middle Easterners they tended to invite business clients to meals and to give extravagant presents 'to your wife' to British administrative officers if a favour was required. They, in their turn had instructions to return gifts of exactly the same value.

Teresa was expecting a second baby when I met her. She suffered a lot during her pregnancy. I was with her the morning the pains started. The doctor was summoned and told her she had several hours still to go. Neighbours crowded in immediately, keening over her. Soon she started to shriek and moan. Jamil decided to take her to Jericho Hospital. I heard later that she did not stop screaming until they gave her an anaesthetic. When she heard a baby boy, Francois, had arrived she vowed to dress him like a Carthusian monk for the first year of its life as a thanks to the Virgin Mary for her help. Sure enough, when I went to visit a few days later, the wee white faced baby was wearing a long brown tunic and fawn girdle over its nappy!

Reverend Alayande did not think too highly of the Syrians and Lebanese, claiming that they did not plough enough money back into the community. 'The only exercise they take,' he said, 'is to open up the tills in the morning and count their money at night'. The same might have been said of the Indians working in Chellaram and Chanrai, who were excellent salesmen, always ready to give credit for a radio, a clock, trousers, shirts, electrical equipment and other goods on sale but they were too busy or too immersed in their own community to mix much socially.

My evenings were spent preparing school work, reading and writing letters home saying how wonderful everything was. It was foolish to walk along the dark, unlit

By-pass after sunset. Hardly a soul passed by outside. I had my main meal at night: chicken, or meat stews, or offal with vegetables and fresh fruit for dessert. Once Peter had washed up, he would bring in the Aladdin lamp, say: "Good night, madam" and disappear till 6.30 the next morning when he brought me tea. About 9 pm the watchnight would call "Good evening, madam" through the window, patrol the compound noisily a couple of times and disappear to sleep under a tree. He was poorly paid and probably had a day job as well. No wonder he was tired.

Unless the Rosijis happened to call I was alone from 3 pm to the following morning with no radio or telephone. The evenings often seemed rather long. I felt cut off and the presence of a 'watchnight' did not help overmuch. Hardly a soul passed by outside. It was difficult to get to sleep with the non-stop stream of timber lorries thundering towards Ijebu, lighting up the walls of the bedroom as they passed. What a contrast, in England, someone had always been around to welcome me when I came home; parents or flat mates or dear old 'Ma' in Sheffield. I was alone in the house, yet never afraid. I had never met a Nigerian who was unfriendly or unkind so why should I be?

Chapter twelve
Yoruba friends and functions

My loneliness lasted a very short time since the Rosijis seemed to know everyone on the By-pass and made sure I did too. There was Mr Animashaun, a giant of a man, who managed Gottschalk's, Mr Masteroudis, a Greek trader, Reverend Solaru who was the Nigerian representative of the Oxford University Press, and a fair share of lawyers including, Khalil, Dibbo, Sam Ighodaro (whom I had known in Croydon), Akerele and E. H. Lambrou.

Lambrou was the only expatriate lawyer in Ibadan specialising in commercial cases. He and Ayo were partners for a time, but he neglected the clients and they split up. There was something unpleasant about this flabby, aging Cypriot who had lived abroad too long to have any memory of kith and kin. He would 'paddle in the palm' of the hand of every lady he met, make suggestive remarks and gloat over the naked pictures in his bedroom, which the visitor had to pass on the way to the bathroom. I was too naive to realise he was all talk and a bit lonely. Generous, hospitable and very caring to Gbemi when she was pregnant, in hindsight, I think I judged him too harshly.

John Humber, the Rosijis' next door neighbour was another man who lived a bit outside the pale. He had worked in many countries as a mining engineer before coming to work for Odutola tyres. He had taken a Nigerian mistress, which was common, but defied tradition by marrying her and settling down for good with their four children. The hoity toity European community did not approve. This 'going native was simply not done'.

The Principal had known Irene Ighodaro in his Fourah Bay days and caught up with her again in London after her marriage to Sam. I remember her lectures to the grammar school boys on, 'medicine as a career' and other related subjects. Like many Sierra Leonians, English was her first language. Her sing song, direct, speech interlarded with wisecracks and 'oh' appended to her sentences made the most brilliant ideas simple to understand. She had received countless accolades for her contribution to world health and womens' rights, but still loved to speak of her early life in her parents' compound when she had to sweep and fetch water before going to school.

Apart from visiting people on the By-pass with the Rosijis, both they and the Alayandes introduced me to their friends and families. Invitations to functions and parties soon followed. The dances were the jolliest. They were held at the university, in colleges, in halls in the town and in the West African Club. In Britain, the girls had waited anxiously to be invited to dance. 'Highlife' was the most popular dance in Ibadan then and no one needed an invitation to do that. The fattest, the thinnest, the oldest and the youngest swayed their hips, kicked their legs and gyrated to the loud music of a band or gramophone. Head always upright the couples worked their bodies down to the ground in rhythm and worked them up again. It was an exhilarating experience. Gbemi remembers me gliding haltingly across the floor to the booming beats of the frenzied highlife, 'tall, sedate and bemused in the twisting, jostling throng'. Fortunately she concludes thus: 'eventually waltz, foxtrot, highlife seemed one to her. She had scaled the wall.'

Crossing social bridges was easy at the early stage, but it took time and trouble to understand all that constitutes Yoruba culture. I learned it simply by joining in. To quote Gbemi again: 'Jean showed real interest in all that was going on. My parents liked her very much.' Mr Mann, her father had settled in Ebute Metta after he had retired from the railway. We visited his second wife and family when we were in Lagos for a weekend. I generally stayed in the mission house near the Cathedral. They were used to visitors and welcomed me warmly.

It was also a chance for Gbemi and myself to shop in the Kingsway Store which was the largest emporium in the Western Region. Besides selling everything imaginable, it had a hairdressing department. Mrs Prest, the wife of Chief Arthur Prest, (Tommy Ogbe's cousin), worked there and knew exactly how to deal with my thick, black European locks. A great relief after my first hair cut in Ibadan. Unable to find a hairdresser, let alone a salon, I had asked Peter Steward's advice. 'I know a fine barber past all', he said, 'Expart in all hairs'.

This man had sat me on a chair in the sitting room and got to work with a pair of clippers. It felt all right and looked all right in the mirror in the bedroom, but when I used my compact mirror to see the back, I got a nasty shock. The 'expart' had literally tonsured me and I had to wear a headtie for weeks until the hair grew again!

Thanks to Mrs Prest I was able to face Gbemis' relatives with confidence. Mr Mann was not always well in health. Once he sent an SOS to Ibadan. He needed to go to hospital and the registrar was demanding fees up front before admitting him. The driver was told to take Gbemi and myself down with the money since Ayo had to go on tour.

His mother and father lived in Abeokuta, their home town, and we visited them often, sometimes staying the night, sometimes returning the same day. Alake Ademola had been driven into exile by mass demonstrations of the people in Abeokuta led by Mrs Funmilayo Ransome Kuti, wife of the doughty headmaster of the Abeokuta Grammmar School. Neither Alayande nor Ayo supported Ademola's exile and they both campaigned vigorously for his restoration. They won the day and we went down to congratulate him. The venerable old man was tremblingly jubilant. Not only was he back in power, but his new young wife of sixteen had just given birth to a baby boy! We broke kola nut with him and offered him a bottle of whisky to celebrate.

Family gatherings were festive. Each occasion had its particular rites and was always well attended. This was because the family throughout West Africa was an extensive unit. Ayo Ogundipe, Head of the Dept of Sociology & Anthropology at the University of Benin explains: 'In the fifties the full family would include grandparents,

parents, children, cousins and the most distant kinsfolk. Everyone within that structure would feel obliged to help the rest. It was part of the duty of the members who had succeeded in life to set them up in a trade, give them an education or subsidise them when they fell on hard times. If one member had something to celebrate, everyone would be invited. The strong family influence served as a deterrent to what people did in terms of fearing what would happen to their families.'

When their friend, Olusola Solanke, became engaged to Bola Adigun, an ex-student of United Mission College, the Rosijis were invited to the Gage (engagement ceremony). Gbemi told me all about it.

'It's the first formality before a wedding. Bola's grandfather, the senior member of her family, officially handed her over to the Solanke relatives. Both families were then formally introduced to each other even though many had met before. Traditionally with us a marriage is a contract between two families, not just between two people. At the Gage, the girl is absorbed into her fiance's family and vice versa.

Introductions over, the official ceremony began with the exchange of gifts. Then symbolic foods were passed round: water to sooth and calm; oil to smooth over disagreements; spirits (usually Schnapps) for everlasting preservation; kola nuts for mutual regard; alligator pepper with its uncountable seeds for fertility and a "oja", a belt for health and ability to bear children. As usual the evening closed with dancing and drumming.'

'What happens if the couple don't make a go of it once they are married?' I asked.

'The family steps in at the first sign of trouble and settles any problem before it develops. Marriage is for ever, you know, and there is no going back', she replied.

The wedding of Olusola Solanke was to take place in Ibadan about two months after the Gage. Olusola was tied down in his legal practice in Abeokuta and had to leave the bulk of the preparations to the Rosijis. Ayo was to be MC and best man. Gbemi, heavily pregnant, cheerfully got busy organising the reception which was to be held in their compound.

Since I had to go down to Abeokuta once a week in February and March in order to take a university extra mural class in English for Robert Gardner, I was able to deliver messages to Olu Solanke and he would send me back with instructions and crates of booze and soft drinks. He was a friend of the manager of the Blaize Memorial factory which produced orange, lime and lemon squash from local fruit. The imported Kia Ora fruit drinks cost twice as much and tasted insipid in comparison.

Olu knew the lime squash was my favourite and used to have it ready with ice for me when I called. It was a welcome relief to see him after coping with a motley lot of students in a run-down school building. We used to talk about Britain, where Olu had served in the RAF, and listen to records. He had a complete collection of the songs of Phil Harris and played 'Cigarettes and whisky and wild, wild women' over and over again. I shall always remember those visits in view of what happened later.

To return to the great day itself. True to Yoruba tradition the Solankes were quite obviously expecting a long and happy life together as they posed for a wedding photo outside Kudeti Church on 25 March 1952. Holding a bouquet of flowers picked earlier from the UMC flower beds and lovingly arranged by the missionaries, Bola stood prettily confident, in a full-length, white lace dress with a small train. Two minute cousins, dressed up as page boys in white satin suits, held up the train as if their lives depended on them keeping it off the ground, whilst a gimlet-eyed Yoruba aunt hovered near them to see that they did so!

With her hair rolled into symmetrical corkscrew curls round her face and a dainty fan-shaped lace headdress topping her bridal veil, Bola looked as if she had stepped out of a chic fashion magazine. Olu was also very smartly dressed in a cream palm beach suit of superb quality, a black tie and a white shirt. Ayo, Godfrey Amachree, a mutual lawyer friend, and six other chaps wore exactly the same. Their erect, solid bodies suited Western clothes. Nigerians who had been abroad often continued to wear them after their return, especially if they led a professional life. They would instinctively revert to their own robes for any social occasion, however, and, as the independence movement increased its momentum, many rejected the European style altogether.

This fashion of dressing alike, 'aso ebi', was and is very popular among the Yorubas and other Nigerian peoples. Originally confined to relatives, the idea spread to friends, associates, members of a club or a particular group.

Bola too joined a dozen of her lady friends in 'aso ebi' once the wedding formalities were over and the reception was under way. They had chosen a rich blue brocade and were wearing it, Yoruba style: a fancy white blouse falls over a wrap-around skirt made from a really long piece of cloth called 'lappa'. It was fascinating to watch how they used the additional, extra length of material, the 'ipele'. It rarely stayed long tied around the 'lappa'. It would be adjusted, rewrapped, hitched up, retied higher or lower, flung over the blouse (buba) or just trailed. Were these movements significant like the language of the fan? Did they emit mysterious female messages to those who understood the code? The ladies laughed when questioned but never explained!

Lots of gold jewelry and a large heavy headtie completed the outfit. Bola's outshone everyone else's. Her headtie was a veritable Eiffel Tower of rich blue satin. The Europeans at the assembly, including friends from the mission, the banks, the administration, the Bar and many others could not compete even though everyone had made the supreme effort of donning ties, stockings and even gloves for the occasion!

Two hundred chairs had been hired to seat the guests in the garden and the lounge. As more than that number arrived so a pile of mats was produced to help out. Some latecomers who had travelled from afar expected to stay the night. Poor Gbemi! She had to use all her tact to persuade them not to dump their suitcases in the shining clean reception rooms.

As at the gage party, oil, honey, kola nuts, alligator pepper and an 'oja' had been handed round as a prelude to the reception. Gbemi and her helpers had worked like Trojans to provide the main meal. It was a feast to end all feasts! Huge bowls of groundnut, chicken and other peppery stews had been prepared, not to mention jollof rice, sausage rolls, roast chicken and turkey. There was boiled rice, peppers, tomatoes, mixed salads of lettuce and diced vegetables and boiled potatoes to go with the meat, plus 'fufu, '(pounded yam), 'amala' (small cakes of yam dipped in flour and fried golden brown), 'egusi' and 'ewedu' (stews based on spinach, melon seed and other ingredients).

The dessert was equally toothsome: trifles with cream, fruit salad, large and small cakes, all home baked and, pièce de résistance, a three tiered wedding cake iced and decorated with sugar flowers. This was at a time when an electric stove was a rare luxury and most things would have been cooked on a wood burning stove or even in a kerosene tin, converted into an oven. Drink flowed — champagne, whisky, gin, schnapps, beer and palm wine for drinkers, squashes and fizzy drinks for the teetotallers.

An orchestra played for people to dance and when the players paused for breath, drummers took over. Everyone talked to everyone else. Laughters mingled: the 'ha! ha!' of the Europeans, filtering through the deep, rumbling 'ho! ho!' of the Nigerians. It was a day when differences were put aside and all that mattered was the common enjoyment that comes from seeing two people, two families, happily united.

Olu Solanke had suffered from blood pressure for some time but had not thought it serious. He had been working very hard in Abeokuta before the marriage and admitted to Ayo that he was very tired just as he was leaving for his honeymoon. He and his wife returned full of high hopes for their future together in Abeokuta. It was not to be. Six weeks after his wedding he died of a heart attack. Grief stricken and bereft, Bola was left with one consolation. 'I am expecting a child', she told Gbemi and myself when she came to Ibadan on a visit. 'It will remind me always of him.'

We did not actually attend the naming ceremony of Bola's child as it took place in Abeokuta, but Gbemi remembers us naming the baby of the son of a friend of theirs: 'Those present were mainly women and the ceremony took place in the parent's sitting room. Actually this was quite a modest event. Mother sat the baby on her lap and brushed his lips with every symbolic morsel of food handed over to her before she chewed and ate it herself. The salt, honey and water was passed round and we all had a taste and a sip. Then came the actual naming. Everybody stood up, dropped a coin in the water and pronounced whatever name they wanted for the child. Some were repetitions, but Jean, of course had to be original. She named the lucky little boy "Olatokunbo" the one who has come from overseas' — the name given to babies born abroad. "I simply love that name" Jean insisted. In fact, "Tokunboh" was accepted and "Toks" he remained, signed and sealed with the drop of a coin.'

Thirty-three years later in London, Chief Ayo and Gbemi came to congratulate my son, Richard, on the birth of his son, Jack, named after my husband (who had lived with me in Richard's flat before his death in 1986). They gave him a Yoruba name BABATUNDE. (Father has come again) and Tunde he will be to the family and relatives even if he is plain 'Jack' at school.

Chapter thirteen
Move to Molete

In January, 1951, because of the congestion caused by the ever increasing student population, the school moved to a new site in Molete where Alayande had acquired sixty acres of land. As his biographers observe in the book, 'Legacy of Service': it was a courageous and bold initiative because some people had criticised the rationale behind the movement, in particular those who lived around the old site. The new site was situated at the end of a stoney, winding lane leading off the By-pass just before it veered round towards Ijebu. A narrow bridge over a stream half-way was a hazard for day boys and traffic alike in the wet season as it often flooded. It took at least ten minutes to reach the school gate with the sign IBADAN GRAMMAR SCHOOL spanning the road and a few minutes longer to reach the school itself standing on the brow of a hill called Oke Ado.

My own bungalow was at the bottom of the hill, five hundred yards beyond this gate. Set back a little from the road, it had parking space for a car in front and a small garden. The boys' quarters were at the back and there was just enough room on the terrace to sit with friends when it was cool enough and watch people visiting the school on the other side of the road or making their way up to the principal's new one-storey house.

His house was also on the left side of the road, but built on the very top of the hill. Up there he was 'monarch of all he surveyed' and the whole school complex was a kingdom indeed compared to the previous site in Oke Are. Everything was bigger, better, brighter and more spacious. He could see my house at the bottom of the hill and the two staff houses opposite on the other side of the lane. Behind them came a line of dormitories and the bathrooms. Further up came the dining room and facing his new one-storey house was his office and two good-sized stores. Behind them came two rows of classrooms, furnished with new shiny blackboards and solidly built single desks complete with roomy drawers for the students' books. A grassy compound lay between the classrooms and stone walkways with strong corrugated iron roofs giving shade when it was hot and protection during the rainy season. A large assembly hall linked the classrooms at the end. It, too, had new chairs for everyone and the added bonus of an excellent stage platform.

Chief Akin Delano used to clean the principal's house: 'It is now a historic monument. The reception room, dining room and other rooms were on the ground floor with an internal staircase leading to the upstairs landing, bedrooms either side and another reception room. The floor was made of wooden decking upstairs and it was my early morning job to keep it polished. I enjoyed doing that and got a good shine going. Mrs Alayande was very kind to me, giving me little snacks and tea. It was better than cutting grass although I was used to doing both tasks at home.'

Akin also enjoyed working on the school farm which was situated at the end of the buildings beyond a stretch of uncultivated ground: 'We grew small peppers of all sorts, maize, yams, tomatoes and spinach. No need to plant pawpaws. They were there already. My efforts were not the best. The people who came from small villages were more used to farming and got the highest marks. I didn't mind. It was a day off.'

Akin and the rest of the school were happy about the move. I was the only one with reservations, fearing my friends might find it too far away to call. Balefully the day I moved in I put the name of Siberian Cottage on a board outside. Of course, all my good friends followed me up there including the Rosijis, whilst the Morgans, Bishop Akinyele and his wife dropped in often on their way to see the principal who still continued to include me in many a function or social activity. Within a fortnight a sign board saying SANS SOUCI (without a care) was placed in front of the flower beds of zinnias and balsam I had planted and the 'Siberian Cottage' board joined the piles of weeds and stumps the boys had helped to clear away.

The 18th century French author, Voltaire, who had lived in the original Sans Souci — a house in the grounds of the palace belonging to the German Emperor, Frederick the Great — could not have been happier than I was. My new home was a bright, snug, comfortable nest. It had a bedroom and bathroom on the left, a long room in the centre doing service as a sitting room and dining room and two smallish rooms at the end serving as store rooms and spare bedroom. To begin with I had the same furniture from the flat on the Ijeba By-pass, but brought back a few knick knacks from after my first leave in the summer of 1951 home and a wind-up gramophone.

As an inducement to return for a second tour, the diocesan council had not only given me a grant for kitchen ware and cheerful new floral curtains, they had loaned me the money for a car to be paid back in monthly instalments. This put me on a par with conditions in the government service except that I paid my own mileage.

What a joy it was to switch on the electric light and forget about lighting a Tilly lamp! What a relief to say goodbye to creepy torchlight walks past the kitchen in order to spend a penny at night! I had a real bath too, and a hand basin in a biggish bathroom, a step across from the bedroom. Electricity also meant I could have radio diffusion installed, which was musical company although the teachers opposite had theirs on full blast and it was still playing the self same tunes I had heard during that first breakfast in the principal's house in 1949.

The Ibadan schoolboys were also pleased to have improved boarding facilities. Many day boys in fact, envied them. Again I quote Chief Akin Delano: 'You had to go home after school if you were a day boy and if there was a compulsory debate or meeting in the late afternoon I had to walk back four miles in the afternoon heat. It was very tiring, even with a bicycle. I was pining to be a boarder. Fortunately, this wish came true a year after the move. My father was posted to Ifo with the family so I had to board. It was the better life all right. There was something to do all the time. I certainly did not mind the early morning work. We had to do that at home. . . .'

Akin also found the washing facilities at the boarding school far better than his home: 'In the early days, before the water works were built in town, only people with wells had constant water.

We used to chat to the neighbours round the taps in the street. That's how I met my first girl friend, Dayo, we were both fourteen. We wrote notes to each other, but the only time we met was when we were filling up our buckets. We slept ten to a dormitory in the school, which had two pipe-born, treated-water taps on the lawn outside. We could also bath in a corrugated iron enclosure containing two more taps. The school provided washermen as part of the boarding service. Ignatius was one. He used a flat iron, filled with charcoal, and his pressing was excellent.'

Prayers and the morning jobs of cleaning and grass cutting took place before the boys washed and changed into their school uniform.

Never shall I forget that early morning scene: sipping early morning tea on my verandah I would watch the lads coming out of the dormitories in dribs and drabs in order to do these jobs. I hear again the sounds of those early, bright, pleasantly warm tropical mornings the chirping of a thousand crickets, the distant throbbings of a village drum, the music from the rediffusion, the swish, swish, swish of the machetes cutting through the grass and the barking cries of the principal as he chivvied the boys, lunging at rather than touching them with a branch snatched from a tree. 'Come on! Come on! Aha! Aa! no laggards. Get on with it.'

It was less pleasant having to listen to the daily beatings taking place in the teachers' house before morning assembly. Knowing that this punishment was part of the job, in their eyes, I had to accept the situation.

Samuel Charles, the senior tutor, remained mild and pleasant on the personal level and often dropped into Sans Souci for a chat and a beer, a drink he enjoyed immensely, sometimes to the point of excess. He was trying to arrange for Sylvia, his girlfriend from Freetown, to join him. He had been too poor to offer marriage when they were younger and family pressure had forced her to marry someone else. She had not been happy and was now seeking a divorce. It came through, eventually and the two lovers were united in a new house next door to Adesina and the other two boarding teachers. She was a very pleasant lady and loved popping in to Sans Souci, opposite, for a gossip.

I formed an even greater friendship with Ebun Alayande now that we were neighbours. We had also got together during my leave in England when the British Council had arranged for her to work in two separate boarding schools as a matron in order to learn their methods and improve her English. I had met her at the station on arrival, helped her buy European clothes' invited her home and went to visit her in her schools which were in the depths of the countryside. The post of assistant matron in the first establishment was considered unimportant to say the least and she did not get the respect a lady of her achievements should have received. She was too good a Christian to complain but I found out later when she commented on the warmth and friendliness shown to her at the second.

Sadly, diabetes has caused this capable, clever, buoyant, jolly lady to go blind and deteriorate in health. When we met in January 1991 after nearly forty years she grasped my hand and chatted about days past for a moment. Then her thoughts wandered and our body contact had to replace the words of gratitude I wanted to express for all her kindnesses and understanding. She had the same humility and genuine Christian faith as her father, the Bishop Akinyele. When she died, in 1995, hundreds of mourners expressing their grief attended her funeral and the procession of mourners, paying their respects, continued at the house for weeks afterwards.

To return to 1951, the principal sent a letter to me in London dated 6 September 1951 from Lagos, 'whither I have gone to see Ebun off'. Discussing recruitment of another expatriate teacher he said 'male or female, please, and graduate in arts and science'. Unfortunately the expensive advertisements I placed in the Times educational supplement produced a number of candidates, one less suitable than the other. By a trick of fate he, himself, received and accepted two unsolicited applications soon afterwards.

The first was from Hugo Mentor, a West Indian from Port of Spain, Trinidad, where he had worked as a journalist before he joined the american army. After the war finished he took advantage of a four year training scheme to study for a maths degree and diploma in Paris where he mixed with French, american and other students from abroad. Once he was qualified he was reluctant to stay on or return to Trinidad and when a Nigerian fellow student suggested he write to the Grammar School, he jumped at the idea. He came to Putney the day before I was leaving again for Ibadan and seemed a pleasant enough fellow, without any problems about changing from one country to another.

Agnes Judd, daughter of a senior United Nations Organisation official was the second new member of staff. Her father had chaired a conference at the Ibadan University where he had met the Principal who had shown him the school. He was so impressed by what he saw, he begged him to take on Agnes as history teacher. It took a few months to sell the idea to the authorities and, also, to build a house for her (next to Sans Souci), so she arrived several months after Hugo. She proved a conscientious teacher who mixed well with everyone and had a good sense of humour.

Hugo was given lodgings in a house and money to buy a bicycle, which he rode bolt upright as if a stick were tied against his back. He settled in quickly, establishing an informal relationship with the boys, chaffing the teachers during the recreation breaks and taking everything in his stride without fuss or palaver. As a rule he did not have a lot to say at the monthly staff meetings. However, when something came up which he felt was unfair, he would give vent to an impassioned speech of protest which took us all aback.

The principal had given me a grant to buy new books for the library and Hugo was very helpful when it came to cataloguing them. We used the Bliss System on the advice of the university librarian, John Harris, who felt it offered a more logical sequence of subjects than the better known Dewey classification. His wife, who ran the University Bookshop, could have stepped straight from a Pre-Raphaelite painting with her long orange-red hair, white skin and slim, almost frail, body. She was a mine of information concerning books suitable for the boys and she was prompt in obtaining them if they were not on sale in Ibadan. She also gave me a special liquid to dab inside books to prevent ants eating the paper. Library periods were inserted into the time table and the idea of reading for reading's sake gradually took on.

Students from my classes often dropped in to Sans Souci in the evening to listen to my records or peruse my own books for pleasure or for their homework. In the two weeks before Cambridge Certificate, some of the boys tried to work all night and a special teacher patrol was set up to insist on them returning to bed.

Whilst I sweated for hours planning my library periods and correcting the interminable essays on english and history, Hugo Mentor appeared to get through his marking in no time and did not agonise one bit about lesson plans. Yet in the principal's words, 'Mentor has revolutionised the teaching of mathematics. The boys work at it now with great enthusiasm, they really enjoy his teaching. The good examination results at the end of the year have proved his efficiency'.

As Hugo lived too far away to go home during the day and there was no staff room where he could sit down to relax, the principal asked me if I would provide lunch for him. It was a pleasant change to have company after so many solitary meals. He was a good listener, well read and we used to discuss home affairs and school gossip in equal measure, sometimes in French.

It was awkward for him to entertain me in his lodgings where the other tenants were noisy and quarrelsome, especially the women who often came to blows when collecting water at the tap in the compound. To show his gratitude he insisted on paying the cost of a good evening dinner in Sans Souci. He would cycle up bearing extra goodies from Kingsway, plus sherry, wine and liqueurs. All very pleasant had he not taken away the half empty bottles every time he came!

The boys ate and drank very differently from Hugo and myself! They were given water during their meals and tea with their breakfast of *eku* (porridge with corn) or *moyin* or *akara* or bread and butter. For lunch they had rice, or amala (from yam flour) or *eba* (from garri) served with vegetables like egusi and stews of onions, tomatoes, pepper and meat cooked in groundnut or palm oil. Supper was lighter *eko* wrapped in leaves with vegetable stew. Eight students sat around each table and the food was dished out from a large container by the senior student. Chief Adigun said 'Akin Mabogunje divided it so meticulously that each student had exactly the same quantity of food. He was so good at it and so fair. I am happy he rose to the level of professor of geography after school.'

The wholesome food purchased by the school was sometimes badly cooked. One stifling hot day just before the rainy season when tempers frayed and disputes occur for the smallest of reasons, the boys suddenly went on strike. They sat themselves down on the grass in front of the dining room entrance and refused to eat until something was done about the quantity and quality of the meals.

The Alayandes, Mr Charles and Mr Adesina stepped in to discuss terms. Eventually — and quite amicably — an improved diet was suggested and approved of by the strike committee. A staff meeting was called to put us in the picture and we were all asked to join the boys in the dining room for a month at least. Dutifully, Hugo and I joined them and tackled the stews. It was most embarrassing. We had both eaten with African friends but they must have told the cooks to go slow on the strong peppers! School fare tasted hotter and hotter as we chewed and our gums felt as if they were catching fire. The solution was to swallow every mouthful quickly, chew on nothing for a moment smiling and praising the 'haute cuisine' (or rather 'hot' cuisine!) and continue this process till the dish was empty. The boys were so polite they would insist on prolonging our agony even more by giving us any food that remained in the container.

Fortunately the new menus were accepted peacefully and there was no more trouble in that direction.

Chief Adigun remembers eating in the school dining room: 'The arrangement made in the school for the mid-day meal was superb as all students mandatorily had to lunch in the school and an opportunity existed for inculcating table manners'.

I found the boys good mannered all the time even if I did not always know what they were thinking. When they were found out for some misdemeanour or when a situation embarrassed them they would fidget and click their fingers. One young lad whom I hardly knew really surprised me one day. He stopped me in the compound and asked: 'Miss Jacoby why are you so beautiful?' This was the first and last time anyone spoke like this and I suspected he had been dared to do it.

As for the teachers they were unfailingly polite to me. They would tease each other, however, and make jokes I did not always understand. I certainly missed the fun my colleagues and I used to have in the staff room in Battersea, London. Although we all felt deeply about comprehensive education we never let on we did, whereas the Nigerian teachers took themselves very seriously indeed, often sermonising and moralising to each other. They were firm and fair with the boys but it was not done to fraternise too much.

It is hard to appreciate other people's loyalties. The enthusiasm felt by boys and teachers alike at the Aionian sports matches played at home in Ibadan or away in Abeokuta or Ondo etc. was nothing compared to the attachment they had to the four school groups labelled 'houses' in the public school tradition. Akin Delano remembers belonging to Olubadan, the title of the traditional ruler of Ibadan. The other three were Olubi a famous warrior in Ibadan history, Irefin who had been an Olubadan, and Akinyele after the founder. At my first inter-house sports day I was asked to pick out the first boy in the hundred metre running race, Mr Ayeni was to pick out number two and Mr Unuigbe number three. To my amazement they denied my choice and produced boys from their own house instead! A terrible row broke out and Mr Charles had to step in to settle it.

Similarly when it was a question of your family (meaning extended family) the attachment went even deeper. The Italian writer, Moravia, stated: 'In Italy the family accounts for everything, justifies everything, is everything'. The Nigerians were the same and I was surprised by the lenience they showed to their kith and kin compared to others who were not related to them.

Another difference between us was our sense of humour. Laughter is used very differently in Africa from Europe. I certainly found the West Africans I met from Sierra Leone, the Gold Coast (now Ghana) and Nigeria basically cheerful and unself-conscious about laughing louder and longer than the British. People everywhere may giggle when they are nervous or get hysterical when the situation is not exactly funny but West Africans seem to take this further. Certainly I have seen Nigerians laugh when I expected them to be horrified, shocked, grieved, excited or afraid.

This was particularly disconcerting when we went to see a film in Ibadan. We had two cinemas to choose from, both open to the sky. One was a rope affair in the heart of the town with broken down seats and a broken down projector to match. The reels kept breaking and the projectionist did not always return them in the right order. The other was quite a well run set-up at the end of the By-pass. The programmes changed daily, alternating between very old melodramas like the 'Perils of Pauline', and

Indian films full of shaky scenery, dancing girls, heartless villains, soppy looking heroes and luscious heroines — caught constantly in near-death situations and invariably rescued in the very nick of time. Saturdays was the day for European films.

Whatever happened on the screen, the Nigerian spectators reacted to every twist and turn of the plot loudly and expressively. They had a field day one Saturday when the film of Hamlet began to turn. Whilst the Europeans, togged up in best evening clothes remained po-faced and respectfully solemn as poor Polonius was stabbed, the Nigerians ah! ah!s of mirth filled the cinema and when the swords flashed and corpses littered the stage in the last scene, their hilarity knew no bounds!

Alec Dickson who was responsible for the Man of War Scheme in Eastern Nigeria told me he also received an unexpected reaction from a group of Nigerian men who were shown a film graphically depicting the terrible effects syphilis has on the body. It was greeted by roar upon roar of laughter!

Although the staff and principal did not always have the same sense of humour, we remained on the same wavelength when it came to the importance of good moral principles based on the Christian ethic. Overall, discipline was good and when cases of stealing or cheating did occur, (Chief Delano comments) 'such incidents were generally the work of one small group of miscreants'.

Since a number of boys were well past school age it was hardly surprising they fathered children in the town. It was known but ignored. Unfortunately for me, a very quiet Benin boy called Osunde, who had worked for Peter Steward in the Wedding Cake flat whilst I paid his grammar school fees, had got a girl pregnant. He told me he had taken her for private lessons (his words) and the situation had got out of hand. Unfortunately when the principal was holding a Governors' meeting in his office, this pupil had interrupted them to demand maintenance for the baby in her arms. This was unacceptable and Osunde was expelled. I sent him to Onitsha to live with Emeka and paid through the nose for his education in a private school — finding out, too late, that the teachers were so bad that most students depended on Rapid Results courses to get them through their examinations.

After leaving school Osunde went into the Post and Telegraph service and did well, sending me Christmas cards, even though he was a Muslim, which got bigger and bigger year by year as he rose in the department.

Let Chief Adigun have the last word: 'There was a large dose of Christian practices and ethics in the daily routine both in the boarding house and the school itself . . .'

Chapter fourteen
Social circles

Bit by bit my social life had extended beyond these very enjoyable activities. About three months after seeing me in Ibadan, Brenda sent me an invitation to visit them for a weekend in Ondo. Having no car, the only way of getting to Ondo was by 'mammy wagon' and I was determined not to let a little matter of transport stop me from going. The principal drove me to the main lorry park, found a driver he knew and organised a 'first class ticket'. This meant sitting in the front seat squeezed between him and the stoutest Yoruba lady in the Western Region. I had a svelte figure in those days and the two of us looked like those advertisements which picture the same woman before and after taking SLIMFAST tablets.

People who claim that the Gobi Desert is the hottest place on earth have never sweltered for hours in a Nigerian lorry park. The sun beats down on the dusty mammy wagons and transport lorries standing close together like camels in a scorching desert outpost. It was hard to tell who was coming or going. The departing passengers were shouting and yelling as they clambered over each others' shoulders in their haste to get off, whilst those who were starting on their journey were vociferously jostling and pushing each other in their struggle to climb in at the back of the wagon. Once inside, they used their huge bundles of belongings and crates of livestock as battering rams to forge their way through to the benches at the back. The rest had to stand.

The cries of the street traders selling food for the journey; the crowds of people milling about; the loud farewells of relatives and friends bidding 'safe journey' to the travellers; the barking of pyedogs rooting around for scraps; the incessant honk, honk, of the motor horns; and the zoom! zoom! of dicey engines revving up — added to the general hullabaloo.

The supposed hour of departure came and went. Two more hours passed. Oblivious to regulations concerning weight and number, the driver kept taking on more and more passengers and was in no hurry to leave. Eventually, we started out with the wagon crammed to bursting point and a few hardy souls hanging on like grim death to the ropes encircling the lorry. No doubt they had read the sign in front: 'Hope in God'.

My fat neighbour introduced herself as Amina and we chatted happily together as the driver sped through the streets of Ibadan and on to the bumpy road leading to Ondo. We rattled on and on and on for three hours then stopped at a large market where the chaos started again with some descending and more getting in. I was so tired I dozed off, dimly hearing the driver rev up, stop, then start up the engine. When I did wake up and look around I was sure we had been travelling for miles. 'Have we arrived?" I asked Amina. 'We've moved from one side of the market to the other to buy petrol' she replied.

It was dark when we did make the lorry park at Ondo and Jan Invald, presuming I had left, had come and gone. I managed to ring him from the police station and he returned in a sullen mood. This delay was only one of the many irritations upsetting him in his new career. After working with skilled technicians in a well equipped factory in Prague for many years he was unprepared for the haphazard life in the bush with an uncertain water supply, shortages and difficulties in shopping and problems with his labour force. He did not realise that most of his men had no clocks at home, found it difficult to understand his poor English and did not see why they should work hard on very poor pay.

Brenda was delighted to see me and a bottle of Riesling over dinner cheered us all up. The next day was spent visiting Louis Abizakhem's brother, John, at his sawmill. In the evening we went to his house for a small dinner party where I met another forestry officer, a scotsman called Johnnie Horne, who was stationed in Ibadan and on tour for his work. He gave me a lift back on the Monday and we continued seeing each other after that.

The Scots have a long tradition of working abroad and Johnnie was a flexible, conscientious understanding man. He enjoyed the untrammelled peace of the bush, and was ready to find out about the Nigerians working for him. He was soon promoted director of the Forestry School in Ibadan and did an excellent job training the students. I introduced him to Alayande who asked him to lecture to the boys on the 'Prospect of Forestry' as a career. He spoke clearly and persuasively in his pleasant Edinburgh accent and the boys listened well. As usual a few lads, tired by their long walk to school, got up to stand at the back to stop themselves from falling asleep. This disconcerted Johnnie who thought he must be boring them. Not a bit, his lecture inspired several students to do forestry training that year and others were to follow suit in the future.

Johnnie was a member of a dramatic society called the Ibadan Players and had already been chosen for the lead in their next production, 'MR BOLFRY'— by James Brodie. He took me along to the auditions for the other roles which took place in the flat of the producer, Betty Johnson, who was working as deputy matron in Adeoyo Hospital. A blonde, brassy lady she had gone through two husbands and was searching for a third.

Great disappointment! The part of the heroine (also called Jean) went to Betty's best friend and neighbour, Mary. The other two feminine roles were given to Margaret, the University librarian's wife and to Catherine Phillips whose husband, Tony, worked for the P & T Department. Phil Daley and Bill Mutch, forestry officers, made up the cast. Fortunately for me, the following Saturday — at a party given by the Army — Mary succeeded in filching Betty's latest conquest, a stunning major, from under her very nose. The two ladies had an almighty row and Mary resigned from the Players.

Betty called at the Wedding Cake to offer me the part of 'Jean'. 'The heroine is a simple, Scottish girl', she purred. 'Working in a mission school as you do, Jean, the role is tailor-made for you.'

I did not mind being considered drab and demure if it meant being in the play. Bill Gear, from the public works department, was an overwhelmingly enthusiastic stage manager and his colleague, Freddie Foss, ex-colonel in the Indian army, helped Roland Brownlees and Mike Smith, from John Holt's and UAC respectively, with tickets, publicity and other administrative matters. Tony Phillips and another P & T chap called Ian organised the lights. Finally, Bill's wife, Bea, Catherine and a nurse called Vera Gunton produced the costumes. She had first arrived in Ibadan as nurse to an army officer's wife with TB whose baby she had delivered and she had stayed on as extra staff in Adeoyo hospital and was enrolled officially into the Colonial Service, on a permanent basis, a year later. We became very good friends and are still in touch.

The rehearsals started and like all amateur dramatics, took over most of our spare time. A social life, set around the players crowd, soon developed including private parties, curry lunches, Saturday nights at the Club starting with a meal at someone's home, a climbing expedition to Adda Rock, picnics in the forest and a weekend together with the Gallaghers, who were friends of the Geers, stationed in Badagry. The short stay there was a mix of heaven and hell. The good part was having miles and miles of golden sands and sparkling sea to ourselves, jolly company and uproarious parties each night. The bad side was the mosquitoes. They flew in from the innumerable patches of static water in the surrounding marshes, stormed through the mosquito nets and nearly ate us alive. Far more distressing was a sightseeing trip to the old haul, the plain evidence of juju rites and rituals on the creek.

The Gears and I had a certain amount in common. They lived in the Peabody Estate in Battersea where I had been teaching and shared a mutual friend in David Rapoport, my father's lawyer. His practice was also in Battersea and he and Bill had met at masonic meetings. Both they and Johnnie Horne insisted on my joining the Ibadan Club which was a bigger version of the Kano Club with triple the membership. Under the circumstances, it seemed churlish to refuse. I still loathed the excessive drinking that went on there and its colour bar. However, I came to realise that the sports facilities, the entertainment and the chance to.meet each other, laugh together and let their hair down meant a lot to the European men working in and around that vast sprawling town; also with servants to see to the house and the rough work in the garden, their wives would have been lost without it, especially those who did not go out to work.

Bill Gear continued to attend masonic meetings in Ibadan and one day, a fellow mason, Mike Smith, the British chief of police, took him to one side. 'My men have seen you and Bea with that Jacoby woman', he said. 'We've had her under surveillance for some time because of her association with some politically active Nigerians. Also we're not too happy about her, living alone like that on the By-pass has aroused our suspicions. Do you know anything about her?'

'Jean! Yer don't need to worry about 'er, old chum', Bill exclaimed in his heavy cockney accent, 'I knows all about 'er from 'er Dad's lawyer'.

It was ironic that Bill should have been the person to clear my name since I considered his attitude to his workmen and to Nigerians generally, ignorant and offensive. He labelled them 'those comedians' in conversation and did not have a good word to say about them in spite of my repeated rebuttal of his criticisms.

A scathing comment by Erica Powell, erstwhile Private Secretary to the first President of Ghana, Kwame Nkrumah, could apply to many Europeans in Nigeria, especially the non working wives. 'The enclosed community of Europeans in which I now found myself seemed to be trying to cut themselves off from reality, while remaining blind to the existence of the black masses without.'

The forestry lads were more tolerant and the people in commerce tended to treat their Nigerian employees and customers reasonably enough in business. Mike, from John Holt, was unconsciously funny about the women traders who came to do business with him. If the baby they were carrying needed feeding they would offer it their breast. 'It's so embarrassing, Jean, it really is', he confided bibulously one Saturday club night. 'I was at a boys' prep school, then a boys' public school, and came out here soon after leaving, and I'm just not used to that sort of thing.'

Administrative officers varied a lot. Some made a genuine effort to work with the Nigerians, others were high handed and condescending to them and to other Europeans despising the 'commercial types' (their term) and regarding the PWD as the lowest form of animal life on earth. I was even lower than that, I think, receiving a nod of recognition from the governor, Sir Hoskins Abrahall, at very official functions and not much more. His wife formed a group to promote friendship and the administration wives dutifully turned up, tending to talk to each other instead of fraternising. It could be they did not know how to break the barriers. On the other side, the Nigerian action group had adopted a policy of non-fraternisation with the administration. Hence Ayo Rosiji's comment to Gbemi in requesting her not to attend: 'The Governor won't give us our freedom but he asks us to tea! Aha!'

Erica Powell again: 'Unless you "went native" so to speak, the chances of getting to know an African on equal terms were remote. They were not allowed to set foot in a European club, they were rarely present at the functions one attended, and, if they were, they were ill at ease and said only the polite things they expected you wanted to hear.'

Fortunately, the Ibadan university community was far more open-minded. With staff drawn from Nigeria, Sierra Leone, Ghana, Australia, New Zealand, West Indies, America, the United Kingdom, Canada, Germany, Holland and elsewhere it had a League of Nations quality about it. Thanks to the Gardners and their friends, the Karrefa-Smarts, my Nigerian friends, the professors who had come to inspect the Grammar School, the Harris's and Vera who lived on the university compound, I was frequently invited to university functions. Once I had my little Volkswagen car in the second tour it was even easier and Peter Schild who had taught me to drive, or Klaus, one of Vera's boyfriends from UTC garage, could be counted on to see to any necessary repairs.

The university compound had originally belonged to the army and Vera remembers working in Adeoyo Hospital, living with her nursing colleagues in the old army quarters prior to the opening of the new university hospital and working in Adeoyo Hospital. They were virtually shacks with washing facilities at the back and a thunder box. Before we got fridges, we used to bury the butter and meat, wrapped in paw paw leaves, to keep them cool and tenderise the meat. We ate our main meals in the mess with the academic staff which made for interesting, stimulating cocktail parties with the academic staff were held in the open. Once we witnessed the night sanitary man with the nauseous bucket on his head, nonchalantly strolling through the middle of the party. It was particularly amusing to watch everyone trying to ignore him.

To return to a higher plane! A bible study group was organised in the house of a New Zealand university lecturer. Pleased to repay the folk in UMC for their hospitality and kindness to me, I used to drive them there in my VW beetle. One particular evening the rain had been heavy enough to cover the bridge between the school and the By-pass, splashing over the bonnet of the car as I passed. Further on a careless gardener had lit the grass to cut it near to the verge and there were flames on the road leading to the mission house. 'I've come through hell and high water to fetch you', I joked, as they piled in.

A further incident enlivened the evening. The group, about twenty five of us, were deep in purposeful analysis of St Paul's Epistle to the Corinthians, when we were interrupted by an urgent tap on the wide glass door dividing the lounge and the garden. It was a huge baboon and he looked pretty fierce. An American Rhodes scholar, Professor Britton, had gone to the Eastern Region to locate and bring back several baboons in order to research the theory of their link with man because they assumed an almost upright position. One of them had obviously escaped from the strongly fenced garden where it was held in captivity.

A phone call soon summoned the professor. He arrived in a jeep and jumped out thumping his chest and shouting Huh! Huh! and other baboonish noises which the animal recognised immediately and answered. The two of them danced around each other for a minute or so and went off with the professor driving!

I had met the Brittons on the MV *Auriel* going out for my second tour in 1952 and found them an adorable couple. Artistic, charming and tactful, she was for ever guiding her white haired, absent minded husband through everything that was the least little bit practical such as finding his glasses, his pen, his books or the table in the dining room. It was a shock to see his scientific side! Maybe he had humanised the baboon so expertly, it had responded to the lure of Christian prayer!

A regular Sunday service was held in the Grammar School hall at 10 a.m. and the sermon was usually given by a member of staff. In 1953 my turn came on Palm Sunday. I reminded the worshippers that Jesus had come up to Jerusalem for the 'passover' which was an extremely important feast in the Jewish calendar. Commemorating the exodus of the Israelites from Egyptian bondage, it was known as the festival of freedom. The fact that Our Lord was a Jew through and through should never, I insisted, be forgotten and to speak or think disparagingly about the Jews was blaspheming Christ himself. A few people complained to the principal saying, 'They expected a Christian, not a Jewish, sermon!'

Sometimes I attended a Sunday evening service at St Anne's, staying on for a meal afterwards, together with the guest speaker. It was always a cosy occasion and reminded me of home. Naturally I found some members of the mission more sympathetic than others but at heart they were good, sincere women and very kind. Once in my last year they found out I was far from well and insisted on my staying a week with them to give me special care.

The most memorable religious occasion of all was the day Archbishop Vining came to town immediately after his ordination as Archbishop of West Africa in Freetown,

Sierra Leone. Mojekwu had known him in the East and admired him greatly so I was looking forward to meeting him in the flesh. Here is my description written the following day ... Messages were sent to every school informing them where the students were expected to stand along the route leading to Bishop Akinyele's compound. The directive was to meet outside Government College at 4 p.m. Prominent members of the town were waiting in their cars for the Archbishop to arrive. Bishop Akinyele, bowed in body but crystal clear in mind, had driven up with his wife, his daughter, Kemi Morgan and her husband. They were in front and his son-in-law, Reverend Alayande, followed with Ebun, his wife, their two daughters and myself. We were dressed in our finest. The Alayande ladies in blue with huge matching head ties and I wore a pretty Horrocks light-pink and white dress, and, for the first time since leaving London, a pair of nylon stockings. Even more resplendent were Archdeacon Latunde, the chairman of the board of governors, and Chief Agbaje who waited behind us in a Buick car as big as a house.

At exactly 3.30 a small Renault car buzzed up and parked itself outside the college gates. The Principal of Government College, deputed to organise the pecking order, was affronted. He bore down on the driver and harangued him in no uncertain terms. Did he not know that the Great Man himself was due any minute? 'Yes', the driver said 'I know'. The 'Great Man' was actually sitting behind him, snatching a post prandial nap. No swanky cars for this modest archbishop.

He was gently awakened, and welcomed by the principal and by the occupants of the waiting cars who dashed up to shake his hand and hurry back to their cars, hoping to jump the queue once the Archbishop departed. A surprisingly quiet police presence prevented this and the motorcade set off. We smiled sweetly and waved at the schoolboys and girls cheering, jigging and dancing as the motorcade passed. The stall holders along the route, selling limes, kolas, oranges and bananas, gaped and cheered; the Lebanese and Syrian traders greeted us noisily from their cloth shops; the market women paused in their haggling and pointed us out to their neighbours; curious pagans stopped and stared; and some Muslims pointed at me and shout: 'Ya wo re'.

'They think you must be the Archbishop's wife, following dutifully behind your husband', laughed Ebun.

We stopped at every Anglican Church we passed and the Archbishop made a point of getting out to greet every single member of the congregation. There was a ten minute delay at the Salvation Army Citadel. All the soldiers of Christ seemed to be there belting out hymns and beating drums in his honour. (Ecumenism was very strong in Africa long before it started in Europe.)

Finally the motorcade reached Bishop Akinyele's compound where the welcome was equally uproarious. Mountains of sandwiches and cakes were served to the visitors by a group of ladies sporting large badges saying Women's Improvement Society on even larger bosoms. Everyone had so much to say and to laugh about it was hard to get them to quieten down even when the Archdeacon rose to introduce the governor, Sir Hoskins Abrahall.

HA, called thus by his department, may have been an efficient administrator but his speech was so heavily Oxford English it sounded pompous and was drowned anyway by the constant buzz of conversation on the part of the audience. Seeing him pop his notes into his pocket and sit down everyone realised he had finished and applauded heartily. He then stood up again to introduce Archbishop Vining.

His loud voice and forceful personality held everyone's attention. He spoke about his official enthronement in the Cathedral in Freetown by the Archbishop of Canterbury himself and of the huge welcome he had been given in Lagos. The reception in Ibadan had equalled and excelled all other welcomes. All these good wishes encouraged him to undertake this great new task — a task which seemed too large — 'But after all I am the same man' (great laughter) 'and with the help of God I shall do my best'. Official addresses were read out by the Archdeacon and Reverend Alayande amid a general hubbub and presented to the Archbishop. Bishop Akinyele followed this with a vote of thanks. This man oozed faith and integrity so much and was so universally respected the entire congregation was silent as soon as he started to speak.

An enormous reception at the university took place in the evening with more food, more drink, more dancing and drumming. Very much a man's man, the Archbishop ate, drank and mingled with the guests but left the dancing to others.

The highlight of the visit was the service taken by the Archbishop in St Peter's Church the following day. Never in my life have I seen a church so crowded. Sir Chandos Hoskins Abrahall and his lady, all the high-ups in the administration, sweating in their ceremonial uniform of white drill buttoned unbearably up to the neck, chiefs from all over the Western Region, the Nigerian élite, senior officials of all the government departments, the British Council staff, government education officers, Dr Mellanby and his wife, Jean, from the University and many senior lecturers, the heads of UAC, L & K, UTC, CFAO, SCOA, Patterson Zochonis, GB Ollivant and other trading companies, Louis Abizakhem and his associates and every member of the CMS able to travel, not to mention representatives of the other missions had joined the many, many Christian people in Ibadan to show respect to and pray with the very first Archbishop of Nigeria.

He arrived straight from another reception, looking splendid, if overawed, by the newness of his hat and the shining whiteness of his moirée episcopal robes. When the hustle bustle of the huge congregation had died down, and the choristers had filed in, the Archbishop began the prayers. The whole service was an uplifting, inspirational and unforgettable experience.

Our principal had a way of persuading people to visit his school however busy they were. The Archbishop was no exception. He came up the next morning. We teachers formed a guard of honour outside the hall and were introduced in turn, then followed him into the hall where the boys sat quietly, spruced up for the occasion. As usual Vining spoke in simple words everyone could understand.

After the service the teachers stood with their classes along the route down to the By-pass cheering and waving to their own Archbishop as he drove away to attend more receptions and more meetings. A very great man, Archbishop Vining, full of energy, purpose and faith.

Chapter fifteen
Drama on and off the stage

After the Bishop's visit and 'Mr Bolfry', life continued full of drama — on, and off, the stage.

The next play staged by the Ibadan Players was the psychological thriller, 'Gaslight', by Patrick Hamilton. Set in Victorian times it describes how a seemingly charming man tries to drive his rich wife, Bella, into insanity in order to get possession of her fortune. Colonel Freddie Foss had volunteered to produce it and everything was done with Indian army precision. As Johnnie Horne was on leave and Bill Gear, who continued to stage-manage both the play and myself, was now often on tour, Freddie used to pick me up and take me to the rehearsals which took place at the house of Harold, the assistant producer. He and most of the cast lived in the university complex so, at the beginning, this suited everyone. Everyone, that is, except Harold's wife. Once she discovered that Lena, the lady playing the part of Bella's housekeeper — a brilliant if odd researcher of English Literature — had lured Harold into a torrid affair, she refused to let us use the house until the femme fatale was dismissed from the cast and forced to do her research, sexual or literary, elsewhere. A friend of Vera's stepped in as my 'housekeeper' with barely a month to go.

The researcher had a nervous breakdown — recovering quickly when no one took any notice. As for the production of 'Gaslight', we got rave notices and full houses. The chairlady of the Red Cross was so impressed she implored Freddie to put it on again the following Saturday, donating the takings to the Red Cross. Emeka happened to be in Ibadan on business that weekend and came to see the play. As Monday was the start of the school half term holiday, he drove me down to Onitsha on the Sunday. The week together was a happy one in spite of the bitter sweet undertones now underlying our friendship. He was working very hard indeed to establish his practice. What free time he had was devoted to scouting, preaching and education. Unfortunately, the headmaster of the school in Akuma had absconded with all the funds, which meant closing the school. Emeka had turned to other projects including fund raising for a school in a leper colony, twenty miles from Onitsha, run by the Church Mission Society.

We visited this colony together. In order to promote interest and sympathy in the UK, the missions in the UK had tended to stress the terrible effects of leprosy on the body by publishing pictures of sufferers without legs or noses, existing in squalor, shunned and driven away from their villages. The place we saw told a different story. The lepers were clean, cheerful and living as normal a life as possible with their families. Mission workers in the hospital dispensary gave them tablets daily and intensive instruction on hygiene to make certain they kept all their drinking cups and plates separate. Two doctors carried out operations and dealt with serious cases in the hospital. Neither they nor their fellow workers complained about being far from anywhere, about the danger of catching the disease or even about their vocation. They acted like ordinary people conscientiously doing a job; ever ready to laugh or crack a joke. It was inspiring.

On our way back Emeka stopped the car to show me an area where the forestry department had planted small, sturdy bushes in order to prevent the eroded land crumble away altogether. As we made our way over the ridged, dry red earth, full of dramatic gashes, both of us suddenly felt compelled to stop, fearing the sense of something very evil. We could not wait to get back to the car and drive away. We found out on our return that we had been on the site of what had once been a notorious juju shrine dedicated to human sacrifice.

After half term the principal asked me to take on the school dramatic society. 'The Rivals' by Robert Brinsley Sheridan was chosen because it was part of the Cambridge Certificate syllabus. Ian from P & T gave advice on lighting and Bea Gear made up the costumes designed by Jacqui Roberts, a professional actress and an ex-starlet from the Arthur Rank Film Organisation. She also gave invaluable help in coaching the all-boys cast how to speak, bow and curtsy — 18th century style.

She and I had met on the MV *Auriel*. She was sailing out with her baby Paul to join her husband, Richard, who had just started working as an assistant district officer in the bush near Ijebu-Ode. They called in monthly when they were up for supplies. Strange reversal of fortunes, I was financially comfortable by then and able to provide good fare from Kingsway and modern comforts like electric light and (cleanish) running water, whilst they lived in a barely furnished small bush house with no shop for miles, no electricity and fitful dirty water.

When I drove down there for the weekend we would read and recite poems together on the Saturday which was a pleasurable change from the rowdy club dances. As they were Roman Catholics, they automatically went to mass on the Sunday held in a minute church five miles away. Father Patrick, who lived even more simply than the Roberts, gave us breakfast afterwards. He was utterly dedicated to his Nigerian flock and so full of faith, it started me wondering about 'going over to Rome'.

The performance of 'The Rivals' in our school hall had a full audience. The play was a wild success, exceeding all expectations. After congratulating the Dramatic Society at assembly the following morning the principal took me aside.

'Jean', he said, 'you are an inestimable treasure. Next time you give a party I want you to help yourself to one of my chickens'.

I invited the Geers and Vera to dinner the next Saturday and told Thomas, my new cook steward to choose a chicken. (He had replaced Peter who had not wanted to move from the By-pass.) The chicken meat was exceptionally tender and we ate it with relish.

On the following Monday the principal called to see me in Sans Souci with a request from Reverend Banjo, principal of the Government Training College. His students were rehearsing for the 'Barrets of Wimpole Street' — by themselves and they could do with my help. He had told him he would send me along that afternoon.

He stood up to leave, then sat down looking embarrassed. 'I'm sorry to say your boy Thomas was seen taking two chickens, not one, from my hen coop Saturday morning. Quite a few chickens have gone missing recently, Thomas is obviously the culprit. What makes it worse is both chickens were broody'.

I, myself, had already suspected Thomas of being light-fingered when money disappeared twice from a locked desk drawer. This was the last straw. He had to go — and I asked the principal to tell him so. Thomas was called, swore that he had never taken anything else before Saturday and started to bluster.

The principal cut him short. He drew himself up to his full height of six foot two inches and declaimed in true preacher style. 'Thomas, Thomas. You have committed an unforgivable act. You have attacked a hen that was about to give birth. That is as bad as attacking a pregnant woman. Say no more. Take your money and go. May God have mercy on your soul.'

Thomas snatched the money and made for the door where he fired a Parthian shot. 'Me fine, fine cook. Madam will never find boy past me.'

Some months later when I was shopping in town, a cheerful voice greeted me: 'Good morning, madam. Are you well?' It was Thomas, smiling all over his face. This ability to forget old scores was an endearing trait among Nigerians and that is why I mention it. Some of my friends had similar incidents. Vera's colleague, Betty, was actually attacked by her 'boy' when she caught him red handed stealing her clothes. It was her testament which sent him to prison for a year. Meeting her again after his discharge, he greeted her as a long lost friend.

The teacher training students, who were older and more advanced in their studies than the IGS lads, were very friendly and grateful for my help. Their production of 'The Barrets of Wimpole Street', was well under way, requiring only hints on pronunciation, interpretation and movement. Seeing the 'females' galumphing around the stage I urged them to slow down and imagine they were wearing stiff whale bone corsets and layers of petticoats underneath their crinoline dresses. Once I'd unearthed a picture of a Victorian miss from the British Council library, they understood better what I meant and began to wear their long skirts more gracefully.

We differed on one small point: Flush, Elizabeth Barret's spaniel. I advocated a toy dog. They insisted on using a scruffy, collarless puppy. Sure enough it urinated copiously each time it appeared on stage. The audience were too spellbound by the whole performance to laugh. Without a trace of self consciousness the actors compelled everyone present to empathise with their emotions. Not an eye was dry as the Barret sisters pleaded vainly with their tyrant of a father to allow them a modicum of freedom.

On the strength of this success, Mrs Banjo implored me to direct a Christmas concert to be held in December in the British Council Hall. Had the ladies rehearsed the readings as well as the singing all would have been well. Unfortunately, the Virgin Mary was not the only one to be 'with child' that Christmas. We never had a full rehearsal. Every time we met half a dozen different ladies failed to turn up because of morning sickness, pregnancy ailments or actual conception. Dear Mrs Banjo must have been the only one to come regularly. I pinned my hopes on her lovely contralto voice and fine presence to carry every one else along.

'Man proposes...'. Two hours before the concert a note from Rev. Banjo arrived, saying:

Dear Miss Jacoby

My wife was hoping to recover from a fever that has been troubling her all week. It is no better today and as she has also lost her voice, she will not be able to take part in the concert.

How I wish I could forget that afternoon in the British Council Hall! The memory of ladies standing up when they should have been sitting down, chattering when they should have been listening to the readings, and sitting down when they should have been on their feet belting out the hallelujah chorus, is too painful to dwell upon.

'At least I can take it easy now'. I thought slinking away from the hall as quickly as possible afterwards. 'No one will ever ask me to produce anything again'.

I was wrong. Some members of the school dramatic society wanted to do a play in Yoruba and came to me for a possible plot and help in producing it. I gave them a tale we had used with the juniors in the school in Battersea.

A man asks his wife to shorten his trousers. When she says she is too busy, he asks first his daughter, then the grandmother in turn and they refuse as well. That night, the three ladies repent and come downstairs, one by one, unbeknown to each other, and shorten the trousers. When he puts them on the following morning, they've turned into a pair of ragged shorts! The lads improvised every word of the script and the sketch was included in an end of term concert. The boy playing the father uttered all sorts of cracks and observations which made the audience split their sides with laughter. Aterwards the Rosijis told me that the language throughout had been explicit, frank and rude and that was why they had not approached the Yoruba teacher!

Considering Ibadan had no commercial theatre we did not go short of dramatic entertainment. Every educational establishment staged concerts and plays. Gbemi Rosiji has nostalgic memories about the music in CMS school in Lagos before it moved to Ibadan:

Music played a great part in our lives always. Miss Titi Pearse, Mrs Jemi Alade, Miss Robin (Mrs Buckner), Miss Shitta, Miss Evelyn Shepherd, and Miss Wedmore, were some of our music teachers. We learned many secular and sacred songs, not airs and tunes alone but enunciation as well: 'A final voices not the e— as in sweet—'. Miss Wedmore (maths and Latin) gave us the ditty, 'Servos fideles habes'; none in our familiar tongues, but then the clamour for local identity had not yet dawned. We relished and embraced all that came our way.

So did the students in Ibadan. The University College drama group chose St Peter's Church as a venue for 'Murder in the Cathedral' by T. S. Elliot. I had seen it twice in London in a West End Theatre and in the church of St Martin's in the Fields overlooking Trafalgar Square. The student performance was better than both. The dignity and strength of St Thomas a Beckett had to be seen to be believed. The Rosijis and I came out rapt and subdued, feeling that we had relived that terrible scene in Canterbury Cathedral when the four knights hacked the courageous saint to pieces.

Chris Groves was famous for her productions at St Anne's. When Derek Bullock took over the English department at Government College, it was suggested the two schools should put on joint productions. He and Chris did this for many years, eventually ending up by getting married.

Had the principal not taken me to see a play about the Portuguese saint, Fatima, at St Teresa's School on the By-pass I should never have met its producer Eileen McCloskey and her friend, Peggy Cullen. They had arrived three months after myself and were the first expatriate lay teachers in a community of nuns. We clicked the moment we met. Little blonde, chubby Eileen with her sapphire blue, sparkling eyes and the slim, red haired freckled Peggy were full of fun, faith and enthusiasm. They mixed easily in any community and often strolled along to visit the Rosijis with me.

Eileen wrote an article to her local Irish paper about their first week. Both she and Peggy were trying hard to absorb all things Nigerian when a summons came from the Mother Superior.

'I have a great task for you both', she began. What can it be? They pondered. Special lessons in Yoruba? Extra prayer classes with the girls? Hard-going treks to the bush spreading the word of God? Whatever it was, they were ready. They would obey the call. 'Well now', she continued, 'Don't I want you both to organise a party for the feast of St Patrick on March 17th; it's almost upon us, begorrah, and we must have a really good shindig. Father McNally will help you buying the drinks and the sisters will prepare the food. Maybe the two of you can sing some Gaelic songs. Sister Finbar's taught the girls Irish dancing already. Off you go to your classes now and God bless you'.

Father McNally looked after the pastoral needs of the community and lived in his own house on the school compound. He had done pioneering work in the bush up North for years before coming to Ibadan. This had taken its toll healthwise and he had to be transferred to Ibadan. When he was well he appeared perfectly normal and energetic but at times a fever would strike him forcing him to stay in bed until it was over. He saw the fun in everything. I often met him at the girls' house and we all had a hilarious time together.

Occasionally, he walked up to Sans Souci for a chat in the late afternoon — without warning since neither of us had a telephone. Once he arrived in a state of collapse after working two hours on the convent roof in the hot sun. He rallied after drinking loads of iced water. He stayed for a light supper and I took out the car to drive him home. Trouble started on the Ijebu By-pass. The car stalled a quarter of a mile away from the convent gates and no amount of fiddling with the engine would make it start. I had on my long printed housecoat which did service as a dressing gown and had not thought of changing since I expected to drive Father McNally to his house and return without getting out of the car. He was too weak to walk any more. It did not seem politic to wave down a car under the circumstances and the huge lorries ignored or did not see us waving.

The nearest house belonged to an english engineer called John Davies. He had broken the European mould in two ways. Firstly, he had his appointment direct from Chief Odutola to work in his tyre factory, when the usual way was to go through an agency, and to add to that he was living openly with a lady called Mary who was not his wife. They kept themselves to themselves and that is why we had not met. I walked for five minutes through the dark to their house and knocked at the door. They were very kind. John took his car out at once to take Father McNally home, then returned and drove me to my car which he managed to fix. Mary had made me tea whilst we were waiting and was obviously glad to talk to someone. She went out very little and concentrated her life on 'Mr Davies'. Not once did she mention his first name. They went on leave soon after that and did not return. A strange interlude.

I was glad it had not been necessary to disturb the sisters in the convent as they were such warm, friendly, natural ladies. They had furnished a sweet little house for Eileen and Peggy who arrived to find a pile of provisions in their store, fizzy drinks in the fridge and a bottle of whisky and brandy on the sideboard. Sister Mary coached the girls in tennis, dressed in her long white habit and Sister Finbar threw herself heart and soul into anything related to drama and music. When the first Nigerian festival of the arts took place in June, 1953, her students were entered for every category.

The idea for this festival had originated with Nora Majekodunmi who lived in Lagos with her three children and her doctor husband, Chief Majekodunmi. With her deep knowledge of drama and music, her own brilliant radio plays, her tireless energy and her efficiency as administrator, she was tailor made for the post of organiser. After enlisting me as Ibadan secretary, she came up almost weekly to see how everything was going and invited me down to Lagos also for a weekend.

I coached the Grammer School students for choral verse and the senior play — a rollicking comedy about a bogus witchdoctor. The boys were very inventive about props and entered splendidly into the spirit of the thing. Choral speech was harder, especially the poem 'The Lake Isle of Innisfree'. The boys knew nothing of linnet filled evenings. No one in their right senses would want to live alone, they argued, certainly not in a place full of bees. Pronouncing 'lake water lapping with low sounds' came out as 'cake water cooking in dough pounds'.

No wonder the Convent girls won that event in the preliminary heats in Ibadan with the indefatigable Sister Finbar to drill them in the Irish cadences. Never mind, the spirited acting of the lads, especially Oguntade, won them a place in the finals in Lagos. Entries had exceeded all our expectations. Seeing how busy I was the principal suggested I stop school for the week before the festival and work every day in the British Council office, dealing with the flood of enquiries, arrangements, arguments and directives from Lagos.

I filled my car with boys and more crowded into the principal's kitcar to drive down to Lagos for the finals. What a great occasion! What a wealth of talent! What disappointments, what arguments about who or who should not have won! It was a weekend to remember. Our boys came second to the girls in Queen's College who richly deserved their success. The Convent girls did well too in the Choral Verse and thanks to Nora Majekodunmi this festival was to be the first of many.

Nora and her family were in Lagos during Festival week. Both she and her husband were anxious for me to be headmistress of a new school he was supporting in Ilesha. That week in the British Council office had given me a taste for administration and I spent a weekend in Ilesha seeing the school and the people concerned who could not have been nicer. In the end, I decided against taking the job, feeling it was too quiet a town after the heady atmosphere of Ibadan.

My leave was approaching; Hugo Mentor had proposed marriage; it looked as if I might end up in Trinidad. I said 'goodbye' to my good friends in Ibadan, met Vera at Lagos airport and we went home together, via Rome, Nice and Paris, where we stayed with my aunt and uncle, Dr Dreyfus. During the war the Germans had accused him of Zionist activities and imprisoned him in Alderney. Paul, that dashing officer son of his, had been rounded up in Clermont Ferrand and shot just before the German defeat, not knowing that his wife, Ritou, was expecting their second child.

Charlie, the second son was a successful surgeon. Yvan had recovered from the strain of the war and was valiantly building up his clinic — at sixty five!

My parents were over the moon to see us and spoilt us beyond belief. After I had said goodbye to Vera at Euston. I thought long and hard during the hour-long bus ride back to Putney about what I was going to do in the future. Little did Vera or I guess that she would end up in East Africa, married to a widower called Jack Kells who had three children and owned a coffee plantation in Kenya, nor that after 18 months, I would be returning to Nigeria, to head a government school in Yola, Adamawa Province. Ilesha was a big city compared to this small town and ten times less remote. How I learned Hausa, established the school and married the right man (at last), belongs to the next part of this story.

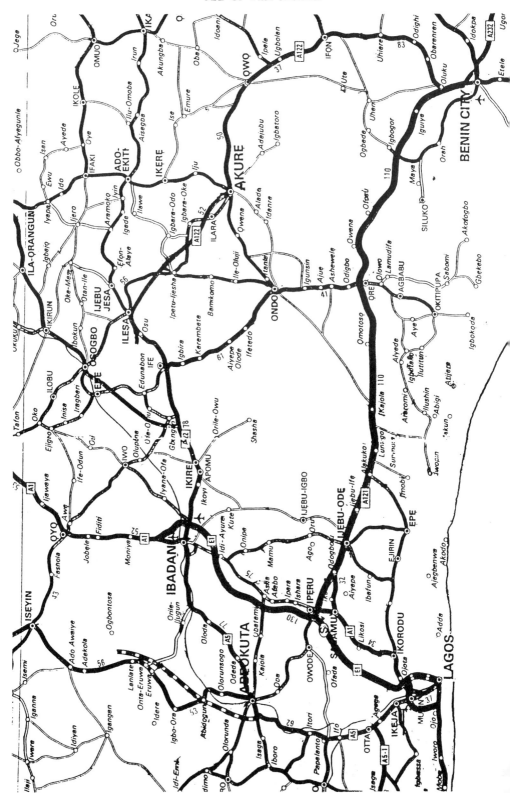

13. Map showing area round Ibadan in West Nigeria.

Signpost at Kano Airport.

Emeka Mojekwu as Scout
Commissioner 1946.

16. Emeka and Author visit Akuma.

17. Emeka (3rd from right, back row) returns, as lawyer,
to his home in Onitsha. Oct 1949.

18. Emeka in Enugu. Sept 1951.

19. Emeka (2nd row, 4th from right) visits his old school.

March 1951. The wedding of Olu Sola and Bola Solanke.

Olumo Rock in Abeokuta.

Ayotunde Rosiji.

Author's first home, 'The Wedding Cake House'. Photo taken 30 years r — now surrounded by traffic.

Christmas Party at the Rosiji's. The author with Esimaje, Funso, Roberta Tukonboh.

25. Group photo, Ibadan Grammer School, with teachers, Linda Gardiner, Alayande, The Author and Samuel Charles.

26. Ibadan Grammar School Staff give farewell party to Odumosu — Aug. 1950.

27. Photo presented to Author in 1952 by two of students. P. Ayande and S Ogunranti, wearing their school blazers.

28. The cast of 'Mr. Bolfr Back row: Margaret Pattic Philip Daly, The Author, Gear. Front row: Mike Ke Johnnie Horne (in front), Gear, Roger Walters and Roland Brownlees.

29. Part of Ibadan Unive

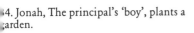
0. 31. 32. 33. Moving on to the new
ite of Ibadan grammar School.

4. Jonah, The principal's 'boy', plants a
arden.

35. Ibadan school dramatic society —Author in centre.

Part three — *Only the best*

Chapter sixteen
A new challenge

Back in London I decided to acquire secretarial skills in order to change direction in my career. The University Appointments Board put me in touch with St Godric's College, Hampstead who offered to give me a nine months' secretarial training provided I taught their foreign students English every morning. After nine months of hard slog, which included three hours travel daily, a punishing non-stop schedule and hours of homework, I returned to the Board proudly waving my secretary's diploma. Now, I thought, I'm ready to face the cosy office world of London. What happened? A string of abortive interviews for office jobs that were either deadly boring and well paid, or interesting and unremunerative. Finally a challenging offer came from the Colonial Office. They needed a teacher in the Northern Region of Nigeria to head the first government girls' school in Adamawa Province, which was presently under construction in the town of Yola on the Benue River.

My first reaction was to refuse. If Ilesha had seemed too small in 1953, surely, Yola, a pin point on the map in the West of the Cameroons, was out of the question. But was it? After all the job description did insist on administrative as well as teaching skills. The conditions in the Government educational service sounded promising and the grade, Woman Education Officer i/c (in charge) certainly had a ring about it. I signed a contract with the Colonial Office and said au revoir to my friends and my parents. This time they were in full agreement with my decision.

'My daughter, a headmistress at thirty two!' Mum exclaimed.

'It's not as if this was your first visit" Dad added. 'And we'll see you on your leaves.' Now I'm much too old to marry I concluded. I wanted to concentrate on an interesting, challenging career.

Once again I travelled up to the port of Liverpool embarking on the MV *Auriel* owned by the Elder Dempster Company which virtually monopolised the shipping trade in British West Africa. It had three other passenger boats: *Apapa, Takoradi* and *Accra* and also carried a few passengers in its large cargo boats. They stopped at the ports along the coast whilst a fleet of smaller craft nosed their way up every single creek and inland river.

It was interesting to see that the pattern of the voyage was the same as before and the passengers did the same things according to their length of service. Leather-faced old coasters, beer bellied and wrinkled long before their time, had taken up residence in armchairs by the bar well before we left Liverpool. Backs turned outwards they deliberately ignored the farewell of the ship's hooter and the sight of the warehouses and large office buildings fading away along Mersey side as we set out to sea. Newcomers clung to the side waving or weeping for a moment, then set about discovering the delights in store for the next fortnight. They enrolled for every dance and bingo night, they put their names down for deck games and tournaments and happily agreed to sell tickets for this and that lottery. The missionaries and hospital matrons dutifully settled themselves in the library; sharp faced bridge addicts annexed 'their table' in the games room and most of us, including my cabin mate, a nursing sister called Phyllis James took things more easily.

A handful of vomiters stuck to their cabins, spewing up without stopping until the turbulence in the Bay of Biscay had given way to the calmer waters off Las Palmas in the Canary Islands where the boat stopped and allowed the passengers to disembark for a few hours. Phyl and I joined a coach group for a drive through its luxuriant pine forests and a visit to the fine, baroque cathedral. A few lechers spent their time with the fancy ladies in the remarkably cheap brothels whilst most of the other passengers bought bargains of another kind in the shops, the markets or from the street traders who pestered them up to the moment of departure.

After that it was 'all systems go' till the boat reached the West Coast and proceeded to drop off its passengers at Bathurst, in the Gambia, Freetown in Sierra Leone, Accra in the Gold Coast, and Lagos, its final destination. My good friend, Peggy Curran had finally married Ted Delaney and they were both at Lagos to meet me and collect the sewing machine which they had asked me to include in my baggage. Before we could arrange a meeting, an unbelievably young education officer nabbed me and carted me off to the home of Tony Hunt-Cooke where I was to stay two days before catching the up-train to Kaduna, the administrative capital of the North. Tony, who was on tour, had been Chief Inspector of Schools in Ibadan and a remote, if friendly face at all official functions. Peggy, his wife, was dumbfounded to find that crazy unconventional girl, Jean Jacoby, was now a government officer. She disappeared to a dinner party in the evening after telling me to expect a visit from Dr Geary, Director of Womens' Education in the North, at ten o'clock the following morning.

That was some meeting. From the moment Dr Geary came striding towards me, I realised that here was one forceful, clear thinking lady. She explained how the British colonial system of Indirect Rule prevailed throughout most of the Northern Region. Government was in the hands of a Native Administration (NA) which was ruled by a traditional chief with a council of elders. Adamawa Province was divided into three: Mubi NA under the Emir and council centred in Mubi; Adamawa NA under the Lamido (King) and council centred in Mubi; and the Numan Federation centred in the town of Numan. This federation represented all the pagan tribes in the area with local chiefs acting as chairmen in turn. All three came under the benevolent if firm control of the British Resident whose HQ was in Jimeta.

After this introduction, Dr Geary went on to speak about education. Overall there were far fewer schools in the North of Nigeria than in the South. In Adamawa this was partly due to lack of resources and partly to the fact that Adamawa and Mubi were predominantly Muslim. Their priority was Koranic training and they saw no reason for providing anything more than basic education for girls since they were often married off as early as twelve or thirteen. She and Grisell Roy, the provincial woman education officer had finally persuaded them to agree to the establishment of the school in Yola but opposition was still latent in Adamawa Council and tact would be needed in dealing with them. Fortunately she had the full support of the Christian missionaries. They were only allowed to operate among non-Muslims so their schools were in pagan areas such as Numan, Bambur and Garkida. They ran mostly primary schools and were delighted at the thought of more higher education for their better students.

Tact would also be needed to deal with George Bell, the engineer responsible for building the new girls' school and his cronies in the PWD (Public Works Department) who were at daggers drawn with the Administration. 'The climate in Yola does not help personal relationships.' She explained. 'Its position on the Benue between two high ranges of hills make it claustrophobically hot especially during the rainy season when storm clouds gather without bursting for days on end.' La Geary paused momentarily for breath. 'Do you like Shakespeare? A group in Yola reads a play a week. Last time I was there, it was 'The Tempest'. Stifling my desire to ask if George Bell had played Caliban, I nodded respectfully as she concluded her briefing by an order to visit three out of the five girls' schools in the North in order to pick up a few hints on organisation and problems: Kano which was well established, Katsina which was comparatively recent, and Maiduguri which was between the two.

Before I could ask where these places were, she stood up to go. 'You'll learn more from Grisell Roy when she returns from leave. I taught her geography in St Paul's.' She gave me a scathing stare. 'I seem to remember you opted for history. I have three meetings to attend before driving up to Kaduna. Good luck in Yola'. Seven days passed before I reached Yola, on 21 November 1954.

I kept a day to day diary from that date until 4 March 1955 and will be quoting from it occasionally from now on.

The first day had been spent in the train to Kaduna. It stopped at Ibadan for an hour. Gbemi Rosiji, my dear friend and neighbour on the Ijebu by-pass had taken the trouble to come to the station to see me even though she was very pregnant with her third child. Ayo, her husband, was on tour and she had left Abimbolu the baby with her sister-in-law, Mrs Ogun. I told her to look out for my children's book, 'Abimbolu' (named after him), which was due to appear in the bookshops any day.

As we were chatting, Ladipo, who had acted as my stage manager in all the plays I'd produced at the Grammar School, came panting up to greet me. Finally a secretary, called Terry, bound for Kaduna, who had travelled out on the Auriol joined me in the carriage after visiting friends in Ibadan.

I needed to spend three days in Kaduna in order to meet officials dealing with my appointment including the Director of Education himself, Tony Shillingford. He offered to sell me his black Austin seven, and to send me a black puppy once it was weaned. The Engineer in the PWD had to check over the car before sanctioning the official government loan and, Director or no, he pronounced the price too high. I felt like Oliver Twist in reverse returning to ask the Director for less, but he had to agree.

My next destination was the large, prosperous, tin-mining town of Jos. Set on a plateau, its climate was exceptionally pleasant and people were glad to be posted there. Although it had several hotels catering for visitors from abroad or on local leave, it was cheaper for the government to put me up privately and pay on a 'government guest voucher'. Rina McDevitt, an education officer who taught household skills to adults was my hostess for another couple of days and I enjoyed being mothered by this bouncy, kindly Scottish widow. With fifteen years of living in Nigeria behind her, she knew exactly what I would need in the way of food and household articles. She took me to a United Africa Company (UAC) department store where we got everything including a credit account from the manager. He told me the government would pay for the cold store to go by air freight on the Saturday and the rest of the goods would follow in a lorry owned by a Fulani trader called Alhaji Bakari.

Elsie Weston, a nursing sister who had been transferred from Jos to Yola and was staying in the flat opposite Rina, asked me if she could ride in my car since she did not fancy going by air. A de Havilland Dove flew weekly to Yola and back. It took six to eight passengers who had to be weighed before take-off and assigned to suitable seats in order to balance the aircraft.

Compared to Yorubaland, the countryside between Jos and Yola appeared very deserted. Gone were the thickly forested roads of the South. The landscape varied be-tween hilly, rocky country and miles upon miles of scrubland. I was glad to have Elsie with me, not to mention refreshments for there were no wayside stalls to speak of.

On arrival, as instructed by Shillingford, I called on Toby Kidd, the PEO. He took me to the Catering Rest House, where I was to stay till I moved into Grisell's house, and invited me and Elsie Weston to dinner. The diary calls it an 'odd evening'. It certainly was. Toby had recently lost a young son and was naturally depressed. So was Elsie who was already missing Jos and her woman friend there. Back in the rest house after dinner someone knocked at my bedroom door. It was the man in the guest room next door, Donald Landeg, an inspector in the Department of Health, requesting an aspirin. This was obviously an excuse to converse which he did for the next two hours, tipsily and in a non sequitur fashion: I was to find out later he had a personality disorder and tended to be violent when drunk.

On Sunday morning my somewhat surreal existence continued. After such a long journey it seemed fitting to go to church to thank God for my safe arrival. St John's, a shabby, corrugated iron building, was the only Anglican church for miles, so I took myself there. The service was ghastly. Apparently in English, prayers, sermon, everything was incomprehensible. The worshippers chattered amongst themselves and when it was time for communion they strolled or jigged up the aisle to the makeshift altar, singing off key in strident falsetto voices.

Later that Sunday Toby took me to meet John Stapleton, the Acting Resident for Charles Wreford who was on leave and Leith Watts, the Senior District Officer. They were courteous, helpful and, thank God, completely normal. Since it was essential for all government officers in the North to pass a lower standard language examination, John Stapleton said he would tell Mallam Bello, his messenger, to give me daily lessons in Hausa. This was the language of the ruling classes in Kano, Kaduna and Sokoto; the medium of instruction in the schools and the lingua franca of the Northern Region generally. Where the Fulanis had conquered in the past they had generally assimilated with the Hausa people in their area but the Lamido and his Fulani people had retained their language, Fulfuldi and this was spoken throughout the province. All the same, with so many different tribes in the province itself, Hausa was still the important language to know.

Mallam Bello resembled an Old Testament prophet with his white beard and flowing gown. He gave the first lesson on 26 November 1954 and continued to come almost daily at 7 a.m. He never knocked. He stood outside the front door repeating: 'Salaam Aleikum' until I came out to invite him in. He would sit down on the floor with great dignity and start speaking. He had little English and no teaching know-how whatsoever. I had a small text book, mostly about Adamu, a Hausa farmer and a doorstop of a dictionary by the pioneer missionary, Dr Bargery. Somehow or other we made sufficient progress for me to pass the written and oral exam three months later and receive the statutory government award of £25. Some government officers like Leith Watts and Neil Morrison in Numan went on to take the Advance exam which paid £40 for each part.

I was able to practise my Hausa greeting when I met the members of the Adamawa Native Council on 28 November. Briefed by Toby Kidd, I told them I was pleased to be in beautiful Yola and very much impressed by the good manners of the Northerners. The school buildings were splendidly sited on the Verre hills overlooking the Benue and the fine view could not fail to inspire the girls to work hard. I thanked them for their support and looked forward to the completion of the dormitory compound and the dining room so that the school could get off the ground. I and my future staff would do our best to train our students to be good wives who would, in their turn, become good mothers of the generation to come.

As time went on I met the officials and teachers who worked for the Native Authority. Mallam Bello Malabu, the schools Manager, was pleasant enough and Mallam Ribadu, the SVT (Senior Visiting Teacher) was an interesting, intelligent man. Mallam Hassan Jimeta, Headmaster of the Middle School for boys, was the most approachable. Later he was honoured with the title of Turaki which was a far cry from his humble origins — he had been found in the bush as a baby by a district officer who had arranged with his messenger to bring him up. He had agreed to have twelve girls at his school pending their eventual transfer to the APGS (Adamawa Provincial Girl's School). They were taught separately and lived in the compounds of the housemasters together with their wives and families. I volunteered to teach English to the boys and to the girls twice a week. This helped me get to know them better. They visited the new site a few times and seemed delighted at the thought of moving there.

When I was not learning Hausa or teaching I worked in the stiflingly hot provincial office in Jimeta. I was in Grisell's office on the first floor which was next door to Toby Kidd's and the ground floor was taken up by the Treasurer, the clerk and the senior administration officer, Guy Haslewood. He was the only one with a telephone, let alone a fan. Grisell's efficiency and foresight cannot be praised too highly. She had already ordered everything for the school and it was left to me to hurry up the suppliers. I kept accounts of any additional expenditure, dealt with correspondence and most importantly, learned the intricacies of government office procedure. Kaduna had to be informed at every step and there was one way and one way only, to write a letter or a memorandum.

When Bill Hogan, teacher in the Middle School replaced Toby Kidd as Provincial Education Officer he asked me to help him with the typing. He was a devout Catholic and his faith and sincerity showed themselves in his work. Down to earth and modest with a wry sense of humour he saw through the veneer of snobbery overlying the colonial society we lived in. District officers proliferated in Adamawa and some of them seemed to think themselves 'God's own people'.

To be fair; both their education and the nature of their work fostered the attitude. Many of them had gone to public schools — which is already a class thing, cutting the fee-paying hoi-polloi off from the non-fee paying proletariat. After school and university, (exclusivity again with a further bias towards the older universities like Oxford and Cambridge), they could well find themselves in sole charge of a vast area containing God knows how many tribes. The Northerners themselves were decidedly aware of rank and prestige. Even their Emirs were divided into first, second or third class emirs. DOs (District Officers) were often given the salute: Sannu Zaiki — hail to the lion, the king of the beasts.

Leith and Peggy Watts hit a happy medium. As a New Zealander, Leith was more detached from snobbery whilst Peggy was completely sincere in her determination to fulfil the duties of a good Admin wife. Her English rose looks and terribly posh accent concealed a tough and indefatigable personality. She went touring with Leith on foot, on horseback or in a jeep. She was a good hostess keeping an eye on the cooking and making sure the guests were seated in the right order of rank. She embellished every house she lived in and made striking improvements to the garden. She kept hens and one year she managed to rear day-old chicks from the UK. A great organiser, she raised funds for the Nigerian Society for the Blind, acted as librarian at the Club and strove, against all odds sometimes, to make its functions as lively as possible. Moreover she did not allow private problems such as hospitalisation in the UK for treatment of amoebic dysentery and the death of a baby girl in Sokoto to deter her.

Whilst Peggy always toed the line, Guy Haslewood, Leith's assistant, gloried in being different. Tall, over forty, with a distinguished bearing, he had started life as an actor and was a walking dictionary of phrase and quotation, especially the works of Shakespeare. I joined the group Dr Geary had mentioned and went to different houses weekly to read a play. Guy was automatically cast in the leading role. I was Juliet to his Romeo and Ophelia to his Hamlet; Donald Landeg would get into one of his truculent moods when he considered his part too small; Gerald Warneford, craft teacher at the Middle School and his wife Marjory gave dukes and duchesses in the history plays a very broad Lancashire accent; and, as we were too few to lay down conditions of entry, two or three 'players' were invariably unintelligible or inaudible or both.

About forty expatriates and a thin sprinkling of Nigerian senior service officers lived on the Government Reservation Area in comfortable houses and lush gardens. Education Officers, like myself, who were actually teaching, lived on their school sites. Since houses always went with the job in government service, occupants could be short of space or have rooms to spare according to the size of the family. My future school house could have accommodated a husband and several children! Two agriculture officers lived at Kofari seven miles away; a few district officers worked out in the bush and so did Howell Davies who was researching tsetse control. Everyone knew everyone and they spent their free time exclusively with each other. They had drinks, meals and parties at home together, or listened to music on LPs or 78 records, discussed plays and films they had seen elsewhere, played dice, canasta and other card games and borrowed each other's books.

Books could also be borrowed from the Club library. Situated in a shady compound facing the hills in the heart of the GRA, it was the focal point of our little Yola community. Unlike Ibadan, everyone from near or far visited it at some time or another and many people went there every day — to drink at the bar, to relax comfortably in the lounge or sit on canvas chairs outside and watch the players on the tennis court. On Saturday nights the terrace was cleared for dancing or for beetle or bingo, or whist drives or similar festivities. Isa, the barman who had worked in the club for years swore that the two wooden deckchairs near the bar had been made for Lord Lugard, the very first governor of the North. Isa also doubled as hairdresser cum barber. He would start cutting your hair on the right side and break off when anyone called for a drink. Then he would return a few minutes later and resume snipping somewhere behind your left ear, repeating the process until he or you cried a halt.

It would be hypocritical to say that I did not enjoy the social life Yola had to offer, but I always felt I was primarily in Nigeria to meet Nigerians and many women working in the government service thought the same. Since the wives of most Northern muslims lived in purdah, family visits together were not part of their culture. We had to content ourselves with maintaining friendly relationships with the Northern men we met at work and at official functions and by visiting their wives in their own quarters whenever we could. The Lamido had already asked Grisell Roy and the health officer, Doreen Rothera, to meet his wives and he extended the invitation to me at a party held in his palace to celebrate his enthronement.

I shall not easily forget that evening. It had an Arabian Nights quality about it. Only senior government officials and 'manya manya' (important people) had been invited. They arrived at dusk and servants, dressed in embroidered coats and trousers, led them into a pink, thick mud walled courtyard next to a house of mud painted in light green. Palm trees planted here and there in the sandy compound thrust their spear-like fronds towards the huge, white circle of the rising moon. John Stapleton, Guy Haslewood, Leith and Peggy Watts, Toby Kidd, Doreen Rothera, Elsie Weston and other Europeans (including little me) mingled pleasantly with the Nigerian guests and hangers on of the Lamido, all dressed in magnificently embroidered rigas (long gowns), whilst the servants handed round kola nuts biscuits, cigarettes and non-alcoholic drinks. The Lamido who was tall and slim looked every inch a king in a pure silk white *riga*, brightly coloured cap and sparkling bead-studded slippers. A gossamer thin cloak lay over his shoulders and a special servant hovered near to adjust it when it looked like slipping.

The palace had a less glamorous appearance in the daylight when I called on the wives in their quarters soon after. Eight ladies were in the room and it was tactless to ask who were the wives and who were the concubines. They seemed glad to see me and after the usual greetings they produced what looked like livid, green, hollow woollen tubes and thrust a pair of knitting needles in my hand. Grisell Roy had been teaching them to make socks for their husband and had left for the UK before showing them how to turn a heel. How do you explain to Fulani ladies with very little grasp of Hausa that you do not know a plain stitch from a pearl? Nor were there any children in sight to provide a topic of conversation.

Mallam Sidi, the NA accountant introduced me to his wives himself. Children were running in and out of his compound and the atmosphere was more relaxed altogether. The wives who all spoke Hausa, took me straightaway to a special room which they had converted into a craft school. Its walls were festooned with embroidered cotton table cloths which also lay in piles on the long table in the centre. Pillow slips filled in the vacant spaces. These were also heavily embroidered with patterns round the edges and telling inscriptions in the centre such as: 'God be praised. Slumber soundly, good friend', or 'Two heads are better than one'. Christmas festivities followed soon after this visit and once they were over I had to do my schools tour as decreed by Dr Geary.

Chapter seventeen
Going places

Christmas Day in Putney had been a quiet affair for many years once my sisters Lilian and Marion had married and gone abroad. The highlights of the day were their phone calls and listening to the Queen's speech. By contrast the Christmas festivities in Yola went on for days, beginning with a Residency party for everyone on the station, private celebrations and special evenings at the Club. Everyone downed tools in the outlying towns and came up to celebrate. I met district officers of every rank including Chris Rounthwaite, David Sorrell, Stanley Pike, Neil Morrison, Russell Gardner and Desmond Wilson. At that stage I was bowled over by their glamour. David Sorrell, for instance, invariably called on his horse and Desmond Wilson had an irrepressible Irish charm.

He and his wife, Lucy, invited me to spend the New Year weekend with them in Jalingo where he was stationed. I set out with my steward, Jongera and Shillingford's promised puppy, Penny. In less than ten minutes we were in the Africa of fiction passing strangely bare hills with stranger shaped stones perched on their summits like drunken storks on chimney tops. The road was practically deserted except for an occasional group of semi-naked members of the Munmunyi tribe who clenched their fists in greeting. The older women were too busy smoking long clay pipes to acknowledge us.

During the weekend Desmond spoke a lot about the different pagan tribes in Jalingo province, including the Munmunyi. The government wanted them to move from the interior and settle on the better land provided. Many of them hated the thought of leaving the villages where their ancestors were buried. They were content to scrape out a living with no one to check up on them and stop them from holding untrammelled drinking parties which often ended in punch ups, even killings.

Unwittingly a young couple in an American Mission had stirred up trouble in the southern part of Jalingo province. Having quickly mastered the language they began discussing 'democracy' with the members of the local tribes, telling them how people 'back home' had equal rights. Result: when a minor dispute arose concerning the payment of taxes (always a sore point), a number of malcontents had risen in revolt, produced guns and demanded satisfaction. Desmond had been sent with a military contingent to restore peace and the 'democratic' missionaries had been posted far away. Strangely enough I met this couple in Kano airport a year later. They were furious at being moved 'for no reason, since we knew the language so well'.

Desmond and Lucy were warm, welcoming hosts. Lucy taught her two young boys every day and ran an efficient household without fuss. Vegetables and fruit came from Desmond's kitchen garden and the 'cuisine' was French. Russell Gardner, his assistant, spent too much time drinking to lend a hand but he was very jolly company. On New Year's Eve, eight of us dined and danced under the stars: Desmond, Lucy, Russell, myself, John and Jean Matthews (from Admin) in Kaduna and Jock, the district engineer with his wife, Isla who were stationed on their own in the bush miles away from anywhere.

Poor Jock! Once Isla left to be with the children in Scotland, he took to the bottle. Far from welcoming Desmond or any other rare visitor, he refused to see anyone. He was transferred to a less lonely station and soon recovered. Another Jock, the Police Superintendent in Yola, also started drinking because he was lonely without his wife. When the drink gave him a fever, he presumed he had malaria and overdosed himself with Nivaquine. The combination of drugs and drink sent him off his head. Because the air service had been suspended that particular week, Guy Haslewood and a government driver had to force him, screaming, into a strait jacket and take him by car to Kano for treatment.

What with the intense heat and this crisis I felt a bit down in the mouth and was glad to see the cheery Russell Gardner when he turned up in Yola on treasury business. One afternoon he invited me to go with him to visit his friends in Numan. The journey took about an hour. Just as we were nearing the town, he was suddenly forced to make a sudden swerve into a diversionary track because the PWD road force who were cutting away the road in order to rebuild a culvert, had failed to place the usual bundle of branches over the road to alert the travellers. Written notices were out of the question since many lorry drivers could not read. After several rather boring drinks (which Russell thoroughly enjoyed) we left Numan as dusk was falling. He was peering ahead anxiously to spot this diversion when he gave a sudden shout.

My God! We're on it. They've banked the bloody road up. If we don't get off, we're done for'. He turned the wheel sharply towards the diversion pathway but the car hit a stone and turned slowly over like a slow motion movie. I found myself trapped under Russell who was calling 'I'll get you out, Jean, don't worry'. In fact, we were both trapped and it was his boy, Musa, who extricated himself from the back window and dragged us out. We could see the tyre marks of the car from the roadside and they were less than two metres away from a sheer drop of fifteen metres at least. Had the car gone over that, the three of us could have broken our necks. When two hours had passed without anyone or any vehicle passing, Russell, who was far more concerned about his car than about me, told Musa to walk back to Numan for help. After cracking a lot of silly jokes for ten minutes he fell sound asleep and did not wake up until Musa came back in a lorry four hours later. All that time I shivered beside him, listening to strange rustlings in the bush, praying and thanking God I was alive.

The next morning I was trembling all over with nervous reaction and drove to the Roman Catholic mission house for comfort where I found Father Power who was both understanding and helpful. I had met his brother and Monsignor D'Alton before at a couple of functions and admired their dedication and humanity. In Ibadan I had already been drawn to Roman Catholicism by my friendship with Peggy, Eileen, Father MacNally and the sisters at St Louis, and the service at St John's had put me off the Anglican church for some time! Fortunately, preparations for the 'schools tour' which was due to begin a week later kept me too busy to brood.

I was seen off at the airport by Grisell Roy who had returned from leave to re-occupy her house and office whilst I moved up to mine on the new site. The Heron plane (which had replaced the Doves) took me to Jos where I had to stay overnight before flying to Kano. Rina MacDevitt put me up as before and I had arranged to see Phyl James, my cabin mate from the *Auriol*, in the evening. She had been posted to the government hospital in Jos and was relishing its fresh climate and social amenities after a previous stint in the bush.

As a treat she took me out to dinner at the prestigious Hill Station Hotel together with an old friend of hers, Vic Ashwell. Set high on the plateau facing a range of hills, this fine grey stone building was the 'most select' of all Nigerian hotels. It was managed by a large, ponderous man called Pop Bowler who demanded and achieved a high standard of excellence in food, accommodation and service. Let the guests lark about as they liked in the clubs run by the government or the tin miners, in Hill Station they were expected to comport themselves with decorum.

Phyl and I dressed accordingly. I had on my best, yellow dress and she looked the perfect debutante in a chic black ensemble with a V neck and a double row of pearls concealing her cleavage. Vic Ashwell was the archetypical district officer and never unbent anyway. All went well until the catch of Phyllis' necklace caught in her hair as the steward was serving the meal. Trying to free it, she snapped the string altogether. Pearl after pearl plopped into the Brown Windsor soup, rolled around the table and scattered over the dining room floor. Many bachelor diners rushed to retrieve them and return them to the blushing Phyl. Then, feeling some pearls lodging themselves on her body, she stood up to shake them loose. At this Vic flung himself face down to field them as they trickled through her underclothes and he was quickly joined by the braver males. By now everyone in that dining room was shaking with mirth and that night decorum had gone by the board.

There was no giggling the next day with Miss Alice Patterson, the head of the government girls' school in Kano. She was a strait-laced middle aged PT teacher who took her duties as headmistress very seriously, ruling students and staff with an iron hand. Some of the younger teachers resented this but the students who were used to stern discipline took it in their stride and remembered her with affection long after they left school. As for me, I was there to learn how to organise a school and in this respect she had much to teach me.

She was outspoken to the point of tactlessness and stories about her gaffes were legion. For example, when Queen Elizabeth visited the school with Prince Phillip, they were shown around the classrooms and the dormitories. 'I understand that when some of your girls first arrive at the school, they have never slept in a bed before?' he commented. 'Yes' replied Miss Patterson. 'But, by the time they leave they are ready to take their places beside anyone'.

Joan Blacklock in Zaria was as efficient as Miss P. but far more fun. She had done marvels in two years and I tried to copy her unfussy attitude when I started off in Yola.

A fortnight later I flew to Maiduguri. The PWEO (Provincial Woman Education Officer) there was Ursula Bozman who recognised me from St Paul's. She had left the school to work with Dr Geary in India and followed her to Nigeria when the political fight for independence made it too dangerous to stay. She laid on a dinner party in my honour, a highly formal affair complete with scarlet hibiscus flowers floating in the finger bowls after the dessert (Shades of the Raj!). Unable to master Hausa because of her deafness, Ursula had still managed to acquire a wealth of knowledge about the North and was a clever, pleasant lady to talk to. In 1951, she had written a booklet for an educational conference in Kaduna on running a library, entitled 'Say, O people of the book'. Clear, simply written and full of practical advice, it became the 'vade mecum' of every would-be librarian in the Northern Region.

The two days spent in the girls' school in Maiduguri, with Marjorie the WEO i/c (Woman Education Officer in charge), were inspiring. Everything went smoothly on the neat pleasant compound and her handling of the children was unique. The wrong side of thirty and not much to look at, her whole face lit up and made her beautiful when she started speaking. She exuded love, genuine old fashioned, charitable love, and staff and children alike adored her. Like Bishop Akinyele in Ibadan, she did not scold; she just made people ashamed when they had done wrong or sorry if they had let her down.

On the last day, Ursula Bozman drove me out to the Womens' Training College. Unusually, it accepted married women with their babies as well as unmarried girls and its first year course was designed for nurses in training as well as for potential teachers. Because Bornu was a province ready for educational progress and because it was brilliantly run by an ex-nursing sister, Alex Cooper, and an open-minded principal, Miss Ann MacGregor, the experiment worked. Ann universally known as 'Our Annie', was a law unto herself. Socially she looked and behaved like a golden haired floosie and was the life and soul of every party. Yet, work wise, she was splendid, combining scholarship with practicality to the nth degree.

Government officers were expected to sign the Resident's book wherever they travelled. It was kept in a small hut outside the Residency gates and shown to His Excellency every day. He might invite the visitors to a meal or drinks according to their status. Thus I met the Resident in Kano, Zaria and Maiduguri and returned to Yola with a collection of new acquaintances whom I often met again since the government service, like the army, was subject to innumerable, often irrational postings. With hundreds of miles between us and erratic telephone and postal communication, we education officers managed to keep in touch through visitors, Kaduna HQ and bush telegraph. We learned who had been posted, engaged, married or blotted their copybook, licking our lips over the news of Our Annie's latest exploits which were naturally exaggerated in the telling!

Gossip prevailed in the women's coffee parties, in the club or at any social gathering. We also talked a lot about the state of the roads which were bad to appalling. What else was there to talk about? Shopping? Hardly. The market in Jimeta was small, scorching, and scant in produce. Its crummy main street consisted of a few shabby street stores, the SUM bookshop, and minor branches of UAC, SCOA and John Holt. All these catered mainly for the Nigerian taste, with the exception of liquor, which required an official permit from the provincial office.

Nor was it easy to chew over the usual topics of the day since our access to information was severely limited. The main British papers were available in Kano, Kaduna, Jos and the large Nigerian towns but they never reached Yola and the small stations. The enthusiastic reader could order expensive, airmail editions which were a mixed blessing. The scant air service meant they arrived in bunches and had to be placed in date order before they could be read. The Nigerian newspapers mentioned important European news in passing, but concentrated more on indigenous news. Incidentally, a free airmail edition of the London 'Times' was sent to the Resident in every province. We picked up what news we could and exchanged magazines like 'Life', 'Time' or a late weekly edition of the 'Telegraph'.

Letters from home were a help and visitors from abroad also brought us up to date. If they were VIPs like a judge, advisors on education like Freda Gwillyam and Sir Christopher Cox from the Colonial Office, or even the writer, Richard Pape, an official drinks party for the station would be held in their honour. When Charles Wreford, who had returned from leave, was told that the Minister of the Foreign Office was due in Yola, he had everyone running around in circles organising a cocktail party to end all cocktail parties. Alas! Kaduna had made a cock up. This was no minister. This was a very, very boring, very, very minor official on a fact finding visit who did not merit so much as morning coffee.

Compared to life in the bush, Yola was one mad, social whirl! Grisell Roy gave me my first taste of it soon after I returned from Maiduguri. She needed to go up the Gongola valley to check on the girls coming to school the next term and to select a second batch for a second class. Having covered most of Adamawa during her previous tour she was an excellent mentor and guide. Our stewards Jongera and Ibrahim loaded up her kitcar and my Austin with luggage. Their personal bundles were microscopic compared with the clutter of essential articles we needed.

Here is Grisell's list:

BEDDING: canvas beds, mosquito nets, cotton sleeping bags.
FURNITURE: canvas chairs, picnic table.
COOKING REQUIREMENTS: saucepans, cutlery, a water filter, chop boxes containing tinned foods, bottles of water and squash.
PERSONAL: a suitcase containing clothes, books, paper, Paludrine, anti mosquito cream and stomach powders.
A LONG STRONG ROPE AND A HANDFUL OF NAILS, (Bush rest houses were usually empty and, slung across the centre this would act as a clothes line).
A LAVATORY BOX.

Our first stop was Numan where we stayed two days in the Resident's round, mud rest house overlooking the river. It had windows which shut, a door which did not and a thunder box in the bayan gida (toilet) outside. These three luxuries were missing in the subsequent rest houses so our 'fersonal' (the boys' pronunciation) toilet proved to be a boon!

Breakfasting early on the verandah we could see people arriving to bathe themselves and wash their clothes. The cool morning sun casting a strange creamy glimmer on the parched sandy banks would soon hot up enough to dry them. Mallam Akila, the gentle, competent Schools Manager in Numan federation joined us as we were finishing our coffee. He was loud in his praise of the Bachema people who formed the largest local majority. 'They are outstandingly vigorous and go ahead', he told us. 'They were not beaten when the Fulanis overran the rest of the Adamawa province and thanks to their industry and the richness of this area, they remain proud and independent. We like the Fulanis', he continued, 'but if you allow them into your town or your society, they will want to rule'.

We left him to visit the primary school in Numan which was, indeed, full of very bright Bachema children. We then proceeded to Dong, nine miles south along a terrible road. The classrooms stood side by side in two long wooden buildings with corrugated iron roofs and were joined at the end by an office, and two store rooms. To give the children somewhere to play and to avoid the risk of snakes, rodents or mosquitoes, the compound had been stripped of every blade of grass. In spite of a couple of trees that had been left standing to shade the occasional car or lorry, the school and compound were as hot as hell by midday.

The word had gone round that we were coming. The stones in front of the office had been whitewashed and the school had been cleaned up. The young headmaster greeted us, with the usual ritual, of signing the visitors book. We went into class 1, 2, 3 and 4 in turn. Each time the children jumped to attention, shouting: Good morning, SAH!' The two infant classes were writing on slates with chalk, copying from a shabby, scratched blackboard. The older pupils were luckier. Most of them had an exercise book and a pencil and the luckier few had shabby, dog-eared Hausa and English text books to read.

A minor crisis occurred when Grisell split her skirt on both sides getting back into the kitcar. We had to return to the school for help. Fortunately, the first year lady teacher had a bobbin of thread and scissors and a wrapper for Grisell to wear whilst she repaired it. 'It was lucky they had a pair of scissors', she commented as we drove off. Basic school equipment can be down to a minimum in the very bush areas, not to mention classrooms. It is not unusual to find the infant class drawing and writing letters in the sand in the shade of the school building. As for books, there is seldom one for every child and once I visited a newly opened village school of two classes operating in grass huts where class 2 was having a reading lesson with only two copies of the Hausa book 'Ka Koyi Karatu'. One was in the hands of the Mallam (teacher) and the other passed from child to child as each one read out a sentence'.

Kiri and Shellen followed Numan. Grisell made her inspection in each and we both tried to pick suitable students for the next intake. Not easy when you had to judge the age by the faces and the exercise books tended to look alike. Just occasionally we could spot some talent, neatness, a proliferation of ticks or an extra bright face. The results of a simple test Grisell had devised and sent out helped a little and so did the suggestions of the teachers. The recommendation of a chief might be suspect. He was often pushing his own daughters.

We finished about two o'clock and repaired to the rest house for lunch. Umaru had found vegetables in Kiri market and the local chief in Shellen gave us fresh fish and honey. However hungry we were on this tour and others we made in the future, the routine was the same. The boys would never serve anything to eat until they had hooked up the clothes line, hung up our clothes, carried the lavatory seat out to the bayan gida outside, made sure it was free of snakes, made up our beds and boiled fresh water.

A siesta after lunch would leave us soaked with sweat but refreshed. After sitting a while over afternoon tea, complete with pretty tea cups and tea pot, we might pass the time with an occasional visitor: a chief, perhaps, a district head, or a district officer passing through or an engineer like Jock. Otherwise we would take a stroll in the bush with the sound of the birds or an occasional villager for company. The evening had a quiet about it that was hard to imagine: the sky seemed to have double the stars we saw in Yola, the birds were hushed, and the villagers were asleep in their huts. We'd talk a while about the day, our families, books or music, have dinner and turn in early, lulled by the gentle rumble of distant drums.

After seeing this truly African Africa, I felt more confident about dealing with the future students once they joined me at the new site. Equipment-wise everything had been organised and Mallam Lepatel who had replaced the Turaki as headmaster of the Middle School had helped us purchase corn in bulk and store it. Two questions remained to be answered: when was the school going to open? who was going to staff it?

We had a good labour force under a willing energetic black James Cagney look-alike called Bage and little else. Jiddah, the clerk was totally incompetent and my one and only assistant teacher at that time suffered from recurring attacks of VD. Both of them had received notice of dismissal. Kaduna, the NA Education Office or Grisell would have the task of replacing them. They also needed to appoint a teacher of general subjects, a Mallam and a missionary to give religious instruction to the Muslims and the Christians respectively, a craft instructor and a matron. The surly George Bell assured us that the school would be ready by August. In order to be back in time I was sent on leave earlier than expected. Leaving Grisell copious handing over notes I left Yola on June 3rd. Once again I flew to Jos, then on to Kano where I stayed three days in the Airport Hotel waiting for the plane to London. The wheel had come full circle since December 1949. This time Kaduna and not the Ibadan Diocesan Concil was paying the bill!

I met Jack Spicer in the dining room an hour after my arrival. He was principal of Bauchi Teacher Training College and had frequently passed through Yola on his way to Mubi Training Centre. A clever, warm, efficient, talented man he was one of the brightest stars in the educational firmament. After years in the North he knew a lot of people staying in the hotel and introduced me all round.

After lunch next day I was heading back to the chalet for a siesta when a voice behind me called: 'Jean Jacoby. Surely, it's Jean Jacoby'. I turned round and found myself facing Vic Ashwell: friend of Phyl James and recoverer-in-chief of falling pearls, that riotous evening in Hill Station! He was with a heavily built man of forty or so whom he introduced as 'John Evans but everyone calls him Jack'. The two of them were stationed in a one-horse place called Gombe where Vic was district officer and Jack managed the branches of London and Kano Trading Company in the region. Vic had driven him to Kano in order to put him on the down train to Lagos prior to sailing home on the *Auriel*. 'I've no wife waiting for me in Liverpool', he told me, 'so the boat trip is better than a cruise'.

Not to mention Las Palmas and all that goes with it, I thought cynically. Since both Jack and Vic visited Bauchi frequently on business, they automatically joined Jack Spicer, me and his friends (mainly men) in the lounge after dinner. At 10.30 Jack Spicer would stand up, firmly extricate me from whoever was chatting me up — with or without lustful intention on their or on my part! — and paternally escort me down the dark path to my chalet in the compound. After making sure I was firmly locked in, he'd call out: 'Good night, Jean. I leave you to your virginal slumber'.

'Good night, Jack', I'd call out and listen to the trudge, trudge of his mosquito boots taking him back to the hotel.

Chapter eighteen
Teething problems

The early beginning of Adamawa Provincial Girl's school were decidedly shaky.

Problems arose on the first night when some girls resented having to sleep on a bed in a room for two in a stone dormitory building. Considering they were used to lying on a mat next to their sisters in a mud hut without doors and windows, this was hardly surprising. Wanting to feel 'cabin'd, cribb'd, confin'd', they locked the doors of their rooms, kept the windows shut to stop 'fairies' breaking in and urinated on the floor.

The second night I was called out at 2 a.m. because a Christian girl called Lucy Dong was having hysterics on the bedroom floor. My diary notes that 'I eventually softened her down and we read the Bible together until she fell asleep'.

The following morning I assembled them all in the dining room at the end of the dormitory compound and, as usual, addressed them in Hausa. 'This new school of ours must seem very far from home. I am sure you will soon settle down and enjoy the many good things it offers you. I am a stranger too, and together we must learn from each other. Please do not be frightened at night. Remember that you are well protected. Bage will lock the compound gate every evening at sunset. The watchman patrols the school grounds throughout the night and your matrons, Hadija and Titi are within earshot in their little houses outside the wall behind this very room. Finally I promise you that I will come to say good night to you this evening and every evening after that.'

I kept this promise faithfully until I left Adamawa for good, three years later.

The girls all agreed that the 'best thing' about the school was the constant supply of running water in the toilets and showers strategically placed near the dormitories. A few girls who came from villages where water had to be fetched from one single tap or from a nearby pool, began using the toilet as a bath and the shower as a toilet. They soon learned their mistake and joined the others in using them constantly. Hadija, my very sensible, strong-minded matron had to prevent them from washing their uniform too frequently as it was wearing out the cloth.

'Hankele a hankele' (gently, gently,) the school got under way. Bage and his labourers worked well cutting the grass and tending the newly planted neem trees dotted over the compound to give shade. The cooks in the kitchen seemed to know their jobs, and Pawa the school messenger, an ex-army sergeant was a reassuring if surly presence. John, the new Igbo clerk, had soon learned government office procedure and was gradually learning filing and accounting according to the laws of St Godric's College, London.

Unfortunately, Titi, the assistant matron cum instructress was as feeble as Hawa was strong. The girls took little notice of her because she was more childish than they were. She had been the concubine of an important chief who had sent her to us to get rid of her. My good friend, Doreen Rothera, had met her in his compound when she was giving his women a medical check-up. I asked her to examine my girls and she came up twice during the first two weeks. I joined her the first time in order to learn the use of the contents of the dispensary that Grisell had thoughtfully provided. Suddenly, Titi barged in, pulled up her blouse and presented her bare stomach for inspection. After this, any time Doreen came up to the dispensary or to my house, Titi would rush up and go through the same pantomime.

Doreen had seen how basic life in the villages could be and was not surprised to find that many of the girls had worms or dysentery or bilharzia. She suggested sending all the girls down to the hospital in Jimeta with samples of their urine and stool in case they had anything else. It seemed an excellent idea. I rooted around for tins and empty bottles and decided I would send six at a time to avoid them missing too much school.

She also discovered that two girls had leprosy. It was not the infectious variety and they had brought medication with them from the colony in Garkida. Provided they went to the hospital once a month for a check-up and for further supplies they should be all right. I thanked Doreen profusely for her help and she disappeared on tour for a month.

Sending the girls off to Jimeta hospital became part of the morning routine. The matrons woke the girls at 6.45 a.m. and at 7 a.m. they assembled in two lines in front of the double gate locking the compound. Since many had the same surname — the name of their birthplace — I had decided to give each one a number.

'Good morning girls', I'd say importantly. 'Good morning, madame'. They'd shout cheerily. 'Number off'. 'One, two, three....', and so on. In this way, it was easy to find the absentees. I'd call the names of the hospital brigade, give them a tin and a bottle each and wait till they returned with them full. The rest of the school were sent to the playing field with hoops and skipping ropes until I joined them for PT.

Quite often a girl or two would come back with empty containers. 'Madame. Madame ba na iya! Ba na iya' (I can't do it). They'd pipe. It might have been true, it might have been because the walk to the hospital was long and hot. I was too pressured to care. 'Nonsense, girl', I'd snap. 'Go away and get on with it'.

I'm ashamed to say, they were too frightened of me to disobey! They did 'do it' and Hawa would lead them down to the hospital, carrying the tins and bottles on their heads.

Since the girls sometimes needed to go twice to the hospital, I decided to stop the small brigades and send the samples of every single girl down with Pawa. The doughty old soldier would have none of it: such a job is beneath me. Madame must take it in her car.

Seeing his point, I piled the lot on a tray with a ridged edge, put it in the car boot, securing it with newspaper and drove off. Just my luck a Fulani herdsman happened to be leading his cattle across the drive and their jostling forced me to make a sudden stop. Result, I found several broken bottles and spilt tins when I took the tray out.

'Damn and blast!' I said aloud. 'Never mind if they do miss school. I'm sending all the rest with Hawa to the hospital tomorrow', which I did and very soon the girls got better. I stopped collecting bottles and tins, the hospital brigades were no longer necessary and I could relax. However, when Doreen returned from tour and reopened the dispensary she found that practically everyone in the school had scabies. The clothes they had brought from home were infected and they had infected each other. She rushed down to the hospital to collect a huge jar of Lorexane cream, ordered the girls to strip and got me to help her rub cream on the inflicted places. Their clothes were put to soak in huge bowls full of Dettol solution and they were forbidden to dress in clean ones for the next hour. The Christian girls thought this tremendous fun, they laughed at the splodges of white ointment on each others' bodies and ran about the compound singing and jigging. The Muslim girls were more circumspect. They skulked in their rooms looking miserable. I was sorry not to have spotted scabies before it got too bad but I had been up to my eyes working without adequate teaching staff. Dr Geary had expected Betty, wife of Tom Walton from the Middle School to join me after her leave. They resigned at the last moment. Grisell had her hands full running the education office single handed as Toby Kidd had been summoned home because of illness in the family. She did manage a couple of days teaching, however, which was a great help.

I needed one senior service education officer and one trained Nigerian teacher to manage. The only person I had was Mwapa Jarafwu who occupied one of the two junior service houses standing at the head of the drive. Her husband was still at college and would join her once he was qualified. Mwapa had trained as a grade two teacher in Garkida and did her best with class two in spite of being six months pregnant. (I had not wanted to put her health at risk by asking her to work in the dispensary). A pleasant, competent lady, she was to do further training in the years to come and ended up as Principal of the Womens' Training College, Azaria, N.E. State.

Realising our plight, the Turaki sent us a Fulani lady called Hadija as a temporary measure. Tall, languid, willowy and hesitant, this Hawa had trained as a teacher and left after six months to marry a man with a very unsavoury reputation indeed – rape being one of his lesser crimes. She moved into the second staff house and he joined her at weekends when he could. A veritable Niobe, Hawa wept when he did not turn up; when her efforts at teaching were unsuccessful; when I asked her to do anything; and when she felt like it.

After a month of Hawa and general pressure, Mafeking was relieved. Jean Cole, a bright, young education officer was posted to us from Sokoto and took up residence in the house next door to mine. She had opted to learn Fulani which she knew well and this helped her establish a good rapport with Hawa. She would convey to her what I required and we had less vapours and a spot more work. Poor Jean had health problems in Sokoto and the Yola climate sometimes rendered her unfit for work. She made up for this weakness by co-operating in every other way. She got on well with the staff and the girls, her teaching was good and she had a genuine interest in the welfare of Northern women – especially in the field of nutrition. I gave Hadija and herself the menus given to me on my Geary tour and between them, they planned a suitable diet sheet for every meal.

This was done and everything went satisfactorily for a week. Then a small delegation of Bachema girls appeared at the doorway to the office and were invited to come in.

They addressed me in the usual way, kneeling, head averted and voice pitched high. Could the corn at breakfast be sifted from the bran? We would be glad to help if the cooks found this too much work?' I readily granted their request and Hawa was asked to tell the cooks to organise it immediately. Such a familiar activity would, I felt, make the school feel more like home.

I myself loved hearing the thud, thud of the pestle on the mortar in the bush villages early in the morning. It was the one time it was cool before His Majesty the Sun cast his blazing rays over the fields, the houses and his wilting subjects. That was why government schools, including mine, had followed the example of government offices by starting at 7 a.m. After PT the girls were taught the two most important subjects, English and arithmetic and then we had breakfast break from 9-10 a.m. Jongera used to prepare a beautiful meal of fresh orange juice, home made rolls, scrambled eggs, toast with marmalade and coffee.

Two days after the girls had come to me with their petition, I was lingering over this feast when Hawa interrupted me, all of a fluster. 'Madame, maza, maza' (Come quickly). 'The girls have refused to eat their breakfast. The dining room is in uproar.'

I sent for Jean and we hurried over. It was all too true. The girls had stirred the food, then left it cold and unpalatable on the tables. The cooks were moaning and groaning with wounded pride. Titi had joined Hawa in her weeping and the girls were standing up, shouting: 'We want to go home! We want to go home'. It took a minute to find out the immediate reason for all this clamour. Contrary to my instructions, the corn had not been sifted. Looking back, I realise the girls were just reacting to the sudden changes in their lives.

They calmed down as soon as I started to speak: 'There has been a misunderstanding. I assure you, the order was given to sift the corn and I am repeating it now. All the same, it is a very bad thing to spoil this good, expensive food which you have managed to eat since the beginning of term, and you must be punished. The whole school will stay in the compound next Friday instead of going out with the matrons'.

I could hear a certain amount of grumbling but having experienced worse, I ignored it and took Jean to check the store next to the dining room, expecting them to settle down. When we came out, the girls were still there and they started to shout again. They had taken off their uniforms and placed them in piles outside the dormitories. Realising the situation was getting a bit nasty, Jean and I made our way to the gate meaning to call the Manager. The girls surged forward trying to stop us and I had to call Hadija to fetch me a branch to ward them off. They all drew back at the sight of it except Asabe Mubi who had never been anything but difficult and hostile. She lunged towards me and I hit her in self defence. She gave a piercing scream and every single girl joined her in hysterics. Hadija and Titi pushed their way through the crowd to reach us at the gate. They managed to ease it open enough to let us through. As they were trying to relock it, the girls advanced in a body to stop them.

Talk about Horatio at the gate of Rome: 'But those behind cried "Forward", and those before cried "Back"'. There were Jean and myself, shoulders against the gate trying to close it from the outside and there was this yelling mob inside determined to get out. Hearing the commotion, Bage and his labourers came running up to help, then John the clerk, then Pawa. Extricating myself, I ran back to the house to fetch my car and drove like mad down the dirt road to the Provincial office in

Jimeta hooting loudly all the way. Grisell was out but Guy Haslewood was there and he responded to my alert immediately.

'Keep calm. I'll send a message to the Manager in Yola and phone him as well. It's nearer the school, he should be there before you'. He sounded like a Yankee general sending in the cavalry to quell the troops. 'Please God, let the Manager get there in time', I prayed as I drove back to the school. 'It will be disgrace and demotion for me if those damn girls run away'.

Would you believe it? I found the compound gate locked and the girls were working quietly in their classrooms. Jean Cole left her lesson to report.

'It was incredible. For no reason at all, the girls quietened down a few minutes after you'd left. Maybe their throats were hoarse with shouting. Hawa told them to put on their uniforms and get on with their school work'.

I let sleeping dogs lie and repaired to my office. Ten minutes later up drove the Turaki, the NA legal advisor and Grisell Roy who had been working with them in Yola. The girls were summoned to the dining room and soundly berated by the Turaki.

'How could you be so ungrateful to your teachers when so much has been done for you? You had only to mention the matter of sifting the corn once again to Miss Jacoby and none of this trouble would have taken place. She and Miss Cole have left their homes far away to help the children of our country and this is how they are repaid. The matrons and the cooks have worked hard to look after you. Are you not ashamed?' And so on and so on in the same vein until he had reduced a number of them to tears. 'I want you to say you are sorry'. He concluded, 'this must never happen again'.

'Na tuba. Na tuba'. I'm sorry. I'm sorry. The girls replied and filed out submissively.

I had expected the Resident to be furious about the incident. Instead he sent a very nice letter congratulating me on the 'superb way in which you dealt with the situation'. Mallam Lepatel, the headmaster of the middle school, came up specially to commiserate. He popped up in frequently after that to chew over our problems together. We had both come fresh to the job of 'headship' and derived comfort and help from each other.

There was one particular problem, however, which I hesitated to mention. Too many male visitors were turning up at the school during the PT period before breakfast. They would tell John, the clerk, they had business to discuss, then disappear to take a walk to the playing field. They knew (and probably John knew too) that the Muslim men were seizing their chance to inspect possible brides who could otherwise have been tucked away from view until the day of their marriage. Other males were simply interested in seeing 'Les Girls'. To be blunt, I had not realised that they, the girls not the males, were not wearing any knickers under their uniform. Instead they had on a sort of wrap around, cotton slip and when they were doing handstands, somersaults or exercises with hoops, balls or skipping ropes, they were showing too much flesh.

I got Jean Cole, who was a competent dressmaker, to make up a pair of knickers as a pattern. She cut out two triangles of baft, put a gusset at the apex and joined the two wide sides together. We had to order the elastic needed to go through the hem at the top as there was none to be found in Yola. This is the reason I wrote the following ditty:

LAMENT OF A LADY LEOPARD HUNTER—
I love hunting leopard in darkest Afrique.
I don't miss TV or the Giggle Boutique.
In my little bush hut with no books at all,
I'm having myself a whale of a ball.
I'd stay on for ever in this baking clime,
Except that I can't buy elastic in the local market and my pants go slipping,
slopping, slithering down my legs
Throughout this adventurous, exotic, memoir-making time.

Elastic, bolts of baft, white thread and Jean's sample were given to the tailor with
instructions to make ninety pairs of knickers, thirty large, thirty medium and thirty
small. Stony-faced he set to work at the sewing machine which we placed on the
verandah of my house. Without pins or tape measure machine, he finished the lot in
five days and each girl received three pairs.

To my surprise, the men continued to stroll up to the playing field. I asked Hawa
why. 'Ah, madame. The reason is simple. The girls are not used to these new fangled
garments. Sometimes they forget to put them on. Sometimes they cannot be bothered'.

'Now I understand', I said. 'All the same, this is an important matter and I am going
to make sure they do bother in the future'.

I did make sure, in this way. After the routine greetings and the numbering off at
the morning assembly in front of the locked gate to the dormitory compound, I would
shout 'Stand to attention everyone. Right. Lift up your skirts.' As they stood like
cancan girls at the Folies Bergères, Jean and I went up and down their lines on knicker
inspection. Those who were not wearing them were sent forthwith to their dormitories
to put them on and I refused to allow anyone to go to the dispensary or to the playing
field until every single girl was be-knickered.

To make assurance doubly sure, Barge and a labourer were posted at the top of the
drive to prevent cars or pedestrians from entering the school whilst PE was in
progress. When it was over, Pawa was sent to tell them that: 'Madame is back on seat'.

Most of the Nigerian visitors to the school were connected with education or
government. I did not see many parents at the school itself but I did go to the homes
of the students when I was touring and so did Grisell, Doreen, Dr Geary and many
others. It was, and still is, not uncommon to send your child to live with someone else
in Nigeria. When Grisell told a certain chief that his daughter had been accepted, he
replied: 'That is good. Madame, from now on I give my child to you.' This said it
would be wrong to say the parents did not care. Gubboni Numan's father, for
example, rushed over to see me in Yola as soon as he heard she was in hospital with
amoebic dysentery.

My diary recalls:

I could see he was worried stiff over her. An ex-army sergeant, he went on and on,
interspersing voluble Hausa with incoherent English expressions. 'I think I should take
her home to the doctor in our village, madame', he concluded. 'Let us go to see her
in the hospital first', I suggested. I took him to see Dr Attah in the hospital who told
us that Gubboni was throwing away the pills he had prescribed. Her father agreed to
leave her there after I had promised to visit her daily and make sure she took them.
As we were leaving I caught sight of her mother sidling into the ward with bowls of

food. The pills worked well and we had Gubboni back at school within a week.

'Mens sana in corpore sano'. I was responsible for the souls of the girls as well as their bodies and that meant contacting Mallam Bello, the Organiser for Arabic studies and Mr Jensson, the pastor of the Sudan United Mission.

Chapter nineteen
Never a dull moment

Mallam Bello, the supervisor of Arabic studies took life at a leisurely pace. Grisell had taken ages getting him to supply the Arabic text books we needed before I arrived. Seeing them lying in the store at the beginning of the term, I wrote asking him to come up quickly to translate the titles so that we could distribute them properly. A month passed before he came up to do this. He told me then that he was looking for a teacher and two more weeks passed before he returned to say that he had found one.

'I have chosen this man he said gravely, because he is old and he is calm. Your Muslim girls are at a marriageable age. It would not do to put temptation in their way by choosing a younger man.'

'I understand', I replied, trying not to giggle. 'He can start tomorrow. I will come next month to see that all is well. Sei wata rana' (until another day). The girls could never, ever have been tempted by this Mallam Bello. Dressed in a shabby riga, tall, skeletal and shaky, he was senile rather than old. In one sense, I was relieved. Matron Hadija had her work cut out chaperoning my nubile students and this man had obviously outgrown his sexual urges. I led him into the book store and showed him the Arabic books. Our conversation went like this:

'This one is for class one, Mallam.' I handed it to him. 'Toh. Toh. Madalla' (Yes, yes. Thank you). 'That one is for class two.'

'Toh. Toh. Madalla.' 'And the third one is for the third class which will start next year. Dai dai?' (All right?). 'Dai dai, madame. Dai dai'. His wrinkled face was covered with smiles as he left, carrying the badly printed books as if they were bound with vellum.

Although courteous men were common in Adamawa, the manners of this old man stood out like a beacon on a hill. He never lost his temper and the girls liked him very much. Steeped in the Islamic tradition, he made sure they said the required prayers and declaration: 'THERE IS NO GOD BUT GOD AND MOHAMMED IS HIS PROPHET' five times a day: at dawn (fayri), at noon (zuhr), in the afternoon (asri), at sunset (maghrib) and in the evening (isha). It was impressive to watch them at worship. After washing themselves they faced towards Mecca in the east, bowed, then prostrated whilst praying. After the various crises we had gone through in the school, this discipline calmed us all down. Mallam Bello used the time-honoured teaching method of chanting and the girls responded whole heartedly since they had learned this way as children in Koranic schools in their villages. Where money was not available to build a school, the teacher and children had sat outside in a circle, chanting and writing in the sand. Once, when I was called away urgently, I asked him to take over for half an hour. The girls were practising the poem Solomon Grundy — which was part of the entertainment planned for Dr Geary's first visit to the school.

Solomon Grundy,
Born on a Monday,
Christened on Tuesday,
Married on Wednesday,
Took ill on Thursday,
Worse on Friday,
Died on Saturday,
Buried on Sunday,
This is the end,
Of Solomom Grundy.

My business took half an hour longer than expected and when I returned the girls were still repeating the poem!

It was Mallam Bello's task to keep me informed of any special day in the Muslim calendar to make sure we did the right thing. This was especially important during the month of Ramadan when every good Muslim was expected to go without food and drink for a month from sunrise to sunset. He and Hawa arranged for the meals to fit in with this requirement. Going without water in the heat of the afternoon was a great strain. In and out of school, most Muslims I knew adhered to the rules. The appearance of the new moon signalled the start and finish of Ramadan. It was not a question of the Iman seeing it in Yola, the announcement had to come from Kaduna.

My diary details the Ramadan programme of 1956.

— WEDNESDAY, JULY 17th. The Turaki sent me instructions to buy a ram and 200 kola nuts for Sallah, so drove Bage and Mai Chaffine (someone from the mosque) down to Jimeta market to buy one.

— THURSDAY, JULY 18th Hadija, Agatu and I bought biscuits and presents in Jimeta market. We'll give them to the girls, the teachers and the labourers after the general Sallah in Yola she said. Bage asked me to come and see the ram slaughtered. I refused politely saying I was sure he could do it most competently without me.

— FRIDAY, JULY 19th. All the girls were up, spick and span and much too early. Contrary to my instructions, Hadija decided to give them a little food, just before they got on to the lorry sent by the Manager. Why do we plan? A very nice thought, anyway.

Sallah was unforgettably impressive. The huge crowd of worshippers bowing full length in prayer simultaneously is a sight I shall not easily forget. All the expatriates in or near Yola were there. Rich or poor, white or black, everyone was dressed to the nines. The Turaki was stunning in flowing layers of yellow cotton and a sky high turban. As for the Resident, and the senior district officers they looked like 'pukkah sahibs' attending a durbah in India. Their uniform seemed designed to stifle them: their thick white jackets were fastened stiffly at the neck; a wide leather belt with a sword dangling at the side constricted their waist; and a sweat trap of a helmet came down to the eyebrow.

Back in the compound the girls ate a huge meal beginning with kola nuts and followed by ram stew, cooked vegetables, rice, fruit and biscuits. After this the presents were distributed and they sang and danced for the rest of the evening.

Hawa came over to my house the following evening to chat about it all. 'Ah, ah. The girls were so happy!' She laughed, 'I said to them: you've had meat, kola nuts, a ride to Yola and presents, was anything lacking? "No! No!" They all shouted. 'Nada da nada' (Nothing at all)'.

The Christian girls had gone down to Yola with the rest. They had sat with the teachers to watch the prayers, and, naturally, joined in the celebrations afterwards. It was my job to arrange religious instruction for them as well as for the Muslims. I knew Mr Jensson through my dealings with his wife in the bookshop and wrote to him. When he did not reply immediately, I left it for the moment thinking he must be on tour. The SUM people never came to the Club because they disapproved of drinking alcohol, and, like the American Baptists in Ibadan, their social life was mostly within the Mission.

About three o'clock, one unbelievably scorching afternoon, I was flat out, asleep in my bedroom, when I dimly heard the sound of someone tapping at the open front door. Jongera had served lunch and gone back to rest in his quarters. Realising that whoever was tapping did not intend to go away, I heaved myself off the bed, slung an African cloth round me and staggered to the sitting room where I propped myself against the door — like Dorothy Lamour, bare shouldered in her sarong.

A wispy, insipid little man was standing on the verandah. 'I am Mr Jorgensen and I am replacing Mr Jenssen who is on leave'. He said stiffly. 'I have walked up in order to see someone concerning the Christian education of the girls in this school.' His tone implied that a half-clothed woman like myself could not possibly know anything about such a hallowed subject. 'Oh, er. I'll be with you in a minute.' I got dressed quickly and the two of us sat down in the sitting room. He had chosen the chair furthest away from myself and seemed distant and uncomfortable throughout the interview. It did not take long to arrange for the classes to take place in the classroom next to my office. Realising he must be very hot after his long walk, I said: 'Would you like some tea, Mr Jorgensen?'

Just what this colourless, unattractive missionary thought I meant by this well meaning invitation, I do not know, but it brought him sharply to his feet, blushing like a girl.

'No, no. I am having tea with my wife' he snapped. He said 'wife' as if it was a crucifix and he was a Christian brandishing it before the fiend, Dracula.

The girls started attending his classes as planned and in early December, he wrote asking if he could take two extra Sunday afternoon meetings as a preparation for Christmas. I thought this a timely idea and gave him the go-ahead. The drive home took me past the office and the first Sunday I thought I saw him coming out of the dormitory compound. This was 'lèse majesté' indeed and thinking I had been mistaken I checked with Hawa the next day. She swore the girls had told her I had given permission to go into the dormitory compound. They had entered the room, shut the door and started to sing hymns.

I told her she should have known better as a good Muslim, scolded the girls separately and then sent for Mr Jorgensen. This time I was the distant one. I dressed in a dress that buttoned to the neck and kept him standing as I spoke to him in the office.

'I've called you here, Mr Jorgensen to explain why you changed the venue of the class without consulting me.' 'Er. Well, the girls thought it a good idea.' 'I am amazed by your ignorance of the country where you are teaching' I continued. 'As a married man you must realise that sitting with a group of girls in a closed room would be considered the height of indiscretion by the councillors of the Numan federation. As for the Lamido and the Muslim community, if they heard that you had invaded the privacy of the school's dormitory compound which is guarded and out of bounds for any male visitor, your head and mine would be on the block.'

The man's mouth was opening and shutting like a dying fish. I decided to frighten him even more. 'Missionaries are not that welcome in the North as you must know and your blatant disregard of Muslim custom could do immense harm to the Christian cause. I shall not report the matter this time but if it happens again . . .'

'No, no. Never'. He was off before I finished the sentence. He kept his promise.

In the same school he and Mallam Bello spread their separate faiths. Coming from such different backgrounds, it was hardly surprising to find the girls arguing and quarrelling at times. The staff were generally able to smooth them down and reported to me if they came to blows. One evening I was called out to the dormitory because five bullies from one tribe (term for ethnic group in the fifties) had decided to set upon a little girl from a rival tribe, reviving some ancient rite. She had collapsed with fear and hurt and fainted. Thinking they might have killed her, they had woken Hadija up and she had sent for me.

I went down to see the Turaki about it the next morning and he came back with me immediately. He told the bullies off in front of the whole school and ordered them to go with Hadija to be beaten. They came back looking quite cocky but it must have been bravado as they did not bully anyone again.

As their health improved and everything was done for their well being, the girls gradually settled down to a steady routine of work and play with supervised homework every night. Each Friday Jean and Mwapa brought me their scheme of work for the following week. It was no good asking Mallam Bello! The girls were so happy with him I did not even think it was necessary.

I was in for a shock. Always dilatory, Supervisor Bello did not return for two months. The moment he entered the classrooms he found out that our Mallam Bello had given each class the wrong book. Asked for an explanation he said that I had made the mistake and he did not want to argue with me. The books were distributed correctly and I started to relax. Not long after that Mallam Bello asked for permission to go to hospital for rheumatism. I felt sorry I had ever thought badly of him and sent him to the doctor with a note from me — in German, because he, the doctor, came from Hungary and we sometimes spoke it together.

'Lieber Herr Doktor. Dieser arme, alte Mann ist krank. Was ist los? (This poor old man is ill. What is wrong ?) Back came a short note: 'Tell him to return for treatment. Er hat VD'.

I dispatched the 'poor old man' with a note to the doctor, saying: 'Es wäre Zeit dass seine Lebensgeister ausgeloscht wurden'. (His lustful days should be over by now).

The doctor replied with feeling: 'Lebensgeister kann man niemal auslöschen'. (Man's lust never cools).

When Doreen Rothera heard what had happened, she split her sides laughing. 'You are a little idiot, Jean. Everyone but you knows rheumatism is a euphemism for VD.'

The arrival of the United Nations Commission to visit the Cameroonian Trust territory in December 1955 gave me ample chance to speak German and French although English was the official language. The Mission itself consisted of four delegates — M. Dorsinville from Haiti whose English was not so good as his French; M. Shevven from Belgium; a charming, intelligent American called Patrick Mulcahy; and Liu Yang, from China. These four were accompanied by a bevy of journalists including the Foreign Editor of the Daily Mirror; a British brigadier; someone with a beard claiming to be an expert in economics and two liaison officers. Each one had his own secretary. My diary describes their entourage.

Denise Wyn, a big blonde woman who acted as the brigadier's secretary was billeted with me. It was obvious their liaison had got her the appointment. Not the ideal guest. Her conversation consisted of complaints. Yola was too hot, too full of mosquitoes, the round of social events was wearing her out and the brigadier was too demanding. She was especially cross when he insisted on her joining the delegation in their visits to the school, the hospital, the prison and the waterworks. In previous places she had taken refuge in a swimming pool, but the only one in Jimeta belonged to the Resident and was out of order.

The town of Jada went one better than Yola by staging an agriculture show. Jean Cole and I went in my car, whilst the matrons and our girls joined the middle school boys on their lorry. Jada was choc a bloc when we arrived. Grisell and most of the Jimeta GRA had arrived very early. Entertainment, static to frenetic, was the order of the day. There were eye-catching craft displays of raffia mats, baskets, terracotta pots, calabashes whose patterns had been etched in by burning and cornstalk models of lorries, bicycles, animals and people.

A demonstration of the use of a decorticating machine for groundnuts deafened the ears of anyone approaching.

The Fulani had driven in their cattle and their mooing vied with the horses in their woven cloths and fancy saddles waiting for their riders to stage the dramatic charge towards the platform of chairs where the Commission and VIPs were sitting under huge umbrellas. Most of us had seen this charge before ending in an abrupt halt inches away from the spectators. It was the first time for the lady secretaries. They were terrified and Denise fainted.

Once the dancing and drumming began it was hard to concentrate on anything else. Most of the performers came from pagan groups and the whistle summoned each group in turn. A second whistle told them to stop.

Some dancers wore grass skirts, some feathers, some had their legs covered with bobbles from ankle to knees. Others had plaited hair or rope pigtails sticking out in all directions. One dancer was hidden altogether by his mask of wood depicting a bird and a skirt of thatch. The bird represented a spirit (dodo) and a young lad was prancing around him poking him with a stick. Age was no disqualification. The dance of a small old man whose cap kept falling off with his exertions had the audience clapping and roaring for more. The cameras and the cines of the Commission clicked and flashed hysterically all afternoon.

Determined to put the new school on the map, I had instructed the tailor to make the girls new bright yellow and green dresses with headties to match. Guy Haslewood who openly disapproved of the government spending good money on girls' education called them a 'lot of bloody canaries'. Fortunately, the Resident and the members of the UIV Commission thoroughly approved, congratulating Grisell and myself on the demeanour of the girls and the general progress of the school.

John Chamberlain who had replaced Toby Kidd as PEO was equally encouraging. Realising I needed a break after such a hard term, he insisted I take two weeks local leave over Christmas. I arranged to stay with my very good friends, Eileen and John Skevington who had been transferred from Barclay's Bank, Ibadan, to Gusau in the Northern Region. They had been married three years and had two little girls, Anne and Margaret. Grisell arranged for me and Jongera, the steward, to travel to Kano in her kitcar which needed a service. After making certain the driver had taken it to the garage, I could continue to Gusau by plane. Then as now, drivers were often tempted to use their vehicles as taxis, given the chance. I had known several ladies in Ibadan sprinkle the seats of their cars with sand before sending their drivers off alone on a long journey.

Any journey west of Yola automatically started at the river's edge. The ferry boat crossed the Benue two or three times a day according to the whim of the ferryman. It had room for two vehicles and was open ended. The ferryman knew every inch of the river and poled the boat across in a series of zig zag curves to avoid the currents and sand banks under the water. Once across, Grisell's driver decided against taking the comparatively good route via Biu because he said it was too long and suggested the shorter road. He did not tell me it was nicknamed the Thirty Nine Steps because it was so hazardous, with pot holes and rocks hindering progress every minute of the way. Except for a hospital and a school belonging to Sudan Interior Mission we did not see a large building until we reached Gombe, a hundred miles away. The occasional village we did pass consisted of a collection of small compounds, nothing more. I knew Jack Evans was stationed in Gombe and decided to look him up.

To be honest I hoped he would provide a toilet and a hot drink! Contact between us since we met in London had been tenuous, to put it mildly. In October he had sent me a picture via his friends George and Betty Cockhead who were driving through en route for Yola. It depicted an African village and looked like the work of a mentally deficient four year old. Since Jongera was constantly nagging me to help him find a new tyre for his Raleigh bike, I did acknowledge this unwelcome gift. I had brought the bike from England and sold it to him for five shillings a week as I had found Yola too hot and too hilly for cycling.

I wrote:

Dear Jack

Thank you for the picture. It was a kind thought. I wonder if you deal in tyres for a Raleigh bicycle. If so, could you possibly send me two for my steward? They are unobtainable in Yola. All the best.

Jean.

Jack replied a month later. 'We don't stock that make of tyre. Silly girl that you are, you sent your letter to a remote village near Mubi called GOMBI and I am stationed in a town called GOMBE. You were lucky it arrived at all. If you are ever my way do drop in.'

The L & K building was easy to find. It was next to the Barclay's Bank in the principal dusty street of Gombe which combed out into a series of dustier, noisier alley ways. Jack was delighted to see me walk in unexpectedly. He stopped work for the day and took me to his house for tea. He had organised the building of this house himself without a plan or a drawing. What a contrast! Boozy, bluff, casual Jack turned out to be a born home maker. His chairs and curtains were made of pretty cretonne material, a huge Belgian rug covered the red painted floor and shelves round the room held books, photos, ornaments and an interesting assortment of beer steins which he had been collecting for years.

His northern homeliness was a welcome contrast from the la-di-da conversation of the Admin types in Yola. He persuaded me to spend the night in Gombe Rest House which was run by Tom Bowling, Jack's assistant. We discussed our separate jobs, our families, books and I don't know what else that evening. Over breakfast the following morning he made me promise to stay for a day at least on my way back and to return to see him for longer whenever I could.

The next day we drove to Kano via Jos and left the kitcar in the garage as planned. The flight to Gusau was pure joy after a day and a half on the road. Eileen was at the airport to meet me with her very lovable little daughters. It was heart warming to feel part of a family again. We chatted endlessly. She shed a little tear about the death of a baby son and I told her about meeting Jack again. 'He sounds dependable. Somehow I feel he will be a very good friend indeed', she said.

She and Skev were extremely popular and I was included in the hectic round of Christmas parties held in their friends' houses and in the club as well. I particularly enjoyed the party given by an important Lebanese entrepreneur called Jamil Akkare and his Nigerian wife, Mary. This letter describes their hospitality:

Different dishes appeared every hour, too many to name. We had delicious patties filled with tomatoes, minced beef, onion and garlic; chicken with crispy chips; mouth watering bowls of mixed salads; meat rolls; peppery stews; roast meats – goat, chicken and turkey; and a huge Christmas cake made by Mary. The drinks were equally lavish, any you like to name and whenever a guest said 'no' to champagne and covered their glass to show they meant it, Jamil poured it over their fingers till they removed them.

He was more respectful to Monsignor Lawton and his three companions from the Dominican mission who were there with him. The Lebanese invited him to all their parties. He mixed easily without ever losing his dignity. His approachability and spirituality made him an ideal priest and it was a pleasure to be in his company.

Jamil's house and business were situated on a good tarmac road called the Beach, together with the banks and the usual big canteens. A small community of Lebanese and Syrians had their shops selling material further on. The name Beach had nothing to do with water. It harkened back to the first traders who had set up their trade on the banks of a river. The tarmac road led out of the Beach at one end to the Club, the railway and the GRA. At the other it joined crossroads leading to Sokoto and Funtua. The scenery was drab, scrubland in every direction except for the village of Bungude. Situated on high rocks above a river, a number of trees had grown high above it and it made a good place, the only place to go for a picnic.

This was how I saw Gusau for the first time. When I said goodbye to Eileen and the children at the airport at the end of the holiday, neither they nor I guessed I would be back there in 1958.

Chapter twenty
A school at last

1956 began with a whimper and finished with a bang. The journey back to Yola from Gusau did not go according to plan. My letter home on 3 January 1956, addressed 'On the roadside, somewhere in the North', describes it.

Darlings

Travel in Nigeria is always an adventure. At the moment we are stuck by the roadside with battery trouble. The kitcar is just out of the garage and God knows why it should go wrong. The flight from Kano was so turbulent the pilot was as sick as the passengers and the chill early morning harmattan haze has made matters worse. Once we did get started, the driver said we must take the long road to be on the safe side. Poor Jack! He will wonder what has become of me . . .

The following evening —

We waited three hours yesterday before an empty lorry appeared. The driver and his mate helped push the kitcar and we started off once again. The road got bumpier and bumpier and our average speed dropped to five miles an hour as a result. It improved eventually, and Isa put his foot on the accelerator to make up time lost. Evening fell and he kept going at the same breakneck speed. There's a strange fascination about zooming through endless bush in the pitch dark, straining to see the next bridge or culvert with not a village or person in sight.

Suddenly, the headlights lit up a huge wild, grey sow with a litter of piglets. She scampered into the bush, leaving the piglets. Before I realised what had happened Isa charged into them and killed them all. He leapt out shouting with joy and bundled their corpses into the back. He was so excited he could not stop chortling and chuckling. Jongera had to tell him to shut up and concentrate on his steering. Funnily enough it was the money he would get selling the piglets which thrilled him. As a Muslim he would never eat them.

I was relieved when we reached a rest house, or empty building rather, without furniture or any facility. Jongera is a born boy scout. After cutting up four ropes with a stone, he hung a mosquito net over my camp bed and managed to bring me tea and biscuits. It was bitterly cold, I snuggled into my sleeping bag wearing two skirts and two sweaters. . . .

The rest of the journey to Yola was uneventful. Relieved and happy I called at the

Education Office to report. John Chamberlain and Grisell gave me a frosty reception. 'You're lucky to have a school to return to', Grisell stormed. 'A bush fire started about fifty yards away from the school buildings two days after Christmas. Barge and his men got to it just in time.'

'You were told to get them to dig a fire trace round the periphery of the school grounds before you left, Jean,' John added. 'Why didn't you do so?' 'Barge was told. We went round the compound together to mark it. Maybe he did not hear the measurements properly', I replied. 'We were speaking in Hausa after all.' Barge's goodwill was all important. I persuaded Grisell to give him the benefit of the doubt and we let the matter drop. Soon she was absorbed in finding examples of local craft, faifais, burnt calabashes and cornstalk toys and artifaxes for a group of our girls to show at a large display in Kaduna on the Occasion of the Queen's first visit to Nigeria. They took part in the procession at the end of the show, together with girls from all over Nigeria and were thrilled to bits when Her Majesty spoke to each of them personally.

This term the girls appeared happy to be back at school. Realising that a number of them would have returned from homes where the water was contaminated, and reluctant to single them out we established a health routine for the whole school. Two large tubs of Dettol solution were waiting for them in the compound. As each one arrived she had to give the clothes she was wearing to the matrons to soak, shower with medicated soap and go to the dispensary to be rubbed down with Lorexane. When they were dry they put on the uniforms they had washed and dried before the holidays. This prevented the onslaught of scabies or similar rashes. Cases of worms, bilharzia, or dysentery were dealt with as before with the ludicrous pantomime of urine and stool samples being head-loaded down to the hospital.

Jean Cole had gone on leave before Christmas and was posted to Maiduguri where she married an old friend, Trevor Tudor. Her place was taken by Mary Pearsall, who had already taught a year in the girls' school in Kano, under Alice Patterson. She was competent and efficient in every way and I was able to leave the dispensary to her.

Everyone, including the staff, was ill at times, but overall we had only one surprise in 1956. Fatu Jalingo, one of the younger students had to be rushed to hospital yelling with pain, after eating sand to cure her stomach ache. She blamed the Yola sand, swearing that the Jalingo variety never failed. By a stroke of luck, Mary who never missed a club night, met Jim, the new doctor the evening he arrived. He was most interested in what she told him about the school and arranged a visit. In no time he took over the duties of a school doctor, giving monthly examinations, keeping a closer eye on our two lepers and making personal calls if anyone had a fever. With such a kind caring man to turn to, I felt like Christian shedding his burden in the book, 'Pilgrim's Progress'. Nor did we have any more major crises scenes about food or accommodation. At last! At last! Mary, Agatu, Mwapu and I could concentrate on extending the frontiers of the girls' education through school work, sport, fresh activities and travel. Basically, the yearly grant was sufficient to cover whatever we wanted to do. Better equipment replaced anything that did not work. Ink, for instance, had arrived in huge bottles and, however carefully it was poured, it invariably slopped over the inkwells in the desks. We replaced them by fountain pens, biros or pencils. The teaching staff were given Ursula Bozman's book on keeping a library as a teaching aid and the classes had their own library. The girls were expected to keep a notebook describing the books they read in a couple of sentences and each had to compile her own dictionary. I still have Aishatu Fufori's, dated 16 July 1956: under the letter 'F' she has written: friend, fail, four and few!

All the teachers threw themselves into their work. Mary did a particularly good job dealing with the different standards in the top class. Agatu established a close rapport with the students from Numan division and towards the end of the term, she formed an impressive girl guide company. Mwapu did her very best until she went to Garkida to have her baby. She was to return with her husband in 1957 and both continued as teachers for a few years. He did not like having a woman boss very much and was inclined to go his own way.

I taught each class English twice a week which kept me in touch with the girls' progress. In order to understand the problems of the staff a routine was established whereby all of them, Nigerians and Europeans alike, handed me their lesson notes every Thursday and discussed them with me the next day. They really appreciated this extra 'training' and told me it helped them tremendously. Monthly tests were held to keep the students up to scratch and these were followed by a staff meeting.

Inevitably the girls who came from homes where education was encouraged had better results to begin with. The Muslim girls, however, did not want to lag behind and worked hard to catch up.

There were two notable exceptions. Fat, voluble Dudu, the daughter of a powerful, reactionary Fulani chief could not be bothered to work whilst the gorgeous, bronze skinned Mamadaso had her mind centred on men. Some in-built mechanism in her body alerted her to the arrival of every male. If one came to the office, she would be draping herself by the door as he arrived. If he and I had to go somewhere in the compound, her slinky figure would materialise with a concocted reason to see me.

Never mind. She came into her own on the playing field. Enthusiasm for the comparatively new games of rounders and netball was rife throughout the school and Mamadaso excelled at both. Her lithe body sprang so high in netball, she seemed to deposit, rather than shoot the ball into the net. When she played rounders, no one could catch her out as she streaked from post to post. It made her day when Mary Pearsall persuaded Jerry Rees, a district officer friend, to form an all-male rounders team and challenge APGS. The match was hilarious. The men whacked the ball tremendously hard but, ignorant of the rules, kept running themselves out and the girls won. In spite of its success this event was a one-off. When the opponents of girls' education heard about 'the male invasion' of the school on the hill and the fact that Mary and I had been wearing shorts, they sent a strong protest to the Provincial Education Office in Jimeta. When we told this story to Jerry he countered it with one of his own.

On tour in the bush near Mubi he and Jean, his wife, had called at a remote Roman Catholic mission station run by two priests from the South of France. With their grey beards and faces wrinkled by years under a tropical sun, they looked like saints in a stained glass window. It was the hot season and Jean had on a pair of white shorts which were sticking to the canvas chair she was sitting on. The shorts rose higher as she tried to detach them.

Feeling a little embarrassed, Jerry said: 'I hope you will excuse my wife wearing shorts, Father Pierre. She suffers so much from the heat.' 'Please do not worry yourself, Monsieur', said the father with a shrug and a smile. 'After all, I am French.'

Yola was even hotter than Mubi, and anywhere else in the Adamawa province. Returning from a conference in Kaduna, Grisell wrote: 'It was disappointing to find how quickly mental activity, gained when visiting Kaduna or Jos, subsided on my return to the oppressive climate of Yola'.

The nights were as bad as the days in the hot season. Like most of the folk in the GRA, I slept outside in a 'Rumfa'. This was a temporary room, made of matting with a lap-over in the fourth wall to allow for entrance and privacy. As no one was around I took my nightie off before going to sleep. Jongera had perfect manners. Unwilling to surprise me in the buff, he used to cough long and loud outside the entrance when he came with morning tea, to give me time to put it on.

This idyllic bedroom under the stars had two snags. Snakes and storms. First; how do you spend a penny when the house is fifty yards away and snakes lurk in the grass outside? Easy. You put down 'chamber pot' at the bottom of the next shopping list for Paul, the UAC manager in Jos. It came in a few days. Alas! Presuming I had spawned a baby girl, he had dispatched a minute, pink pottie.

I returned it with the following note: 'Although I take PT daily with my students, I am reluctant to perform urinal acrobatics in the middle of the night. May I ask you, therefore, to replace this with an adult size?' A large, enamel chamber pot arrived within the week. Paul had scribbled this sentence on the bill: 'We apologise for the error and trust this will be a better fit. Paul.'

As the dry hot season was drawing to a close, heavy tropical storms (the second snag) started to erupt during the night. It was impossible to sleep in the rumfa with the rain plummeting on to the mosquito net and I moved inside. Without a fan, the heat was still intolerable, and after a week's lull I decided to sleep on the covered verandah near the door. That way I could nip inside if it did rain. At 4 o'clock in the morning a storm to end all storms exploded. It lasted two hours. Torrential rain soaked me to the skin and ear-splitting claps of thunder set me burrowing under the pillow with fear. Worse still, I dared not leave the bed because forked lightning was running up and down the bedposts. Two houses lost their roofs that night, so it was a good job I had stayed put.

After the rains, the weather was quite perfect. Taking an evening stroll along the rocks near the house was a veritable river symphony. Exotic birds twittered in the lush vegetation below, a light blue haze floated over the river and fishermen chattered and laughed as they mended their fishing nets by the shore. Now the water was deep enough for boats of 1,000 tons or more, their crews could be seen oiling the engines, loading the cargo and setting out for Garuwa in the French Cameroons. The mornings were equally pleasant. The girls seemed happier about getting up and their breakfasts were enhanced by the appearance of an endless supply of brownie pink mushrooms springing up all over the compound.

The weather was both good and bad when we took the girls to SUM Girls' School, Numan for a three day half-term holiday. Phoebe Frensen, the Danish headmistress and I had spent hours preparing the programme beforehand. She was a sweet, young-looking dedicated lady and full of fun to boot. Here is a shortened description of our stay:

On Friday the older girls got up at 1.30 a.m. to clean, but Hadija had refused to allow them to leave the dormitory compound till Mary and I appeared at 6.30 a.m. Whilst Agatu took the girls for team practice, Hadija and Matron Titi packed up the equipment Phoebe had asked us to bring — kettles, cups, blankets, plates, cutlery, cleaning materials, kerosene and bush lamps. (Numan school had no electricity.)

As usual the lorry came half an hour late. In theory the classes were supposed to line up and climb on. In practice, they struggled and fought so fiercely they were pushing each other off. Mary finally turned to me and, quoting a jocular phrase of the time, suggested we follow 'a policy of masterful inactivity' by leaving them to it. After a ten minute coffee break in her house, we returned to the lorry and, sure enough, we found staff and girls happily ensconced and ready for off. We were to pursue this policy many, many times after that and it always worked!

The lorry set off and Mary and I followed in her car. The girls sang lustily all the way to the school in Numan. Their girls were stationed round the flagstaff in the compound and started cheering and clapping as we turned into the drive. Phoebe and her staff came forward to add their welcome. After the Adamawa girls had helped unloading the lorry they were given new uniforms. This time, we had opted for specially woven green and yellow material from a government-backed textile mill in Sokoto. It was much better quality than imported prints, stood up to endless washing and lasted much longer.

We had no trouble getting the girls to bed that night. Many had fallen asleep before Phoebe and I went round the dormitories to see that all was well. They were full of energy, however, on the Saturday morning and everyone pitched in cleaning the compound and grinding the corn. It was a joy to see members of different tribes and religions working in harmony together. After breakfast, the two schools went to see the sights of Numan. They visited the SUM bookshop first, then continued on to the Boys' School. There was nothing to write home about either, but our girls were not used to anything better and enjoyed every minute.

The tour continued with a visit to the Central Office of Education where they met the Director, Mallam Jonah and Chief Mbula who both gave overlong speeches. Going round the SUM maintenance workshop was more lively. Mr Vortoft, the engineer, was quite a personality. Warning the girls not to touch, he set machinery buzzing, whirring and spinning so that they ran away screaming and then crept back, shamefaced to have a peep. The afternoon was devoted to sport: athletics, rounders and netball matches. These were disturbingly hostile events. Far from applauding their opponents, each school clapped their side only and screamed insults at each other on and off the playing field. Numan won at netball, and Adamawa at rounders. Overall Numan scored the most points and carried off the prize — a huge tin of biscuits. Result: the Adamawa teams burst into tears and demanded to go home forthwith. Agatu and I had to speak to them seriously about team spirit and it took an hour to calm them and persuade them to remain. We learnt our lesson and delivered a pep talk about being good losers before setting out for any inter-school competition in the future.

By contrast the atmosphere round the camp fire in the evening could not have been more congenial. Impromptu plays, tribal songs and dances followed each other in quick succession. The girls went to bed laughing happily and were too tired to complain about the swarms of mosquitoes penetrating the ill-fitting windows of the dormitories.

Sunday morning the Adamawa girls who were Christian went with the SUM girls to Church, meeting their parents there who were visibly impressed by the change in their appearance. After lunch everybody, girls and staff, had a picnic by the river. They played ball games, built sand castles and paddled in the water. Little, big-eyed, Rukatu Yola fell in and had to be fished out. Nigerian and English games followed including 'Nuts in May' and rather irrelevantly considering the number of bare foot people in the province, 'Cobbler, cobbler mend my shoe'. Reluctant to join in, a few senior Muslim girls sat stiffly apart on the stones on the river bank. Then, tired out by all this exercise, we sat down on the sand in three large circles for a break. The Numan girls served us tea, boiled up with milk and sugar in the same large cooking pot, accompanied by long sausage-shaped cakes baked by Phoebe's cook. We drove back to Numan in the gloaming, to another evening of games and tricks. Rukatu, this time, had us all laughing as she and Aishatu Mubi chewed on either end of a piece of string to get to the lump of sugar.

It was raining hard the next morning whilst we were packing up. After an hour's chase from house to house looking for the key to the school gate, we finally located it in the cooking pot and were able to drive out. Once again the entire school sang throughout the journey home. It had been grand to see the students mixing together. The sweetest sight to me was Muslim Dudu hand in hand with Christian Ruth. Whatever their religion, in fact, the big girls of both schools had taken the little ones under their wing. On the Tuesday we excused them homework and games. When classes resumed they were asked to write their impressions and were glad to do so. All, without exception, expressed a wish to return to Numan.

After this weekend we continued providing 'education beyond the classroom' on a smaller scale by local excursions and talks given by people living in Yola or travelling there on tour. Mother Magdalene, a devoted Catholic nursing sister, showed the girls round the hospital and the Turaki arranged for them to spend a morning in the magistrate's court when it was in session. We never knew how the talks would be since we had to take whoever happened to be in Yola without hearing them beforehand. However bad the entertainment, the girls would listen politely and without fidgeting. The worst evening was a show by a Nigerian film unit who put on three stale news films, a short unintelligible Pakistani drama, and three Nigerian coronations, the content and colour of which had faded with the years. Other speakers included Mr Baraimian, a visiting judge; Dr Bunny Moore, the chief medical officer; Freda Gwillyam from the Colonial Office and Mr Thomas, an electrical engineer in ECN and the only Nigerian on the GRA. Finally, Jerry Rees gave an excellent talk on government.

It was he who had introduced me to David Adams from the Nigerian Broadcasting Corporation at a party. He agreed to broadcast a short story I had written called Thomas the Terrible — came to the school to record it and later agreed to give a talk, himself, on broadcasting. He was so pleased and impressed with the girls' questions and reaction to what he had to say, he suggested they do a broadcast themselves. They wrote the script with the help of Mary and myself and it went on the air from Kaduna in December 1956. The whole school assembled to listen to it and were laughing and nudging each other at the sound of their own voices.

In the normal course of events, the girls would make their own entertainment after the afternoon games, just as they would do in their own homes. They would chat and tell each other stories as they sat plaiting each others' hair in a dozen twists and whirls or washed their clothes. A number of them planted little gardens in front of the dormitories, where they grew flowers, peppers and corn. One day a week the Numan girls went to Agatu's guide meeting and another day Mary held a sewing group and taught them to make things and do minor alterations. Poor Titi did some raffia work with them which was so terrible, we could not tell what it was! She was dismissed after eighteen months for general incompetence and her post was taken by a far more responsible older lady called Hajara. The girls were under constant but discreet supervision during the daytime. Hajara and Hadija would keep a watching brief on them from their houses just outside the compound in the evening, Mary or I would always be there to see them last thing at night and from then until dawn the watchnight would be patrolling the grounds. The highlight of everyone's week was Friday. Once the dormitories had been cleaned out and clothes given an airing the girls were free of school. Hadija took the Muslim girls to the mosque and the Christian girls went to the market with Hajara.

Hadija and I worked very well together. She came round most evenings for a little chat and sometimes she asked me to lunch with her. My letter home described the occasion:

I dressed in my native cloth and she had donned the Marks & Spencer's skirt and sweater I had given her at Christmas. We sat in her house which she had cleaned till it shone. We ate off leaves instead of plates, Fulani style, hunching up our knees so as not to be too greedy. She had prepared an excellent chicken stew with rice and we finished with tea boiled with milk in the same kettle. Hajara joined as we were finishing, and the three of us started to smoke endless cigarettes. It was like a Greek play. Hadija held the stage with tales of a dangerous youth spent with 'the terrible people of Bornu': I was the young innocent listener, clicking my tongue, exclaiming 'Aha! Aha' and Hajara was the obligatory figure of doom, deeply intoning phrases like 'That's life. Fate willed it so'.

Dear Hadija. She was my sounding board, my informant and my advisor. I would have been lost without her.

Chapter twenty-one
Love and courtship

Trained to respect her elders, Agatu came to regard me as a combination of mother and counsellor. Too bashful to speak to me in person she handed me a letter in August, 1956 to say she was engaged to a boy from her home in Garkida. They had both attended The Church of the Brethren schools there and he was presently training as a teacher in Gindiri College. She probably knew that I had arranged to visit Garkida at the end of the month on school business and was hoping I would take her with me. I was only too pleased to have a local guide. We were relieved to find the road open on the day we travelled to Garkida as it was often closed for hours after heavy rains. We stopped at Little Gombi (where I had sent that first letter to Jack) to fill up with petrol. Also I needed to find out what had happened to a junior student called Fadimatu who had failed to return to school after the holidays.

We saw the Wakili (village chief) at the praying ground and asked him where she lived. Telling us to follow him he led us through a jigsaw of narrow mud tracks until he came to her mother's house. A crowd of relatives were kneeling at the open doorway, peeping into a room where Fadimatu was lying down with a large bump on her knee. It had caused her trouble at the school already, and Dr Jim had cured it in a few days. 'Why did you not go to a dispensary or a hospital?' Agatu asked her. 'Mother said there was no need. She has put fire on it and that will soon make it better', Fadimatu replied. 'Fadimatu dear, it looks worse than it did last term'. I said. 'Let me take you to a hospital in Garkida.' Fadimatu started to cry and her mother and relatives began to wail. 'No, no. Leave her in peace. It is nothing to do with you'. The Wakili shooed them away. 'This is women's talk', he said contemptuously. 'I will speak to her father when he returns from the farm this evening. He will agree. Fadimatu will be ready to go with you on your return'.

We continued on to Garkida, almost hidden by field upon field of corn. It turned out to be even lovelier than Yola and without the searing heat. The missionaries, who all came from America, had built their houses on the mountains overlooking the town and the river. Agatu took me straight to the house of Mrs Baldwin, Director of both the primary school and the leprosarium. She had arranged for Agatu and myself to stay in a many-roomed rest house called St Michael's and her fiancé was waiting in front, smiling broadly.

After they had taken us to Salima Garkida's house they went their own way. We had sent her and Esther Demsa to Kano Girls' School to continue their education. They had been excellent class students and deserved this promotion. Salima looked well in herself but was downcast over her first report. 'Everything was so strange, madame'. She told me. 'I did not always understand the English of the teachers. I worked very hard and they did not seem to realise this'. 'You soon will, Salima. Don't worry. It's always difficult to adapt', I said encouragingly, not liking to explain that she came from a backward area where the standard was low compared to other places. She and Esther both did very well indeed eventually and became secondary school teachers.

I was able to discuss her problem and education generally over dinner that evening with Mrs Baldwin and her husband. A mechanic by trade, he kept the mission transport in order, ran a canteen for the mission workers and supervised the store. The next day she took me round the primary and secondary schools. They seemed better funded than the schools belonging to other missions. The buildings were solid and the classrooms were quite well equipped with books, stationery and educational pictures on the walls supplied by Mr Grimley, the art teacher. Combining artistic creativity and technical skill he had carved a beautiful rack for maps and posters and was also responsible for duplicating time tables for the staff and other related tasks. Furthermore the students each had a garden where they grew corn, beans, groundnuts, and tomatoes and were taught how to cook them in different ways.

This self sufficiency spread to the homes. The CBM wives made their own clothes, baked their own bread, cakes, lime juice and jams. I was invited out for each meal and revelled in their homely hospitality. Single missionaries were automatically housed with married couples so the problems of living alone never arose, I was reminded of films about the first settlers in the mid west where the wives had to turn their hands to everything. Their calm, cheerful acceptance of life was most inspiring. The workers in the leprosarium had the same attitude even though they saw some pretty dreadful cases in the hospital wards. Except that the beds were partitioned into wards of four, it was similar to the one I had seen out East with Mojekwu and the leper villages looked like any other village.

The language problem as such hardly existed. The gospel had been translated into Bura which was spoken throughout the province. This, and the fact that most of the missionaries stayed put on their station ensured continuity. 'The CBM provided some of the best schools in the province', Grisell reported and a high proportion of the pupils went on to hold senior positions in the Nigerian government service.

I left Garkida with Agatu full of new ideas and schemes for joint sports matches and half terms together. We were delayed three times on the way home; by the rain, by engine trouble and by Fadimatu who had gone into hiding when we sent for her and needed to be ferreted out. This delay meant we missed the last ferry and had to take a canoe across the river, waiting another hour until someone came to fetch us on the other side. On the following two weekends Mary and I had our own half-term holidays. She spent hers in Kano with her boy-friend Eric, who worked at G. B. Ollivant, and came back engaged. I went to Gombe to see Jack, braving the ferry in my own car, not to mention The Thirty Nine Steps. I had written to him explaining my non-appearance in January and he had replied, urging me to visit him as soon as possible. Our letters often went first to Jos post office, 80 miles in the wrong direction, where they hung about a few days before they were forwarded. Adopting the only feasible solution, we waited until we found someone travelling to Gombe or to Yola and asked them to deliver our letters personally.

Jack was a warm, generous man who loved giving presents, hence the ghastly African pictures. Considering the postal situation and the dearth of any suitable gift in a bush town like Gombe, most men would not have bothered. Not Jack. He sent more African paintings; crate after crate of fizzy drinks from the L & K bottling factory in Kano; and two dozen tinned Christmas puddings, which no one really fancied in the heat of Africa.

He was ready with more presents when I arrived for half-term: a coarse cotton rug and two coloured enamel bowls from his canteen. Under his supervision, Musa had polished and cleaned every corner of the house. Knowing my sweet tooth, Jack had paid the Rest House cook to send over special desserts. We had a wonderful time together and our friendship went from strength to strength. Impatiently we started thinking about our next meeting. Jack was planning to open up an L & K branch in Yola and needed to discuss the idea with the Resident first. I could expect him in the very near future.

Once again, fate stepped in to thwart our plans. The Manager of the Hides & Skins Dept. in Maiduguri had to return to London urgently soon after this weekend and Jack was dispatched North to replace him. He had worked there before and enjoyed the better facilities it had to offer, including a good air mail service. The skins — goat, cattle and crocodile — were sold according to length. Some unscrupulous traders insisted they were longer than they were. Jack had a ruler made to counter this in order to be able to negotiate a purchase at the true measurement.

He wrote me requesting a paper pattern of my feet so that he could have a pair of crocodile sandals made up. These were duly despatched in a lorry going to Yola, together with a big, bulky mystery gift corded up in sacking. Shades of Cinderella, the left sandal was too small and the right was enormous! I was very disappointed because shoes, bags, gloves and handbags made of properly treated crocodile leather were luxury items in Europe and America. Jack dealt mainly with the Surpass Leather Company of the USA, and they were so impressed with his business acumen they asked him to work for them, naming his own salary. Jack refused, he had more scope in L & K, running established canteens, building new ones, buying groundnuts, cotton and other local products and setting up petrol pumps all over the province. Lucky he did. A few years later the bottom dropped out of the crocodile market and Surpass collapsed.

As for the mystery gift, it was the skin of a fully grown lion, given to Jack by a grateful trader. The tanner it seemed had not waited for the animal to die, it stank to high heaven and was spattered with blood stains. I was too fond of Jack to throw it away. Kept in sacking at the back of the house it was unpacked and laid on the front verandah whenever he came to Yola.

He was still in Maiduguri on my birthday on July 28th. Pawa came back from the post office empty-handed. I cheered up when a Government messenger, sent by Peggy Watts, arrived during breakfast carrying a heavy carton. Last time I had visited Leith and herself she had explained that his senior position entailed considerable entertainment and shown me her store as proof. Tins and tins of provisions lined every single shelf and gigantic jars of Nescafe stood cheek by jowl on the top like sentinels on guard.

My box was firmly sealed with this note on top: 'Happy birthday, Jean. I thought the enclosed would be useful'. Without waiting for Jongera to bring a knife, I tore the lid off myself, salivating like a starving tiger. A typed note this time lay on top of the contents: EMPTY TINS AND BOTTLES FOR SAMPLES OF URINE AND STOOL: GIRLS' SCHOOL, FOR THE USE OF. Compliments — Peggy Watts.

At the end of a very gloomy day, Messenger Pawa brought me a telegram posted from Maiduguri. It said:

'TOUTESMESPENSEESSENVOLENTENVERSTOICHERIEJOYEUXANNIVERSAIRE JACK'.

This I eventually deciphered: 'Toutes mes pensées s'envolent envers toi, chérie. Joyeux anniversaire. Jack'. (All my thoughts fly towards you, darling. Happy birthday). To make his message more intimate Jack had asked a French friend to write it for him and it was the post office clerk who, not understanding it, had omitted all punctuation.

My leave in late August meant more separation. My parents liked the sound of Jack and so did the Dreyfus relatives in Paris and the grandparents in Basle. Jack wrote lovingly to me, enclosed a cheque for theatre tickets and asked me to phone his mother and sister Doris in Liverpool. Doris did most of the talking and her mother, who was rather deaf, chimed in with a request to Jack to write home. 'We have not heard from him since Christmas'.

I told him off personally when we finally got together in Jos. I left the UK early in order to snatch a few days with Jack, staying with Rina MacDevitt as usual. I was very disappointed when he turned up with his Assistant, Peter Canelle and told me the three of us had to spend the evening with the new Managing Director, Brigadier Joseph Patrick O'Brien Twohig CBE, DS. He was en route from Kano to Maiduguri where he needed to investigate a small matter of eight thousand pounds fiddled away by the firm's clerk and the Native Authority. Actually, the only daunting thing about the brigadier was his title. Gallant, with a black moustache curling up each cheek, he was the epitome of charm, generous, fun loving and ever ready to have a good time. We started with dinner at his hotel, washed down by pink vinegary wine. After coffee we played liar dice. Jack and the brigadier were past masters of the game and I was right out of it. Then happily mellowed, we got into the huge company limousine and went off to 'The Midnight Night Club'.

This was a very fancy name for a large grubby room with a curtain serving as a door. A few scruffy Africans and gin-sozzled white men hung about eyeing a gaggle of prostitutes standing forlornly by the bar. Strangely enough the brash music playing from a record player and a hearty welcome from the club owner gave the place a certain atmosphere. A cheerful, curvacious girl from Calabar served us with drinks, and invitational winks in equal measure. When she suggested we, 'go upstairs, it is very decent', the men refused. Undeterred, she handed the Brigadier a card saying:

COME AND EAT AT OUR FINE FINE RESTAURANT UPSTAIRS WHERE CHOP BE VERY VERY DECENT. SPECIAL MENU: LETTUCE CHICKEN AND CUSTARD.

After an hour of this we went on to a European Club where we played liar dice again and had a lot more to drink. All quite amusing for a change and I did my best to say the right thing to the Brigadier who, I was glad to see, thought very highly of Jack. It was past midnight when I got back to Rina's flat, flushed and typsy and her presbyterian soul did not make her think highly of me!

The next day Jack, Peter and I returned to Gombe in the L & K land rover. Another party took place at the Crzywon's house on the Saturday where we played mad card games and giggled our heads off. What with people dropping in Sunday morning and Jack having work to do in his office in the afternoon, the two of us were not alone until the evening. Jack was delighted with the presents I had brought him from London: the autobiography of Neville Cardus and a Czechoslovakian beer mug and we talked for hours. I told him off about not writing to his mother and a letter was written immediately.

This time I received a warm welcome from John and Grisell in Yola. Jongera had cleaned the house especially and the PWD had erected a lightning conductor on the roof. I gave Bage and the labourers a red, Swiss Canton cap, bought in Basle and they were as pleased as punch. If I ever had a twinge of homesickness, the sight of them wearing these as they went about their work used to cheer me up. Dr Geary had given the school a good report when she came for Prize Giving at the end of the previous term. 'You have done well under difficult circumstances', she wrote. 'I suggest you start to think about an official Open Day towards Christmas.' No one argued with Dr Geary. It was fixed for November 26th.

Putting thoughts of Jack behind me, I concentrated on preparing for it and every soul on the hill from Fanta Yebbi, the smallest girl in the lowest class to Mary the most senior teacher, was not allowed to think of anything else. Pressured by the Resident, Sid Cole did all the little jobs on the school compound which had hung fire for months. His men also built a platform at one end of the netball court for the main speakers on Open Day, flattening a square of ground in front of it.

Mary prepared an exhibition in two classrooms showing the children's text and exercise books; produce from the garden; scrapbooks and a photo album about their life in the school, on the playing field and in the dormitory compound. She put samples of the girls' craft-work and sewing on a stall near the window and Mamadaso was drilled beforehand to sit by it, actually weaving. This, Mary argued, would serve two purposes. Her beauty would be an added attraction and having to sit still would prevent her from chasing after the male visitors. Doreen Rothera came up to help arrange a display in the dispensary; Agatu's class constructed two models in plasticine. One showed the Benue flowing through the Verre Hills and the other (her idea) reconstructed a plantation in the deep South of America with slaves toiling in the cotton fields and cruel white overseers standing over them with sticks. The entertainment, a mixture of Nigerian and British songs, dances, recitations and playlet was in my hands.

Dr Geary flew into Yola on the Monday plane; and by November 25th everything was ready. She had decided to stay with me to be near the school and proved an unexpectedly friendly guest. Even so, I never called her anything but Dr Geary. We had dinner that night with the new Resident — John Purdie, Grisell, John and the Turaki. He was too shy and I was too exhausted with preparations to say anything. It did not matter, the others had plenty to say on education and similar worthy topics.

The next day I was up at 6.30 a.m. to make sure the labourers had cleared the compound of groundnut shells, orange skins and threads of cotton. Quite unnecessary. It was clean and neat everywhere and Bage's men were in the playing field placing rows of chairs in front of the speaker's platform. After reminding them to leave room in the centre for the entertainment, I went over to the dormitory compound. The children were up early too, spruce and smart in their clean uniforms. In spite of the matron's orders to stay in their bedrooms, they kept darting in and out like rabbits in their burrows.

I rejoined Dr Geary in the house. She looked extremely smart in a light grey ensemble and a pink hat. I hastily donned my best orange linen dress with four large buttons down the front and was putting on my white hat when Sid Cole arrived to pick up a cine camera lent by Peter Swire. We had previously prepared credits for the beginning and end and everything was ready for him: camera, light meter, and tripod. He went over to the playing field to set it up, only to return five minutes later. Might he have a film to put inside the camera? as we could not oblige, he drove quickly to Jimeta to find one.

A few people were beginning to arrive as Dr Geary and I strolled over to the playing field. The Lamido, the guest of honour, with his entourage joined us. Next in rank came various local dignitaries. We greeted Mallam Ahmadu Ribadu and the Turaki. Then there was Mallam Sidi and a wife or two, Mallam Lepatel from the boys' school and several Nigerian chiefs who supported the school. Other Nigerian friends and officials had been invited by the Resident. Mallam Nimfas had come up from Numan and so had my good friend Phoebe from the girls' school. Her missionary colleagues from Yola, Mr and Mrs Jenssen and a somewhat nervous Mr Jorgensen were standing with her. Apart from John and Grisell, members of the Education Department had come from near and far: Don David from the Middle School: Ralph Wingfield and Patrick Bridgewater from Mubi training college; Jack Spicer from Bauchi, and Margaret Burness, the Inspector of Schools, from Kaduna.

I was particularly pleased by the presence of Dr Jim, Doreen Rothera, Monsignor D'Alton, Mother Magdalene, Leith and Peggy Watts, Pam and Peter Swires and their good friend, Howell Davies, a tsetse fly officer. He was more interested in Grisell than the event but who cared? It was gratifying to be in a position to thank them publicly after all they had done for APGS. As usual the robes worn by the Nigerian guests were a rainbow feast of colour. The well-cut suits and sunday-best outfits of the European guests paled in comparison. As for Agatu, I had made her a lovely mauve dress for the occasion in real cotton bought from England. Even the cooks had been given special uniforms in khaki and green.

Dr Geary, the Resident and the Lamido took their seats in the centre of the platform with the Turaki, the Chief of Numan, Grisell, John and myself on either side. Everyone else sat round the square and the school children were sitting on the ground in front. The function began with two speeches, one from the Resident, one from Dr Geary. Both were clear and complimentary to the school. The Resident translated his own into Hausa pronouncing it exactly as he spoke English. A Hausa clerk translated Dr Geary's. It was now my turn to speak. I stood up waving aside the translator and, much to the delight of the Nigerians in the audience, introduced the children in Hausa.

The entertainment followed with the children themselves announcing the different items in Hausa, Fulani or English as required. Gone was the terrible shyness and hesitancy they had shown during the rehearsals. They flung themselves whole heartedly into their parts when they were acting a sketch and stood up as straight as guardsmen for the songs and poems. As a finale the girls lined up in front of the platform, facing the audience and proceeded to give an ear-splitting rendition of the school chant, Only the Best. Finally the whole school stood in single file, bowed to the people on the platform, then marched off to the tune of 'We don't want to march with the cavalry' (which everyone pronounced as calvary).

I had got the girls to write the chant themselves and they were very proud of it. They sang it in groups of twos and threes, with the whole school joining in for the final chorus.

'ONLY THE BEST'

Only the brightest students,
Only the cleanest compound,
Only the fastest runners,
Only the healthiest students,
Only the loveliest gardens,
Only the neatest school-work,
Only the politest pupils,
Only the tidiest dormitories,
        ONLY THE BEST,
        ONLY THE BEST!

Before the guests dispersed to stroll round the school and look at the exhibition, Dr Geary, in true prize giving tradition, declared the next day a holiday.

This, and the success of the day, made the girls very happy and they remained so till the end of term. With the girls contented, we teachers could now relax, which meant turning our thoughts to love! Mary's engagement had fizzled out and the meeting with Patrick Bridgewater on Opening Day rekindled an old flame. Grisell and Howell did their courting over joint photography sessions together. It goes without saying, Jack and I continued to correspond. We did meet twice before Christmas. The first time he was accompanied by Henry Conroy, the General Manager from Kano, a short, shrewd, wart-faced Liverpudlian whose conversation consisted of memories of his early days in L & K, and very silly jokes such as: 'Did you hear about the two strawberries. One said to the other: If we had not been in that bed together, we would never have found ourselves in this jam now!'

The two of them were together from start to finish. On the plus side, he seemed fond of Jack and told me to look him and his wife up if I ever came to London.

The second time Jack came alone but spent more time with John Purdie than with me, discussing the possibility of a new branch of L & K in Yola. Yola was such a hotbed of gossip I did not want anyone to know about this friendship with Jack and they might not have done, had he not fallen off Jongera's bicycle on the last day, when he got back to the Rest House at 3 o'clock in the morning! The noise made as he crashed to the ground and the volley of military swear words woke up the steward boys. They knew that Jongera worked for me and broadcast the news all over Yola.

Jongera was also in love. His first wife had been barren, which was a good reason for marrying again. He found a young girl of fourteen, got her father to agree to the marriage and sent him in advance 23 sacks of grain, six cloths and a calabash full of kola nuts. His first wife was furious and Jongera asked me to persuade her to stay. When she refused he sent her back to his native village. From then on Jongera started to save up in earnest. When the girl's father saw he wanted to marry her quickly, he increased the bride price, which Jongera borrowed from me paying it back in instalments. After paying the final instalment he fixed the date.

One evening, a rather dull staff meeting taking place in my office was interrupted by the sound of loud cries, wailing and shouting. It was the family of the bride coming up the drive after the marriage. The girl's mother was in front, followed by her sisters and female relatives; each carrying a box on her head containing the belongings of the wife to be. They were singing songs, dancing and waddling their hips as they passed the office and proceeded to Jongera's small house at the back of mine, without dropping a single box. Feasting and celebrations went on for the whole evening and so did desperate messages from Jongera to me. 'Could Uwargida (Mother of the house) spare, a bottle of Krola, a packet of cigarettes. etc.'

The fun continued throughout the next day, both in and near his house and in the girl's village nearby. If a moment's silence fell, some of the female relatives would start howling, as if they were mourning, not rejoicing. In the evening as the sun was setting Jongera and I went to fetch the bride in my car. A pretty little girl, looking much younger than fourteen, came out of the hut, dressed in a bright blue cloth with her head veiled in white. She cried and struggled as her mother and aunt put her in the car. I had to be firm about the number of women going with her. At least fifty seemed to think it was their right.

She cried until they were out of sight of her house, she cried until her mother nudged her and told her no one could hear. Then she switched off, like a bad wireless programme. Mother nudged her again as they neared the school, and the tears were switched on again for the benefit of the new husband. He must realise she was leaving a good home.

On went the dancing throughout the night. The next morning Jongera asked me to call on his new wife. He did not go with me. Womens' meetings are to be avoided. I found the little girl, dipping her hands and feet into Henna dye to stain them red. She was too well mannered to do anything but greet me, and would not look me in the face. She told her sister to give me a raffia mat. She was proud of the bright enamel bowls piled up one on top of each other against the walls, and prouder still of a crooked, red bookshelf nailed high up, also full of bowls. Cloths and raffia mats were hung up too instead of pictures. I thanked and praised, praised and thanked, pressed a bag of shillings into her hand and took my leave.

I counted the days till I visited my loved one, Jack, in Gombe. We had a wonderful Christmas together and on New Year's Day he proposed marriage. He and I wrote to my relatives in London and his relatives in Liverpool. Knowing that engagements made by tropical moonlight and followed by marriage in Nigeria often came to nought, we decided to say nothing to anyone in Nigeria for the time being. He managed to find reasons to come to Yola a couple of times on business but his work prevented him from doing more. The week before I returned home he took two days off to come to see me staying in the Rest House as usual. He came to dinner the first evening and we discussed plans for the wedding in the UK. It was magical, marvellous, dreamlike and for me the saying 'Floating on Air' became a reality.

He came up for breakfast the following morning. We were gazing into each other's eyes over the scrambled eggs when we heard loud shouting coming from the direction of the dormitory compound. We could see flames shooting up through what appeared to be the roof of Hadija's house. I rushed over there, with Jack in tow, somewhat breathless as he was rather heavily built and trying to keep up with me. I went first to the office to collect the hydrant which I thrust into Jack's arms, saying, 'Follow me quick, quick'.

At this point, the girls, who had been changing into their uniforms when all this happened, were so scared they rushed out of the gates, semi-naked, to get away from the fire, screaming hysterically. Remembering my first aid lectures at Girl Guides, I started to slap everybody's faces to bring them to their senses. This achieved, I shouted to Jack to follow me quickly to Hadija's house. Here we found the cooking pot on the fire outside her house blazing and just about to ignite the walls. Seeing Jack messing about with the hydrant, which he had never used before I shouted to him, 'Don't bloody well stand there, put it on the fire'. The poor man was so terrified he opened it and sprayed Hadija, me, cooking pot and himself with the foam which did the trick.

We returned to our breakfast. I tried in vain to recreate a lovy dovey atmosphere, but it was not easy and we continued the meal without talking. A shout from the compound broke this silence. Back we ran to find a lorry drawn up in front of Hadija's house. A load of policemen, carrying truncheons, had been summoned by Pawa and were piling out of the back of the lorry like Keystone Cops. They had nothing to do except thrash kettles, saucepans, stools and everything in sight with their truncheons. Admittedly they did not touch the girls, but they ran purposely around the compound and were almost impossible to move as they were enjoying the sight of so many semi-nude, teenage girls, the Nigerian equivalent of the Folies Bergères. My patience was exhausted and I shouted, 'Get out of here. You have done the job. I give you three minutes to get out.'

It says a lot for Jack's devotion to me that he remained as devoted as ever despite my performance and our marriage took place on 29 June 1957.

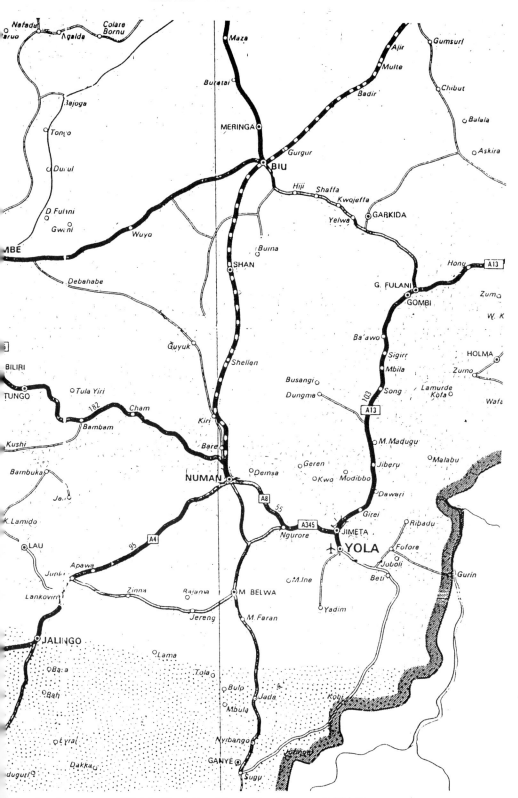

Map showing area round Yola in North East Nigeria (then known as British Cameroons)

37. Author's gardener, Baba.

38. Author & Russel Gardner in Jalingo.

39. Ostriches at Damatu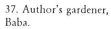

40. The ferry man crosse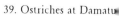 the Benue River.

41. Bob-a-job boy scouts washing author's car.

42. Waiting for the ferry

43. Women washing in ⬛ Benue River.

44. Author with husban⬛ to-be, Jack Evans.

45. Author with Matron Hadija and Hajara her assistant.

46. Nomadic Fulani women by the river in Numan.

7. Author by Kano swimming   48. Fulani men in Numan.
ɔol.

9. 50. Examples of Nigerian Art.

51. Opening Ceremony.

52. The girls listen.

53. The girls entertain the guests.

54. Some of the visitors.

55. Headmistress's final speech.

56. Demonstration game of netball.

57. Seeing over the school.

59, 60. Jack's social life.

. Jack attending a local market.

KANO POLO CLUB

SATURDAY MARCH 3rd, 1951

PATRON

B. E. Sharwood-Smith Esq C.M.G., E.D

GRANDSTAND **5/-**

RACING 3.00
TOTE—SWEEP OPEN 2.30

KANO POLO CLUB RACE MEETING
3rd March, 1951.

PATRON
Mr. B. E. Sharwood-Smith C.M.G., E.D.
Resident, Kano Province.

VICE-PATRONS
Mr. F. P. Mackenzie O.B.E.,   Mr. S. Raccah,
Mr. V. Aouad,   Mr. S. Noujaim, Mr. Akle

STEWARDS
Messrs L. E. T. Evans, Fradet, Boudet, J. Minaise,
D. A. Pott and Lt. Col. A. W. Martin.

JUDGES
Messrs A. H. Barr, G. G. Elgar, J. Holiday,
J. Vaughn-Williams and M. Jazzar.

HANDICAPPER Mr. A. H. Barr	**STARTER** Mr. Brouin
TIME KEEPER Mr. Rex Raccah	**Clerk of the Scales** Mr. Funsho
Clerks of the Paddock Messrs M. Mettenden & M. Buckman	**Organiser of the Tote** Mr. Walwyn Lott
Organiser of the Sweepstake Mr. J. Motion	**Organiser of the Runners' Board** Mr. Kwanashie
Hon. Medical Officer Dr. H. C. Weir	**Hon. Veterinary Officer** Mr. R. Coulthard
Organiser of the Gate Mr. J. Evans	**Race Secretaries** Messrs F. Dearden & V. Aouad

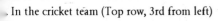

. In the cricket team (Top row, 3rd from left)

62. The L & K vehicle – trouble as usual!

Part four — *Life as a wife*

Chapter twenty-two
Life as a wife

Engagements by the light of the tropical moon, followed by a wedding in Nigeria sometimes came unstuck once the couple returned to the UK. Too often people looked and behaved differently once they were back home and the respective families did not always approve. Determined this should not happen to us, Jack and I conscientiously visited as many relatives as possible in Liverpool, Wales, London and France before fixing the date of the wedding for 29 June 1957. Elsie and Gladys, my sisters-in-law took over from there. We got married in the Congregationalist Chapel which they attended, and the reception took place in the grounds of Greystoke Nursing Home, Aigburth, which Gladys, who had worked for years as a hospital sister, ran with the aid of another retired nurse known as KC. Frank, Gladys' husband, spent his spare time working in the extensive grounds surrounding Greystoke. His energy was unlimited. Thanks to his efforts, patients had new laid eggs and a constant supply of fresh vegetables. Arthur, Glad's lodger and an old police friend of Jack, was responsible for mowing the velvety, weedless lawns. Glad had converted the top of Greystoke into an enormous flat which easily absorbed John and Joan, her children, Frank, Arthur, KC and herself. Sister Elsie who managed the nursing home accounts, occupied an exquisite converted cottage in the grounds with her husband, Cliff and their two children, Keith and Bev.

Ritou, Paul Dreyfus's widow came from Paris to be my bridesmaid, accompanied by Dr Yvan Dreyfus. He had been sent to a public school when he was a boy and finished off in Oxford. He was very impressed, therefore, by the smoothness of the lawns and the brilliant flowers of Greystoke. We saw him a week later in Paris where we spent the honeymoon. Emma, his wife, gave a big family party and plied Jack with roast beef which her cook had prepared specially for him. It was quite superb, and became, irritatingly, Jack's criterion for the rest of our married lives. 'This beef was good, dear', he'd say, 'but nothing like the roast we had on our honeymoon'.

We had planned on staying in a hotel but Ritou insisted on putting us up. Since he did not speak a word of French, Jack was in no position to argue. This did not stop the loquacious Ritou from speaking to him throughout the day. Even she, however, could not join us in the roomy bedroom with its inviting looking single beds, tactfully placed side by side. The first night, we went to bed early. Jack put out an amorous arm. Woosh! The beds were on castors and mine sped across the room. His did the same when I leant towards him. After seven 'nuits blanches', we left Paris for Rottingdean. The minute Jack placed his overnight bag on the bed, it broke! Back home in Putney, we hoped for better things, especially as my parents had insisted we sleep in their room in their double bed. Unfortunately, Dad had started to be very absent minded in his old age, and very restless during the night. Each time he got up for tea or toilet, he returned to his own bedroom!

With no home of our own then, we were glad when the time came to return to Nigeria as a married couple. Anxious to improve Jack's prospects, the Brigadier had posted him to Kano where we lived in greater comfort than either of us had known before in Nigeria. L & K paid for the servants, the furnishing of our fine one-storey house and the upkeep of the lush garden surrounding it. The district resembled a garden suburb with houses set in their own compounds lying alongside each other but concealed by their hedges and trees. We had a telephone in our home, extensive shopping facilities, and three commercial cinemas which we sometimes patronised. Occasionally too, we had a meal out at the airport to celebrate something special, or as a guest of Cassim, one of Jack's traders. We hardly went to the club at all as we seemed to have quite enough social life already. Nor did we ever mind evenings alone. We would chat for hours, or play canasta or scrabble together.

We had quiet dinner parties with the L & K people who lived close by: Vernon Broad (Commercial Manager) and his wife Jessie, Basil Day (Accountant) and his wife, Edith, and Al and Kay Newlands from the L & K drinks factory. Jock Smith had been posted to Kano having completely recovered from his nervous breakdown in Yola. He and Peggy lived in police quarters and they established an immediate rapport with Jack. The four of us seemed to be laughing every time we were together. Other friends on tour from Adamawa and Gombe dropped in to visit or to say au revoir before flying home on leave. Even Mother Magdalene took time off to have tea with us before catching the plane back to Ireland. She was delighted to hear that I was pregnant and made me promise to let her know the moment the baby arrived.

Jack's old friend, Father Carroll from Gombe had persuaded his sister Betty to sell up the family home in Ireland after the death of her parents and to come and teach at St Louis Convent School for Girls, Kano. A chatty, gregarious lady, she missed the company of relatives and friends in Ireland and adopted us as her 'family'. We were invited to school functions and tea with the sisters who could not have been kinder. Father Carrol would visit us when he could, always with three or more fathers in train. I never knew how many I was expected to feed until they arrived. I managed somehow and we had many a riotous evening together, eating well, drinking hugely and sometimes playing Monopoly, liar dice, and even poker! Father Begley had also moved from Gombe to Biliri, a mission in the Bush and came to Kano quite often for supplies. I found him very easy to relate to, both as priest and human being and we discussed everything together, including the tenets of the Catholic faith. In hindsight, I think it was probably these talks with him which started me thinking about joining the Church of Rome.

I found plenty to do on my own at home when Jack was at work. I would make curtains on a second hand machine he had bought from a friend, experiment with cooking, type endless letters home to our parents and our friends or call occasionally on my Swiss neighbour, Sophie Luthi. It was also a joy to have time to write. 'The

Lady' magazine in London took a few articles on Nigerian life, some Nigerian magazines published my short stories and NBC Lagos broadcast the first of a series of tales about an incorrigible pair of rogues called the Pongi and Mr Tutu. Jack rang every morning from the office to let me know who had written or just to have a chat. Mother sent a weekly letter to all three daughters. To us in Kano, to LiLian, Roman and baby Blanche in South Africa and to Marion, Hugh and son Ian in Australia. As soon as she heard I was pregnant, she sent something for the layette. Most European wives within reach of Kaduna or Kano preferred to go to the well equipped hospitals there to have their babies, so Jack and I were happy to be on the spot.

On March 29th I gave birth to a bonny baby girl of 8lb 8oz whom we called Alice. Her surprisingly pretty appearance and the fact that she had arrived without complications filled Jack and myself with enormous joy. Quite a feat since we were both over thirty five and the only other new mother in the ward was fifteen! Except for the usual problem of breast feeding a new baby, all was fine. Jack stayed till 10 p.m. on 4 April. It was terribly, terribly hot and before leaving he asked the nurse to give the baby plenty of water. I slept well myself and woke at 7 a.m. to find him sitting beside me sobbing. He had been called out at 6 o'clock because the nurse had found the baby dead. The post mortem said it was encephalitis. It was best to accept this verdict rather than raise the question of neglect. Since the parents had received our air letter a day after the birth, the message that she had died, given by an air stewardess, arrived less than a day later.

Our friends rallied round and even the Brigadier and the Conroys who were usually at daggers drawn with each other, buried the hatchet and came over to comfort us. A retired missionary called Doctor Bargery took the service in Kano Cemetery. His simple, direct address touched our hearts so much we asked him over for dinner and became good friends. I have never seen a man eat so much and with such enthusiasm. His simplicity concealed great scholarship. He had compiled 'The Hausa Dictionary', which became the definitive dictionary of the Hausa language and is still used extensively. He was a spry seventy when we met him and still hard at work, preparing a Hausa version of the Bible.

He had come to Nigeria in 1900 and remembered the days when he had to hire donkeys to carry his loads from Lagos to Kaduna and pay for them in cowries brought from Mozambique. He was often short of food and drugs when living in the bush. Once he had saved the life of a fellow missionary, Luke Fisher, who had gone down with malaria. It took his assistant two days to fetch quinine from the nearest dispensary and the man would have died if Bargery had not kept him constantly immersed in water to reduce the fever.

We were not alone in losing a child. Peggy Watts too had lost a baby girl who had been suffering from minor ailments. These had been aggravated by such appalling heat and humidity that Leith and Peggy started to make arrangements to fly her to Kano. Poor wee thing died before the plane arrived. Martin Maconachie, another District Officer we knew, lost an infant son through gastro-enteritis and a measure of medical incompetence. His wife contracted a particularly vicious virus in Lagos which damaged her kidneys and contributed to her death in her early sixties.

Although Nigeria was no longer the white man's grave it was certainly less healthy than the United Kingdom. Jack had intermittent bouts of malaria there and for many years after he came home. Grisell suffered from amoebic dysentery most of the time she was in Yola. In outlying districts with no medical facilities it was inadvisable to have young children.

Realising Jack's potential as an administrator was not being used to the full in Kano, the Brigadier promoted him to Area Manager in Gusau (where I had spent my local leave). This could not have come at a better time and we had no regrets about leaving the garden city life behind and starting afresh in a new and smaller town.

From the outside, the house in Gusau looked like a small shooting lodge. Made of local stone it stood in a spacious, tree filled, compound with a wide drive leading up to the front porch. Henry Conroy had been responsible for its design fifteen years earlier and his capable little Scottish wife, Winnie, had helped to lay out the flower beds and the hedges. Subsequent tenants had changed the flowers but I kept finding roots of old ones which were still transplantable. I sent word to my sister Lilian in Capetown to send packets of vegetable and flower seeds from Kirchoffs. In one corner we made a badminton court and often held badminton tea parties, sitting out under a baobab tree surrounded by saucer size zinnias, thanks to Kirchoffs. Our guests enjoyed the home-made cakes I made and the relaxed 'country house atmosphere' until a snake dropped from a branch into my Dresden sugar bowl one afternoon!

After that, tea was taken indoors in the sitting room, or in the adjoining dining room according to the number of guests. Arches, not doors, linked these two rooms and led into my office and a front room. Windows abounded, latticed with expanded metal. The china steins stood colourfully bright on the mantlepiece in the lounge whilst the pewter and silver mugs gleamed on the pelmets of the windows. The Harmattan breeze made it just cold enough over Christmas to light a fire and I did so once. Never the best of housekeepers I forgot to have the chimney swept first. Result: all four rooms had to be repainted. Jack bought an electric fire and forbade me to try again.

God was kind and within the next three years I gave birth to two sons, John and Richard. We had four servants working for us and like most Nigerian servants they were exceptionally kind and patient with expatriate children. The cook-steward Momon Daya (number one) cleaned the house, delegating the harder jobs to the small boy, Momon Biu (number two). The term 'small boy' referred to his position, not to his size. A 'small boy' could be taller than anyone else in the establishment. It was often used contemptuously in common speech, meaning someone who would never get very far. Umaru, the watchnight, certainly did not. He stayed in one place from dawn to dusk, asleep under the bougainvillaea bush near the house.

By contrast, Abdullah, the gardener worked like a beaver. I gave the suggestions, he carried them out with enthusiasm, adding several more of his own. A man of habit, he did the watering every evening from 5 to 6 p.m. — even when it was raining — he grew onions, tomatoes almost as big as pumpkins, peppers, string beans, radishes, herbs and lettuce in the vegetable garden, had his personal allotment and cut down many trees to let in light at the back where the garden seemed to go on and on. To add a little colour there, we planted yellow flowered gamboge bushes which flourished happily like everything else in that fertile compound.

What I did not know was that gamboge was the favourite food of locusts. They swarmed all over the compounds in the GRA one year going from garden to garden, then flying off, leaving the gamboge hedges completely bare. They did not fill the sky like I'd seen on the cinema but the noise of their chomping the flowers was decidedly eerie. They did not return during the rest of our seven year stay in Gusau and the gamboge recovered to bloom again. Our district officer friend, Martin Maconachie, tells his own locust story. 'When a plague of locusts landed in my district, I sent a telegram to the Resident on the standard approved form:

YOUNG PINK ADULT LOCUSTS ARRIVED FROM SOUTH EAST 1630 HOURS TODAY STOP LANDED ROUND BURMI VILLAGE AND STARTED FEEDING ON MAIZE CROPS STOP CLOUD COVERING AREA APPROX HALF MILE SQUARE STOP NOW COPULATING STOP

The reply came back
STOP COPULATING AND KILL THE LOCUSTS THE RESIDENT

The hot climate of North Nigeria tended to attract insects in swarms. We had been invaded by bees in Kano already and had a spate of black moths in Yola. For two weeks cocoons of moths covered the walkways of the school and the agricultural officer had warned against spraying them with disinfectant arguing that they would only settle somewhere more harmful. When they did hatch, they were ubiquitous. You had only to open a drawer or a cupboard, lift a cushion, unzip a purse, unbutton a blouse, put on a shoe, sit on the sofa, lift a plate, whatever, and woof, woof, woof, clusters of black moths would fly in your face. Ugh! The plagues never seemed to be the same in Gusau. One year it was little coloured beetles everywhere, another year it was gekkos, another stink beetles. Flying moths around any lamp were as constant as they had been in Ibadan.

Momon steward's calm attitude towards these plagues was very reassuring. Nothing daunted him, petty or grave. He was as practical as he was philosophical. He knew how and where to get a painter, a plumber, cobbler or a mechanic. He kept track of the stores, disciplined the servants, was unfailingly courteous and never raised his voice. He told us little about himself, knew about everyone and always professed intense surprise at our news, which he knew already. What is more, he was an excellent plain cook.

I had two kitchens. One was a reasonable room leading off the dining room with a store cupboard, a sink, a table and a Nidogas (calor gas) stove in it supplied by L & K to a few favoured customers. By concocting elaborate dishes in this kitchen I gained a reputation of being a super cook. To be truthful, I often left Momon to finish them off for me, which he did, sometimes in my cooker and sometimes in or on the smoky, wood-burning oven outside, where the floor was dirty and greasy. Momon also used this oven to bake the bread I had kneaded. When it came to roasting meat and potatoes, he swamped the lot with oil. Surprisingly enough, the result was perfection.

When the time came to lay the table for a dinner party, Momon changed into a whiter than white starched uniform. Gleaming crystal glasses, best silver cutlery and Dresden plates were laid geometrically, either side of lace mats on the polished table in the dining room. He was inordinately proud of his white linen serviettes which he fashioned into boats, fans or bishops' mitres according to his mood. As table decoration they would have done credit to The Ritz, as napkins they were useless since they were too stiffly starched to open.

In the Christmas season, party succeeded party for all the people in the GRA, and the Lebanese trader, Jamil Akkare and his Nigerian wife, Mary, whom I had met on my first visit to Gusau, also gave an enormous party. His compound, store and office were next to Jack's and the four of us became great friends. The men helped each other in business. As mother of five, Mary gave me sensible advice about bringing up babies and I repaid her by teaching French to her eldest daughter, Josephine. When she got engaged Mary asked me to buy the complete wedding outfit for her in UK during our leave.

'I do not want people (she meant the Lebanese community) to say that a Nigerian does not know how to dress her daughter.' She told me proudly 'Josephine must have the best'.

Dear Mary, she was admirable in every way, a perfect helpmate for Jamil, loving him, advising him, bearing child after child, cooking, dressmaking and running the house.

After our second Christmas, which had been more hectic than usual, Jack fell ill. Fred Hunter, the doctor in Gusau sent him to Kano for tests immediately. The results showed a delicate liver and Jack was told it was dangerous to continue heavy drinking. He turned teetotal immediately. It was a hard decision and more often than not we refused invitations to parties on a grand scale, making an exception when Jamil gave the party to end all parties for Josephine's wedding.

Since Jack was naturally gregarious we still kept open house to anyone passing through such as Bill Miller and Toby Kidd from Yola, or the Krzwyons from Jack's Gombe days. We played cards, gave dinner parties on a small scale or organised quiz evenings. These were particularly popular with the Dominican priests at the Catholic Mission, Father Nadeau, Father Farmer, Father Sharkey and others. Father Daley who was responsible at that time for the maintenance of the churches and the building of a new one in Funtua, preferred conversation over drinks and came up quite often. Once he joined us for the small Christmas lunch party we gave every year to a few good friends or anyone who was on their own and seemed lonely. We ate turkey, plum pudding and mince pies and played family games like forfeits or tongue twisting word puzzles. Because the meat on a Nigerian turkey was tough, Momon used to pour gin down its throat to soften the flesh. It was funny to see the poor fowl totter around drunk and we never thought of it as cruel. Friendly dashes (bribes) abounded in Gusau around Christmas — alcoholic drinks and materials from the Lebanese and Syrians and turkeys from the local traders. We practically paid people to take these birds off our hands, we had so many. Unlike the Admin department, Jack and his commercial colleagues had few scruples about accepting them.

There were a number of mothers with small children and, give or take, they got on well together. If a wife gave a big party, she knew she could borrow plates, or cutlery, or sugar or anything she was short of. If anyone went to Kano or Zaria or another big town, she automatically collected everyone's shopping list and returned laden with thread, Cow and Gate milk, baby shoes, cinnamon, slices of ham and other items. Quite often, they left their children with a friend whilst they were away. Gossip was rife, of course, and sometimes a couple of wives quarrelled with each other, especially during the hot season. Fortunately, differences were forgotten in a crisis such as sickness, pregnancy, and even death. People then vied with each other to go round to the person in need with offers of food, help, and accommodation for their children, where necessary.

Women being women, cliques tended to form without any special reason. Fortunately they did not apply their exclusiveness to the children and they were all invited when there was a birthday party or similar occasion. Someone would volunteer to make a cake in the shape of a bear, or train or golliwog according to request, and the garden would be hung with balloons. After a big tea of sausages, crisps, jelly and similar childish delights, we went outside to play games and sing nursery rhymes. Unfortunately the bookshop carried a very small stock of toys and the birthday child would end up with four boxes of the same game. In the rainy season the vivacious Jean Sadler, wife of Tony the manager of Barclay's Bank DC & O, and I combined talents to make, write, and act puppet plays to entertain the children in the house. In the dry season the children were able to meet at the swimming pool built in the club compound two years after our arrival. No one actually taught them to swim. They picked it up by themselves and most children were afloat by the time they were four.

The only snag about our lives was that we saw too much of each other. It was difficult to prevent this as we had nowhere else to go outside Gusau. There was not a lot of point taking the children for a drive when Jack returned from work as the scrub scenery round Gusau was the same in every direction. The only beauty spot for miles around was on the river at Bungudu ten miles away which was high on a bluff above the river with rocks covering the banks. We did have occasional picnics there sometimes but the children got tired of going to the same place.

Always resourceful, Jack created a 'treat' out of two very simple activities. The first was a visit to the one-horse railway station which had two lines, and infrequent trains. What made it different was the sacks of groundnuts piled up into pyramids which lay besides the rails waiting to be dispatched to Lagos. Jack had bought these nuts from the traders piecemeal and was responsible for bagging them up and transporting them to the station. He knew exactly how many fitted the base, how many was in the next row and so on till the apex was reached. L & K owned three bases which were highly prized. The august Pharaoh of Egypt inspecting the construction of his future tomb could not have been prouder than Jack watching his groundnut sacks rise day by day to form a pyramid.

When John and Richard tired of counting 'Ellen Kay' sacks (their pronunciation of L & K) they would take a walk past the other pyramids, hand in hand, counting other things: wheels, trees, birds, or what took their fancy. John, ruddy cheeked and fat as the man in the Michelin tyre advertisements, would 'teach' Richard the numbers clearly and loudly.

'One, two, three . . . . Richard, say it after me.'

Tadpole skinny Richard, whom everybody took to be a girl with his rosebud mouth, and soulful grey eyes framed by long, curling eyelashes, would dutifully repeat:

'Un, two, free . . . thix, theven . . . firteen, thixteen, theventeen . . .'.

If the driver of a train happened to be in the station, he would give the two of them a ride in the front seat up the lines. Left to himself, John would have sat as still as a stone. With Richard beside him he had to stop him touching everything he saw: the tender, the lever, and the hot coals feeding the engine. When we went for a drive in the Volkswagen beetle we used for local running, we plonked him in the space behind the back seat where John was sitting, in order to keep him out of trouble. He was rising three when we took him on leave and more of a menace than ever. Those enquiring fingers of his broke Gladys' TV in Liverpool and fused every light in 'Gwanny's' house in London. Scolded for these misdemeanours, he smiled his sweet smile and said, 'Wichie, wichie Evans didn't do that. Charly Brown did that'. This imaginary friend, Charly Brown, who was bigger than God and the owner of a fleet of racing cars, was so real to him, it took a long time to convince him that he himself was guilty. Moreover, his lisp lasted till he was in his teens.

Our second treat was a short drive through Gusua to Sabongari, the district where the Igbos and other Nigerians from the South lived in a completely different style from the Hausas. (I remembered visiting the Okonkwos in Kano's Sabongari.) We would leave the Northern style compounds behind and make our way through narrow streets avoiding pigs, goats, ducks, chickens, bicycles, the people, street vendors, and children. Small, ramshackle shops stood cheek by jowl, their shelves crowded with goods and spilling out on the ground in front. We could buy note-paper pads, pencils, Ovaltine, Vaseline, biscuits, bicycle tyres, zips, shoes, cotton cloth, material and many other articles appealing to the European taste.

The Grand Emporium stood on a corner opposite a leafy tree which was a pleasant, shady place for Nigerians from elsewhere to sit and talk. Mr Thompson, the owner, sold a few European clothes as well as everything else and he used to give Jack a special price, hoping that he would put business his way. After letting the two lads · choose a present each we led them out, sat them down next to one of these men whom we had never seen before, and told him to look after them whilst we returned to the shop to snoop around. We knew he would look after our sons and never had a moment's disquiet concerning their safety.

We found the same friendliness and trustworthiness in the outlying bush villages. If the journey was not too long and the weather cool Jack would sometimes take the three of us to a village where he had business to do. Once again I would leave the two boys with a strange man or woman sitting in the shade and go off with Jack, certain they would be all right. Alas, this happy certitude did not apply to the men who supplied Jack with cotton and groundnuts. The whole system of trading was cockeyed. The firms gave their managers money to buy the produce and it was up to them to find the suppliers. Jack, for instance, began in Gusau with a list of trustworthy people given him by Hep Walker, his predecessor. The majority of would-be buyers came to Jack's office in Gusau at the beginning of the season in order to tell him how much they would bring in once the crop had ripened. Enoch, the clerk, would note the amount in the ledger with their names and addresses. Michael, the cashier, would then pay them up front in shillings and they would sign their names or make a cross according to their literacy. Even though large amounts were at stake, no one asked for a reference of any sort. Anyone could come in and say I want to buy this and that for you. When Jack needed to find new buyers he had to use his finely tuned policeman's intuition to judge their reliability.

Quite a number of suppliers lived in villages and not everyone had transport. In this case Jack went to them in the L & K kitcar, with John the driver in front, Enoch and Michael at the back, sitting beside the shillings packed into strong wooden boxes. Glad to see a stranger, the villagers would crowd round the kitcar when it arrived. The driver, Michael and Enoch, would carry the money to a makeshift office in the house of the chief or village head whilst he and Jack had a drink on the stoop, then the same process repeated itself, a promise to bring in 'x' amount, a signature in the ledger and the handing over of the money agreed.

Mostly, the system worked. When it did not, it was big, big trouble. Someone might renege, someone could be short, or someone could disappear altogether. A lot of them had the same name, and their addresses might just be the name of a village. Jack used to take it to heart when this did happen. He and the driver would be hours driving along roads that were no more than tracks, enquiring for his debtors in remote, primitive villages. Although he was not always successful in his search and lost money thereby, his overall track record was excellent. During the seven years we were in Gusau he made more profit than any other commercial firm. L & K appreciated this and never blamed him for any business losses. A letter from the Brigadier in Kano reads:

May 31 1960

Dear Jack

I should like formally to put on record our congratulations on the satisfactory groundnut and cotton season in Gusau area.

The amount of hard work, firmness and tact required to finish the season with so clean a record is realised.

As a token of the Company's appreciation the Chief Accountant has been instructed to credit your account with £50.

Yours sincerely
J. P. O'Brien Twohig'

Other companies were less understanding. SCOA, one year, threatened to make their manager, Jean Pagnon, pay for the money owed out of his own pocket. Missing his wife who was looking after the new baby in France, and worried sick by his financial position, he committed suicide.

Gusau's position as a railway depot and large trade centre attracted a number of visitors from the North and South. In 1959, my good friend, Chief Ayo Rosiji phoned me from Sokoto during his federal election campaign in the North to tell me he was coming to Gusau in two days time. I invited him to dinner and after exchanging brief news of our respective families, we left it at that, expecting to meet. Unfortunately the organisers re-routed his tour and cut out Gusau so we never saw him.

We had better luck when Princess Alexandra and Zik visited Nigeria to celebrate its Independence.

Chapter twenty-three
Meetings and partings

> *The Sultan of Sokoto and the Emirs of Gwandu,*
> *Argungu and Yauri*
> *request the pleasure of the company of*
> *Mr and Mrs J Evans*
> *to have the honour to meet*
> *Her Royal Highness, The Princess Alexandra of Kent*
> *at the Sokoto Gardens on the 13th October, 1961*
> *1945-2100 hours.   RSVP to the Private Secretary to the Sultan*

These invitations were not handed out lightly. Jack was chosen to represent the commercial interests of Gusau and I was there, 'Because of your services to education'.

At that moment in time my thoughts centred entirely on two less serious matters. What were we going to wear and how should we behave in the presence of royalty? Doris, the engineer's wife in Gusau, had been stationed in Kaduna at the time of the Queen's visit and considered herself an expert on all things royal. Over coffee at our house, I asked for her advice.

'Jack should wear a dark suit, collar and tie, and I suggest you put on the smart green and blue two piece you wore for the Resident's cocktail party in Gusau last Easter', she said. 'That should be fine, provided you wear a hat and gloves with it. Oh, and don't forget to curtsy to the Princess when you are introduced. Not too deep, I'll show you how'.

Panic stations! I had neither hat nor gloves and there was no time to order them from London or Lagos. I asked all my friends in the GRA and drew a blank. Eventually, Mary Akkare, living on the Beach, saved the situation. She produced a presentable white straw hat and a tatty pair of fawn gloves, crocheted by her aunt who had died ten years back. I added a ribbon to the hat and took the gloves to Madeleine Luneau. She had worked in Paris for Carven, the famous dress designer and I had spent many a happy hour with her learning how to cut and make a new dress from scratch. She returned the next day with the gloves looking as good as new.

The next problem was accommodation in Sokoto. The catering rest house had been fully booked by journalists, the Princess's equerry, hairdresser and the rest of her staff. By a stroke of good luck, Tony Krzwyon, Jack's buddy from Gombe was stationed in Sokoto as Agriculture Officer and he phoned Jack the moment he heard of our invitation. 'Ja-ack, Ja-ack', he boomed in his loud, exuberant voice, 'You and the family must stay with us, Peggy insists on you all coming and she wants Jean and the children to come for a holiday beforehand'.

We accepted his offer at once and a week before the big event, Jack, who was up to his eyes buying cotton, arranged for his driver to take me and the boys up to Sokoto. He, Jack, would, in his words: 'Join you in Sokoto for the garden party, come hell or high water'.

Compared to our comfortable home in Kano and the air-conditioned bedrooms in Gusau the house where the Krzwyons lived came as a decided shock to my system. Over ten miles from Sokoto town itself, it stood on its own, overlooking endless scrubland, with no trees or high bushes to break the monotony. The weather was stultifyingly hot, day and night, and the thorn hedges planted round the entire compound seemed to entrap any breeze that was blowing outside. Lack of electricity meant hot Aladdin lamps for the bedrooms and one hotter Tilly lamp for the lounge cum dining room. Tony had a passion for horses and he was never without one, sometimes two. They were so expensive to keep, he did not always have enough money over for luxuries such as extra lamps or mosquito nets, which were full of holes.

John and Richard took all this in their stride and I did my best to adapt. The important thing was the welcome which could not have been warmer. Tony's job invariably meant living in the bush and Peggy accepted everything calmly. She used mainly local food and cooked a lot herself. She also made clothes for herself and the children and cut her own hair. Wherever she was and whatever she was doing she looked as if she had stepped out of a Vogue fashion magazine. What is more, she gave her children, Martyn (eight years) and Nina (five years) schooling every morning. I taught chatty Nina whilst I was there — when I could get a word in edgeways! They played happily with my boys in the afternoon, despite the age difference, and before supper in the evening the two families sat on the stoup outside listening to Tony singing and playing his guitar.

My hat and dress had to stay in the suitcase with the gloves in the small bedroom I occupied with the boys as the only furniture was a chest of drawers full of Nina's clothes. On the day of the garden party I laid them on the bed to uncrease them as I was scared to use the charcoal iron and Peggy's boy was too busy helping her prepare a special meal of welcome for Jack. He turned up about 5 p.m. giving us barely enough time to eat and get togged up for the party. This was not so easy as it sounds since, for the last two days, the kitchen tap was just trickling through and there was no water at all in the bathroom. Tony's driver had fetched two buckets from a brackish well during the day and when it was time for us to change, he poured this water into the bath for the four of us to use, one after the other. Emerging, refreshed if not clean, we went into our bedrooms to dress by the light of a bush lamp and took turns again to use the Tilly lamp in the sitting room to comb our hair. I remember frantically putting on lipstick in Jack's kitcar as it rattled over the dusty, bumpy road to the Sokoto Gardens.

What a contrast! I felt like Cinderella facing the glitter of the ballroom as I gazed at their magical beauty. Fairy lights lit up the trees and the paths were edged by little tins of light made from ground nut oil. We were led to our appointed place along the path, to await the coming of the Princess while a small Nigerian orchestra played jolly music. Over one hundred people had been invited to this gathering, Nigerian and Europeans, and every one was dressed to the nines. I recognised Monsignor Lawton and two women-education officers from Sokoto Girls' School, Mrs Clarke who was in charge and Agnes Wedmore (née Judd) my colleague in Ibadan Grammar School in 1953. A rumble of drums announced the arrival of Princess Alexandra. She was dressed simply but exquisitely in a silk floral dress and looked every inch a princess.

Accompanied by the Sardauna of Sokoto and a few other important dignitaries in the province, she walked along the paths stopping to talk to everyone. John Stephenson, (Steve to Jack and his other friends) was at her side to brief her. When it came to our turn, she asked if we both spoke Hausa, if Jack enjoyed trading and if I was still teaching. She could not have been more courteous or more interested. All the same, I was pleased the dimmish lighting prevented her from seeing our crumpled clothes. Funnily enough, Steve sent a picture of us at this meeting wherein we looked elegant and composed.

The following morning we were allowed to take the children with us to see the durbar. It was like a super sallah with horses charging and different troupes dancing their hearts out before the Princess. We were lucky to sit near her and shared her obvious appreciation of the stirring rhythm and complete absorption of the dancers as they gave their all to impress her. Suddenly, one particularly ferocious looking group, waving knives and spears started to jig towards the chair where the Princess was sitting, brandishing their weapons and shouting loudly. She continued to smile without showing a trace of fear. The audience fidgeted with apprehension until Bob Wedmore, in full dress uniform, approached them calmly and spoke to their leader. He nodded and led his fellow dancers away without demur. Bob told us later, that they had meant no harm. They just wanted to get nearer to this beautiful royal vision!

We went back to Sokoto the following year to see Monsignor Lawton enthroned as the first Catholic bishop in the Northern Region. This affair was equally impressive, not because it was full of pomp and solemnity but because it was not. The ceremony took place outside in the compound of the Catholic church. An altar covered with white, embroidered cloths had been erected in front of rows of wooden seats. The service was conducted in simple English, with a modicum of Latin. Apart from a sprinkling of special guests in the first row, none of the seats had been reserved. The people in the congregation came from every corner of Nigeria and held every different sort of belief. European bigwigs sat next to missionaries of various denominations; Non-Catholic Nigerians and Europeans prayed with a veritable host of Catholic fathers, acolytes, brothers and nuns. Had Monsignor D'Alton, Father Begley, Father Carroll and Father Nadeau not come up to greet us after the enthronement ceremony, we might have missed them in the sea of ecclesiastics.

Those who had been invited to a party to celebrate, including Jack and myself, gathered in the church hall. We sat at random at tables laid for eight, facing the platform supporting the high table reserved for the Bishop and his close friends —

Brother Martin, his vigilant companion, who made certain he did not overtax his weak heart by undue exertion, Father Nadeau and Father Farmer from Gusau and four fathers from Lagos and Sokoto. Finally, much to his joy the two sisters of Bishop Lawton had flown for the first time from Chicago, with another lady friend called Alice, to be with their brother in his hour of glory. Alice was an eccentric seventy year old who told us later: 'I wasn't goin' to miss this. I've travelled most places in this goddamned world and gee! I'd never bin to Nigeria'.

Considering the poor shopping facilities in both Gusau and Sokoto the Dominican sisters in Gusau had re-enacted the miracle of the loaves and fishes by producing an excellent meal for the assembly. They had cooked and prepared everything themselves, including the birthday cake and taken it all up to Sokoto the day before in the mission jeep. A passing lorry had caused it to swerve and land in a ditch. Sister Bernadette had sustained cuts and bruises and had to be lifted out. As Sister Catherine was trying to wipe the blood off her face, Sister Bernadette shook herself free. 'Leave me alone, sister dear', she said, 'look after the cake'.

After saying a short, simple grace, Bishop Lawton thanked the sisters for their efforts and his guests for coming. Then, beaming with inner happiness, he proclaimed: 'This is the day the Lord has made'. During the meal other people got up to make impromptu speeches and an Irish priest, who could have been a professional, sang familiar, old fashioned songs like 'Danny Boy' and 'Her name is Mary' in honour of the Bishop's sister.

I had been wondering about joining the Roman Catholic church since my days in Ibadan and this inspiring day in Sokoto was a further step along the road to Damascus. Jack and I discussed the matter with Father Nadeau who foresaw problems with the children if we supported different churches. That is why Jack and I took instruction together with Father Richard Farmer, Father Nadeau's right hand man. Down to earth and deeply versed in the tenets of the faith, he got on extremely well with Jack. We started go to mass with the family but left it at that. Strangely enough, the advent of national independence caused us to take the final step.

Political freedom had brought commercial freedom in its train. Some firms were taken over entirely by Nigerians, and some, including UAC, that ancient bastion of imperialistic conquest, went bankrupt. The Brigadier's efforts to diversify the activities of L & K had not always been successful and, fearing for its future and for his own, Jack sent in his resignation in May 1963. After all he was forty-eight and knew it might be difficult to get a job in United Kingdom once he was fifty. Young John was rising five and would soon need to go to school in the UK. Finally, the provident scheme provided by L & K would give him sufficient capital to make a fresh start. Government officers could accept the lump sum compensation available under the new set up and many did so.

I might have persuaded Jack to stay on a year or so as he had received several offers of alternative employment, but I was too worried about the health of the two boys to do so. The doctors in Gusau changed frequently, some, like Fred Hunter, were excellent, some inadequate, some often on tour and for a short time, Neil Duncan, the Flying Doctor — who did not actually fly because the two aeroplanes donated to him had both crashed — spent most of his time giving medical advice on the telephone to the dispensaries he had set up in the bush. The government hospital was geared to the treatment of tropical diseases and did not cater for Europeans in any way. Nor did the clinic at the Dominican mission. They were very kind and helpful to me, however, when I asked them for advice and, once, Sister Catherine spent a full hour getting Richard to swallow diarrhoea mixture. The doctor who had come to treat him had stormed out after Richard had first vomited, then poured his diarrhoea medicine over his new cream, palm beach suit. Having to rely on an aeroplane to take serious cases to Kano, and the memory of Alice's death there was always with me, and gave me little comfort.

This last tour John had contracted a skin allergy which was difficult to shake off. He had also had a very serious attack of measles. The doctor attending refused to take this 'childish complaint' seriously. Had we not received sound advice from Mary Akkare, he could have died. As for Richard, his propensity to eat and drink anything he saw, such as mud, flowers, the cat's dinner and the bath water meant he went from one stomach disorder to another. Amusing as this may sound, it was no joke watching him grow pale and thin as the tour progressed. I could not wait to get both of them home where I could be sure of a consistently good medical service.

Employees of L & K had the right to go by boat on their last tour, so we applied for berths on the MV *Auriel* and got the date of sailing for August 8th. With three more months to go, we reckoned we had plenty of time to prepare ourselves. Far from it, L & K went bankrupt in September. As area manager, Jack had to go to every L & K branch in Sokoto province to sell as much as he could before the receiver took the rest. Still, we counted ourselves lucky having our passage home booked. Many L & K expatriates and other friends had been ordered to leave at very short notice. We could not pack all our belongings because L & K was no longer in a position to pay for extra freight on the boat. We sold much that was precious to us in the way of wedding presents and souvenirs. Jack even found a tall, big man to buy his dinner suit. I was glad to see the last of it as it was no longer 'de rigeur', however special the occasion.

Two months before our departure, everyone on the GRA was invited to a very special occasion, a reception in honour of Dr Nnamdi Azikiwe, the President of all Nigeria who was passing through Gusau en route for Zaria. It was held in the afternoon in the compound of Doug Nichols, the district officer, and the whole station was agog with excitement. No one was absent. Touring and business arrangements had been cancelled. People working in the bush had braved the bad roads to come and the administrative officers from Sokoto and the outlying stations turned up in full strength. Following the protocol of official visits, Steve, the Resident, had told Doug to put the guests in proper pecking order. Naturally the covey of administrative officers were in front and behind them came the Dominican fathers, the doctor, the nursing sister, the bank managers, the agriculture officers, and the engineer. As befits people who were 'in trade', Jack and I stood at the back with his commercial associates from the 'Beach', together with the Akkaris and a few chosen Lebanese and Syrians.

Dressed in our best clothes, we stood waiting for Zik. He arrived on time, wearing beautiful flowing robes, accompanied by a small entourage. The Resident engaged him in conversation for a moment, then began introducing him to the assembled guests. Shades of the garden party for Princess Alexandra, I thought, taking a large gin and some small chop off the tray Doug's boy was carrying. This is going to be a long wait. Might as well enjoy myself.

Taking little notice of what was happening around me, I took my first sip of gin and concentrated on the problem of prising cubes of pineapple and cheese off a sharply pointed orange stick. The sound of a man's voice calling 'Jean! Jean! Jean! Jean! How lovely to see you!' made me look up to see who it was.

It was Zik. He had caught sight of me and, cutting his way through the crowd like the prophet Moses parting the Red Sea, he was making his way quickly towards me, arms outstretched. He gave me a big hug and a kiss and began to ask me about my parents and my family as if we were back in their drawing room in Putney. I introduced him to Jack and when he heard that we planned to stay a week in Lagos before catching the boat home, he said: 'You must stay with me at the presidential palace. Let me know the exact date you arrive and I'll arrange everything'.

I shall cherish for ever the astonished, envious, questioning expressions on the faces of everyone there. It made up for the hundred snubs I had received in the past because I was 'hobnobbing with blacks'. No one had the faintest idea I had met Zik, let alone known him as a friend.

Conversation amongst the wives in Gusau tended to centre on roads, gossip children, cooking and similar topics. There were no 'blacks' to 'hob nob' with as such, and because times were changing, the fact that Jack and I often invited the L & K assistant manager, M. Ahmadu and his family to our house excited little comment. The next few days Jack basked in my reflected glory as people flocked to his office asking about our friendship with Zik. The news that we were to stay with him in Lagos became the talking point for days in Gusau.

By the time we came to leave our 'shooting lodge' house in the GRA, it looked too forlorn to arouse emotion. Stripped of the steins in the lounge, the piles of files and papers in my office, the toys in the boys' room and the Belgian rugs on the red cement floors in the front rooms, it had lost all semblance of a home. The Receiver had told us that no plans had been made concerning the house which would, therefore be empty for a considerable period of time. Realising this would be a death blow to the garden, we encouraged our friends to take away whatever trees, plants or shrubs they fancied. Sister Anne came up to fetch the two scarlet poinsettia trees that the L & K manager in Zaria had given to us when we first arrived in Gusau. Seeing that they had started to lose their colour, she exclaimed with an enchanting illogicality: 'They'll go right back to scarlet, now that Jean's a Catholic'.

A frenzied series of farewell parties and gifts, followed by an interesting tour southwards to bid goodbye to friends in Jos, Makurdi and Enugu, did much to banish our regrets at leaving. I had spent a few happy days with Emeka in Enugu in 1950, but he had long since left to settle in Onitsha. This time we were there to see my dear friend, Hilda Ogbe. We had kept in very close contact since our first meeting in 1949. My parents had attended her wedding with Tommy Ogbe in London, and I was able to get to know baby Monu on my next leave and their little daughter, Temi, five years later. We met without fail whenever when we were both in the UK, but distances and circumstances had prevented us from visiting each other's homes in Nigeria.

After spending eleven years together in London, Hilda and Tommy's life in Nigeria had been a series of steps up the ladder of success. Tommy had gone from lawyer, to magistrate, to legal advisor to Shell in the Eastern region. Hilda had diversified her talent as fashion expert by designing and selling kaftans, artifacts in wood, metal, bone and, particularly, jewelry which she registered as Ogbecraft. Every hotel, airport terminal and large shop has Ogbecraft on sale up to now. She also sells it in her own shops and in the homes of accredited agents. Her initiative has never waned. Over the years she has run a craft centre in Benin, cultivated herbs for medical purposes, dabbled in the travel business, set up a training workshop for seamstresses, written articles and broadcast for NBC, and edited a series of simplified law books written by Judge Victor Omage.

We did not see Tommy Ogbe in Enugu because he was away on business in Europe. Fortunately, Hilda's mother, Gertrude Gerson, whom we met for the first time, was there to keep her company. She spent half the year with her son and his wife in New York and the other half with Hilda in Nigeria. Extraordinarily bright for a woman over seventy, she did the accounts and sold jewelry to clients coming to the house. Her subtle sense of humour and sympathetic manner made her an excellent companion and the four of us had a very happy time together, relaxing in the garden surrounding the prestigious, architect designed house and looking at her children playing with ours. In spite of the difference in age, Monu was kind and gentle with John and Richard, Temi less so. When her father was not at home to check her, she tended to be wild and disobedient. It was hard to believe this attractive, little girl with bright, brown eyes and perfect curly black hair could be such a headstrong terror.

Hilda was glad to have a rest from entertaining. When Tommy was at home the two of them were caught up in a whirl of parties. Gracious and gorgeous to look at and wearing long, intricately wrought silver earrings with a native dress of her own design, she looked every inch the perfect hostess.

We did not feel too sad about leaving Enugu since we knew we were bound to meet again in Britain. After a wonderful time in Lagos and at sea, we landed in Liverpool in freezing cold weather. Jack needed to decide whether to live and work in London or in Liverpool. In fact the decision was made for him. My father died a month after our arrival and with my sisters far away in S. Africa and Australia, it was up to us to settle in London to be near my mother. She was as shrewd and helpful as Mrs Gerson. When we eventually bought a lock-up confectionery shop in Kensington, she offered us one of three flats she owned near her house in Putney. The shop did well, the flat was roomy, and my three boys — yes, Joe arrived to comfort Granny fourteen months after our return — were within easy reach of a good Catholic school.

It took time to get used to suburban London life after living such a long time in Nigeria. Jack had his particular chair in the Putney lounge and I would sit on the sofa next to him. Whenever we saw a film on TV, set in Africa, we would both feel weepie and reach for each others' hands. Nigeria had done so much for us, we could never forget it. We could never cease to be grateful.

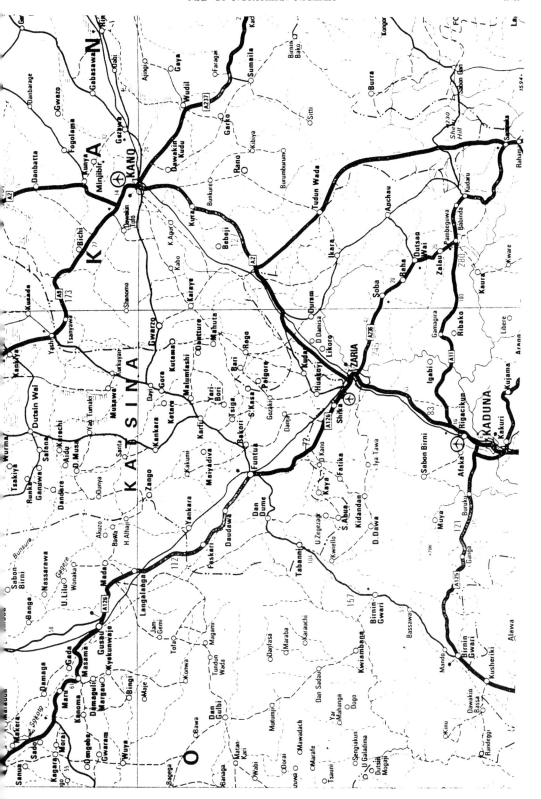

33. Map showing area around Gusau in Northern Nigeria.

64. The Weddling Day in Liverpool U.K.

65. Baby John with 'smallboy' Adamu and our dog Carlos in the garden of our home in Gusau.

66. Author with baby John and the children of Jack's Manager, Mallam Bello.

67. Childrens' Parties.

68. Mrs. Bello with the children.

69. Playing in the garden.

70. Jack with sons, John and Richard.

71. Fr. Daley & Dominican Fathers in Yaba, Lagos.

72. Christmas in Gombe with the Krzwyons.

73. Fr. Begley, Jack & Fr. Carrol in Biliri, near Jos, 1958.

74. Author with the Fathers.

75. Fr. Daley with friends.

76. Outside the Dominican convent in Gusau.

77. 'Dickens is not a bore'.
Lecture by Author to staff of
United Africa Co. in Kano.

Lecture ! Lecture !! Lecture !!!

THE
MAYFLOWER STUDENTS' ASSOCIATION
KANO BRANCH

*will have as a Guest Speaker on
7th December, 1960 a Mayflower
Resident representative*

MRS. JEAN EVANS
B.A. (Hons.) Dip. Ed.

*the well known Author & Broadcaster
She will give an extremely interesting
Lecture on "Dickens is not a Bore"
with Educational film strip of Charles
Dickens at the :-*

INTERNATIONAL HOTEL
30 — 34 ENUGU ROAD, SABON—GARI KANO
from 6 p.m. prompt
AND

*Members of the public are invited
Admission:—* School Children 6d Adult 1/-

M.O. UGHODAGA   G.O. OSUBOR
CHAIRMAN   GENERAL SECRETARY.

78. Leaflet which announced the
'Dickens' lecture.

THE LADY   21st August, 1958

A Trim in the Tropics : By Jean Evans

ON HER first visit to Nigeria, that extraordinary pioneer Mary Kingsley was checking her luggage with a Coaster.

"My dear woman," he cried, "you've forgotten the two most important items."

"Nonsense. I have everything I need," the forthright Victorian replied.

"You've forgotten the gin and you've forgotten the coffin," said the Coaster.

With air conditioning, electricity, water, shops, cinemas, hotels and hospitals in the big towns, you don't need so much now for entertainment and the coffins go out as the prophylactics came in.

All honour to the fearless Miss Kingsley who faced swamps, illness, cannibals, dangerous rapids alone—a resolute woman in a bun, long skirts, sleeved blouses and her shoes.

One experience, however, was left to her surviving successors. A haircut.

MY FIRST haircut was in the university town of Ibadan, which boasts the largest native population in Africa, South of the Sahara. I was teaching in a boys' school, an otherwise all male staff. The nearest European was five miles away.

As the damp heat matted my thick hair, I called to my Boy.

"Onye. My hair. Is there anyone who cut it?"

"Yes, Madam. I go bring you fine fine barber past all. He be my brother from my village, Ugo."

"Are there many people in Ugo? "

"Yes, Madam. They go reach one hundred."

Onye's brother came when Onye was at market. He sat me on the verandah of my twenty-roomed house I inhabited alone, and set to work. I hastily dug out the hand-clipper from my bag. There was no other. Onye's brother worked with a broad grin and neck clippers. We spoke in gestures. He spoke Ugo dialect—period. I pointed, tapered with my fingers. He nodded. The hand-clipper reflected, I thought, an adequate bob. A set price apparently. I proffered sixpence, Onye's brother grinned more broadly and departed.

I GRINNED too, until a week later I happened upon a mirror lying among a pile of dirty newspapers. With that, and my hand-mirror, I managed to see the back of my head for the first time since my arrival in Nigeria. My cry brought the whole of the African staff running. I was tonsured.

A layer of hair as thin as a baby's first covered a round pink patch of skin. The patch was four inches in diameter. Yes, I measured it.

It took six months for my hair to grow. When it did sprout it came in a mass of straight spikes like the end of a school-yard parting.

In COURSE of time I acquired a car. One weekend I drove down to Lagos, the capital, with the wife of an engineer, and her twenty-year-old daughter, Cynthia, out for the University vacation.

Lagos has a port, a beach, hundreds of people, beautiful shops, and, ah luxury! three places where you could have your hair done.

The one that could take Cynthia and me was a little fourth-floor flat just behind the Big General Store, next to a row of corrugated-iron-roofed hovels full of goats, stalls, children, chickens, babies and gramophones. Everything was going full blast.

The flat was in pink (" Heartache Salmon ") and pale green (" Olive Rhapsody "). Plants grew on the balcony, and plants grew inside; there was subdued lighting, flowing muslin curtains, music (muted), coloured combs and yellow carpets. Still, both Cynthia and myself received superb " sets."

A couple of Nigerian plateau women were sitting with their children at the entrance to the flats. They wore leaves only, and were smoking long pipes. They stared at us hostilely as we left, and spat out the quid.

TWO YEARS later, I was promoted to the headship of a girls' school in the Northern Cameroons. We were at the end of the line. The roads shut during the rains, and during the dry season, too—for repair. Mountain storms frequently prevented the air service.

Perhaps it was the dazzling beauty of the blue-grey mountains over the shimmering Benue River, that inspired him, but Isa, the bar steward at the club, was a magnificent hairdresser. He barbered us all—we were about fifty Europeans—quickly, artistically, and with the same unwashed comb and scissors.

" Isa," we would call, " bring a squash and a haircut." We would be done then and there, sitting with everyone else on the club terrace overlooking the river, with Isa leaving off now and then to serve drinks.

If we had forgotten our towels, Isa wrapped the cloth for drying the glasses round our necks. However, he always dusted us off with white powder from an Imperial Leather Talcum tin. Once I taxed him.

" Surely, that is plain flour you put on my neck, Isa."

" Madame. No. Haba! " Isa was most offended.

" Well, what is it? It tastes like flour."

" It is not plain, Madame. It is self-raising."

We were all sorry when Isa left.

AT MY school I had to look after ninety black woolly heads.

The ten Pagan girls wore their heads cropped. They were rough and tough. Their grandfathers had been cannibals, their fathers hunted or drank beer according to the season. Mothers did the farming and earned the money.

The other eighty little girls, half of them Christian, and half, Moslem, were very hair conscious. They would sit for hours, heads on each other's laps, parting with iron or ox-bone combs, then oiling, twisting or plaiting. The styles varied.

You could wear little nobbly twisted bits over your head, you could have it quartered into four sections and plaited. Plaits could also be drawn into a pile at the back, a large

top knot, or divided into two like thick horns. The hair of the light-skinned Fulani girls was exceptionally long, but theirs was nothing compared to the hair styles of their Bush sisters, the Bororo, who used to pass proudly through the school grounds with their cattle—a picturesque, verminous tribe.

The Bororo wore enormously long thick plaits well smeared with grease and bedecked with glass jewels, safety pins and gold rings. The Bororo men also wore their hair long. It made a strange contrast to their scarred bodies, witness to the terrible beatings they had received in public with smiles and laughs, when they had been initiated into manhood.

I MOVED on again—I had married by now —and fortunately heard of a hairdresser through my neighbour; she was the type of person who could always find a " little woman " who sews, or a " little man who does your hair," but she never remembered their names.

" There's a little Turkish woman from Cyprus," she told me, " a name like Turkish Delight."

What joy! Madame Turkish Delight owned a pretty and clean house. She was lusciously attractive herself and had an expert touch. She operated (like Hassan) chez elle. Her husband took the cash.

I relaxed. The scissors snipped. I began to chatter.

" I suppose you still have relatives in Cyprus? "

" Ah, yes." A deep sigh. The scissors hovered.

" Still, they seem to be showing the Greeks they'll stand no nonsense," I said briskly to recall her to her task.

" —!! " A flood of abuse in Greek. The scissors jabbed now. " The Turks. They do terrible things to us poor, poor, Greeks. Torture." The point of the scissors caught me behind the ear. Madame's eyes flashed. She swore, she shouted, and she gesticulated. She was Medea spurned by Jason, Electra urging Orestes on to murder.

" I'm sorry, I thought you were a Turk," I yelled at her above her curses, and slipped desperately from beneath the towel.

SHE HEARD me. She threw her head back and roared with laughter. She pushed me back into the chair, called her husband, told him, and they both roared with laughter. He brought out a bottle of dark Cypriot wine, and insisted on my drinking to the extermination of the Turks with them. In that wine it was a pleasure. I laughed, too, and swayed home very happy.

My husband greeted me glumly. " You'd have done better to have a crew cut," he said. " We've been posted. To Nguru. There are six Europeans, and you will be the only woman."

Nguru's marshes are wonderful for shooting. The fishing is good, too. There are tracks of sand for roads, and three small shops.

After two months my husband cut my hair with nail scissors.

" This was the most unkindest cut of all."

LONDON & KANO TRADING CO. LTD

To
J. Evans Esq.,
Gusau.

From
The G.M's Office,
Kano.

Ref JE-OT/ROS.

Date 21st May, 1960.

Dear Jack

    I should like formally to put on record our congratulations on the satisfactory groundnut and cotton season in Gusau area.

    The amount of hard work, firmness and tact required to finish the season with so clean a sheet is realised.

    As a token of the Company's appreciation the Chief Accountant has been instructed to credit your account with £50.

As I shall be away when you pass through Regards to Jean

Yours *Sml*

c.c. Chief Accountant.

80. Letter to Jack from his Company — May 1960.

The Department of Extra-Mural Studies
UNIVERSITY OF IBADAN

in collaboration with

Ahmadu Bello University, Zaria

invites you to

A BRAINS TRUST

at

GUSAU

On Sunday: the 12th of May 1963

Chairman; Mr. J Evans, Area Manager, London and Kano Trading Company, Gusau.

Trust; (1) Dr. I. A. Shah M. B : B.S.
      (2) Mr. D. Sellwood B. Sc.
      (3) Miss Catherine Gallagher C.R.N.A.
      (4) Dr. N. Duncan M.R.C S , L.R.C.P., D. Obst. R Cog
      (5) Mr. Inimeti
      (6) Mrs Jean Evans B.A. , Dip. Ed.
      (7) Mr. B. O W. Mafeni B. A.
      and other distinguished brains

      (8) *[handwritten]*

Place: N. A Reading Room Gusau

TIME: 4. 30 p. m.

Please send your questions to Mrs J. L. Evans,
c/o London and Kano Trading Company, Gusau, by 11th May, 1963

BERNARD MAFENI
Paramount Printers Zaria   (Resident Tutor, Zaria)

81. A Brains Trust at Gusau.

PLEASE BRING THIS CARD WITH YOU

The Sultan of Sokoto and the Emirs of Gwandu,
Argungu and Yauri

request the pleasure of the company of

.... *Mr. J. Evans* ....

to have the honour to meet
Her Royal Highness, The Princess Alexandra of Kent
at the Sokoto Gardens on the 13th October, 1960

R.S.V.P. to the
1945-2100 hours   Private Secretary to the Sultan

82. The invitation.

Alhaji the Honourable Sir Ahmadu Bello, K.B.E.,
Sardauna of Sokoto, Premier of the Northern Region.

83. The Sardauna.

84. Jack & Jean Evans (Author), Princess Alexandra and The Sardauna at the Evening Presentation in the Sokoto Gardens.

85. Newspaper cutting of the event.

PRINCESS ALEXANDRA EATS TRADITIONAL FOOD AT SOKOTO

WHILE in Sokoto, Princess Alexandra visited the Sultan's Palace and gave a personal message of greeting from the Queen to the Sultan and the four Emirs and Councils of Sokoto Province. The Princess asked to see a display of leather-charming at the palace and was later presented with three leather cushions, four pieces of locally-woven cloth and some Sokoto leather (generally known as "Moroccan leather").

From the palace, the Princess in company of the Premier (Alhaji Sir Ahmadu Bello, Sardauna of Sokoto), drove to the market where she toured the stalls and afterwards was presented with two leather poufs by Alhaji Garba, a well-known businessman.

Her Royal Highness was cheered on her way back to the Residency by many people along the route.

The Princess had luncheon at the Premier's house and partook of traditional food. Sir Ahmadu also gave presents to the Princess. These included ostrich feather fans and a silver-embroidered green "alkyabba" cloak.

During the Durbar, the Yauri contingent, the first to march-past, was led by the Bungawas, famous for "dambe" (a local type of boxing). A feature of the Argungu contingent was a display by four horses which lay on the ground while acrobatics were performed upon them. The Emir of Argungu was preceded by nine gaily-garbed horses led by equally bright-ly-attired grooms.

The Gwandu contingent was led by two dancing groups—the Kwankwamba and the Yaba dancers—and local boxers. The Emir's bodyguard, with brass helmets, coats of mail were next. The Yauri

contingent—the Emir was preceded by 12 gaily-decorated horses with grooms dressed in white with bands of red. The Emir was followed by 21 rows of horse-men in multi-coloured robes.

Leading the Sokoto contingent was a group of men and women dancers and local boxers, followed closely by the Sultan's personal band of dogarai. Then came 12 smartly-caparisoned horses and a camel which knelt on its foreleg as it approached the Royal stand.

The Sultan's party was majestic as well as colourful. It included various types of dancers, snake charmers, hunters and cattle Fulani.

The grand finale was preceded by two camels which knelt before Her Royal Highness, and then came four waves of eight horsemen, one from each Emirate.

86-88. Hilda Ogbe with family and friends.

Hilda Ogbe with family and friends.

Sampler of Hilda Ogbes' Jewellery business, Ogbe Craft, in **Benen City.**

CIVIL WAR — from IFE
Fr. Farmer

Christmas greetings from still another new address. I am now a
Lecturer in the Dept. of Religious Studies and Philosophy at the
Univ. of Ife. There was much to do about applications, interviews,
etc., and the appointment came through Oct. 1.

It is quite a change-occupation, climate, new customs and the like.
But it is a happy change after the events of the previous year.
Here all is peaceful and relaxed. One hardly knows that a civil
war is going on in the country. The students are very sincere-
too serious perhaps. They work very hard and that keep me working
hard as well. I have eight lectures a week in five subjects. I
have never gotten more than a couple pages ahead of the class

I am Chaplain to the Catholic Students as well. This takes up what
little time is left over after classes and preparations. They seem
to have some kind of a do almost every week, and of course the Father
  must be present and give a little address. I also preach at the
general Christian Service once a month. The members of our Dept.
 rotate this job. I really enjoy it.

                              Dept. of Religious Studies
                              University of Ife
                              Ile Ife, Western Nigeria

Hope you are well. Enjoyed talking with
you. God bless you.
                    Fr. Farmer. J.

91. Letter from Fr. Farmer, Ife University regarding the Civil War.

Epilogue

Chapter twenty-four
Return to Nigeria

For over 30 years revisiting Nigeria was out of the question.

A part-time teaching job, three sons to bring up, a husband to feed and my mother to care for took up all my time. We corresponded with many friends there, however, including Jamil and Mary Akkare in Gusau and Father Farmer, who was doing research and pastoral work in the University of Ife. Amongst the stream of people visiting us during their leave were Father Daly, who had been posted to Lagos during the Civil War, Father Nadeau, Dr Fred and Maureen Hunter from Gusau, the itinerant Krzwyons from the North and last, but certainly not least, Hilda Ogbe and her family. In the late eighties, Jack and my mother died within three years of each other. By this time, my lads were able to take care of themselves and I was free to accept Hilda's long standing invitation to stay with her in Benin.

On 15 December 1988, I flew out to Lagos. Hilda was at the airport to ease me through the confusion and chaos which is part and parcel of the terminal. Most considerately she had booked me into the Hilton Hotel for a few days to enable me to adjust to the new Nigeria. Independence had brought with it a proliferation of sky-scrapers, factories, banks, industrial buildings, mosques, hotels, government offices and schools. What had been Carter Bridge had become an insignificant lane, turning into a wide, frenzied, four lane motorway.

Hilda took me to see her friends in Lagos. The wives had often come from abroad and derived much support from their local Niger Wives Association. This was a countrywide organisation, whose only condition of membership was to be married to a Nigerian husband. Many, like Hilda, had carved out successful careers for themselves — no one more so than Betty Okuboyejo. Over a gargantuan Hilton breakfast, she talked about the clothes empire, called 'Betty O', that she had built up from scratch. Her Afro-European designs have colour and shape that can be recognised anywhere. I asked if she knew the Ibadan address of my old friends, the Rosijis, she told me that they had long since moved from Ibadan and were living in Apapa, Lagos. She suggested we contact her friend, Judy Asuni, another Niger wife and a Lecturer in Sociology at the University of Lagos, who would certainly know where they lived.

We left Betty to attend a wedding reception given by Professor and Mrs Fafunwa for their son Babatunde Fafunwa and Huguette Njemanze, friends of Hilda's, who had visited me in Putney several years back. The wedding was at the Federal Civil Service Club in Ikoyi. This was a magnificent, crowded affair, which continued long after we left to call on Judy Asuni who also lived in Ikoyi. She knew the Rosijis' house, gave us full directions and we went there immediately.

Strangely enough, Gbemi Rosiji had been at the wedding with her friend, Dr Nina Mba, and thought she had recognised me over the sea of faces; she was not too surprised, therefore, when we called. Her husband, Ayo, however had attended another wedding. He was asleep when she returned and knew nothing of this encounter. I was overwhelmed with the splendour and beauty of their lovely home, which required a network of telephones to every room as it was so vast. Gbemi rang through to Ayo to ask him to come down to meet a guest and I do not think I have ever, ever, seen anyone so surprised as he was when he saw me, especially as I was bedecked in finery and jewellery from Hilda's magnificent collection!

They pressed us to stay on for a day or so, but we were expected back at Benin before dark and unlike the old days when we had ventured out at all hours in old cars on roads full of potholes, it was now unwise to drive on new tarmac roads after dark. They implored us to call in on our return to Lagos and stay as long as we liked.

On arrival in Benin, I found that Hilda, like the Rosijis, had gone up in the world. Her house was smaller than theirs, but exquisitely designed by herself to incorporate a workshop and an office with a lounge, dining room and reception area. We had a wonderful month together, meeting her friends and spending Christmas in Abuja. We celebrated the New Year in Benin with Victor and Christine Omage and their three daughters. His New Year parties were a feature in the social life of Benin and all the elite of Benin were there. A few days later, Victor invited us to attend the ceremony when his father was made a Chief; a great compliment since these occasions were normally strictly family affairs. The ceremony began in the deceased Chief's village and we all then proceeded, in a noisy, hooting motorcade, to the house of Victor's father, the new Chief, for drinks and celebrations.

Car trouble, in fact, prevented us from calling on the Rosijis on our return, but fortunately they visited the UK frequently and rang me when they came that summer. The years fell away and we became as close friends as ever, meeting practically every year. In 1992, they introduced me to their friend Dr Nina Mba. She had come to London to pursue her researches for the biography she was writing of Ayo Rosiji, 'Man with Vision', and was delighted to meet me because I knew something about his early life. She came to my house in Putney and was so impressed with the amount of material I had concerning my personal experiences in Nigeria that she suggested I write my own memoirs. With Nina guiding me in my research I started to write and this book is the result.

Nina took me to the launch of the biography of the Hon. Tafawa Balewa by Trevor Clark. It was a very crowded affair, but she managed to introduce me to her friends, including her publisher, Joop Berkhout, a genial, outgoing man, always on the alert for new talent.

With Nina as guide, philosopher and friend, I was able to pursue the research in Britain at the Rhodes House Library in Oxford and with Nigerians in England. I visited Nigeria again in 1992 dividing my time between Hilda in Benin and the Rosijis in Lagos, where I was able to meet many old friends and establish new contacts. I was granted interviews by many people, including the Oba of Benin.

Nina also arranged a short trip to Ibadan, so that I could return to the grammar school and visit the Alayande family in their home. We also had an invitation to lunch with her publisher, Joop Berkhout. He said he had thoroughly enjoyed my first book, 'Abimbolu', and I offered the publishing rights to him which he gladly accepted. When I told him I had started another book called 'The Punaku Treasure', which, like 'Abimbolu', was intended as a reading book in school and was set in the north of Nigeria, he said he would like to see it as soon as it was finished. He kept his word and the book was published in May 1994. For the third time in four years, I went out to Nigeria; this time for a reception to celebrate its official publication, given at the home of the Rosijis in Lagos. I also enjoyed meeting old friends and during this visit I attended several concerts at the Muson, the musical centre of Lagos.

It was during this visit that Nina and I were invited to accompany the Rosijis when Ayo went to Ibadan for his installation as Bobajiro. This was a memorable occasion. We drove there very slowly through the old town and arrived with hundreds of other people in front of the Mapo Hall (the town hall), which was next to the Palace of the Olubadan. He was seated on a special carved chair, placed under a canopy with his counsellors beside him. The noise was deafening with the hooting of cars and people arriving. Praise singers, drummers and dancers were cavorting between the VIPs under the canopy, and the audience. People were arriving in their Sunday best clothes to celebrate the making of an honorary Chief. Ayo and Gbemi sat in pride of place among the audience. They were dressed in very expensive cloths, hand woven years ago and lovingly stored between official ceremonies. Canon Alayande, my old principal was there to take the prayers, which were followed by speeches from senior members of the Council. The ceremony concluded with the conferment of the title of Bobajiro (King's Counsellor) on Ayo, whilst Gbemi was given the title of Iya Alaje (the one who promotes prosperity). After the ceremony my old friend, Canon Alayande, came to where I was sitting and insisted on presenting me to the Olubadan. He smiled warmly as I prostrated myself before him and told me he remembered meeting me in the fifties. Following this ceremony a party was given by Chief Daisi for two hundred guests.The whole month of my visit was a glamorous, memorable period for a lady well over seventy and I can never thank enough the people who welcomed me and made it all possible.

92. March 1994. Chief Ayo Rosiji is conferred as The Bobajiro of Ibadan (King's Counsellor) by His Highness, The Olubadan of Ibadan, Alaiyeluwa Oba, E. A. Adeyemo Operinde I, DD, J.P.

93. Chief Daisi, Chief S.L. Edu, Chief Ayo Rosiji and his wife Gbemi, who was given the title of Mamani Iya Alaje.

94. Chief Daisi and his wife give a party afterwards to over one hundred guests.

95. Dr. Nina Mba, Editor of Author's book (on right of picture).

96, 97. Presentationof Author's new book for children, 'The Punaku Treasure'.

98. Hilda Ogbe with Author at Presentation.

99. Chief Joop Berkhout, The Okun Borode of Ife (Publisher) and Chief Ayo Rosiji.

100. Craftsman making a talking drum.

101. Brochure of Independence Celebrations, Sokoto 1960.

02. Examples of Nigerian leatherwork.

03. Women making pots.

104. Stall selling cutlasses.

105. Floor covering for sale.

106. Peppers for sale in the market.

107. Market stalls.